Strategic
Leadership
The General's Art

Strategic Leadership
The General's Art

Editors

Mark R. Grandstaff, PhD
Georgia Sorenson, PhD

MANAGEMENTCONCEPTS

ƒƒƒ
MANAGEMENTCONCEPTS

8230 Leesburg Pike, Suite 800
Vienna, VA 22182
(703) 790-9595
Fax: (703) 790-1371
www.managementconcepts.com

Library of Congress Cataloging-in-Publication Data

Strategic leadership : the general's art / edited by Mark Grandstaff, Georgia
Sorenson ; afterword by James MacGregor Burns.
    p. cm.
  ISBN 978-1-56726-236-0
1. Leadership. 2. Strategic planning. I. Grandstaff, Mark. II. Sorenson,
Georgia Jones.
HD57.7.S7814 2009
658.4'092—dc22

                                                                    2008048110

Printed in the United States of America

10   9   8   7   6   5   4   3   2   1

About the Editors

Mark R. Grandstaff, PhD, is an award-winning scholar, teacher, and facilitator with more than 25 years of experience in leadership development, organizational assessment, and strategic thinking. He has worked with organizations such as the Army War College, Air War College, and the Joint Special Operation Command to educate their senior officers in strategic leadership and thinking, develop leadership curriculum, and analyze and prescribe solutions for organizational problems. As part of his National Service Initiatives, President Clinton appointed Dr. Grandstaff to serve on the first Summer of Service committee, which developed leadership curriculum for those working with at-risk children.

In addition to his work with executives and other senior leaders, Dr. Grandstaff is an associate professor of history at Brigham Young University, and he has taught at the University of California at Berkeley and the University of Maryland, University College. Much of his research involves the uses of history in understanding how national and institutional cultures affect corporate strategy and decision- and policy-making.

Dr. Grandstaff holds a doctorate in history from the University of Wisconsin at Madison, and his fields of interest are American institutional culture, American foreign policy, and organizational development. He also holds an MA in the sociology of religion and community formation and a BS in business management and aviation technology. Dr. Grandstaff is currently a Senior Fellow of the James MacGregor Burns Academy of Leadership and a Fellow of the Inter-University Seminar for the Study of the Armed Forces. He is the author of three books and more than 40 scholarly essays.

Dr. Grandstaff retired from the Air Force Reserve after 24 years of military service, 16 of which he served on active duty in both the Navy and the Air Force.

Georgia Sorenson, PhD, served as Inaugural Chair and Professor of Transformation at the U.S. Army War College in 2005–2006. She is currently a research professor and founder of the James MacGregor Burns Academy of Leadership at the School of Public Policy at the University of Maryland. In 2002–2004, she was the Visiting Senior Scholar at the Jepson School of Leadership Studies at the University of Richmond.

An architect of the leadership studies field, Dr. Sorenson has lectured extensively on leadership in more than 30 countries in the past decade. She was a co-founder of the International Leadership Association and serves on the editorial board of numerous journals, including *Leadership, Leadership Quarterly,* and *Leadership Review.*

Dr. Sorenson earned her doctorate in education at the University of Maryland, and her dissertation, "A Phenomenological Study of Ten Transforming Leaders," is cited extensively. She earned her master's degree in psychology from Hood College and her bachelor's degree in psychology from American University.

Dr. Sorenson is the author of numerous books on leadership and has contributed chapters to several other books. Her most recent book is *The Quest for a General Theory of Leadership*, edited with George Goethals (2006). She is also coeditor of the award-winning, four-volume *Encyclopedia of Leadership* (2004).

About the Authors

COL Charles D. Allen, U.S. Army, is the Director of Leader Development and a faculty instructor in the Department of Command, Leadership, and Management at the U.S. Army War College, where he teaches core curriculum courses and electives in creativity, leading organizational change, and strategic leadership. He has led in a variety of assignments as a field artillery officer, garrison commander, and Inspector General in U.S. and overseas assignments. He has a BS from the United States Military Academy at West Point, a master's in operations research from the Georgia Institute of Technology, a master's in military art and science in theater operations from the Command and General Staff College School of Advanced Military Studies, and a master's in strategic studies from the U.S. Army War College. He is completing PhD requirements in organizational behavior at the University of Maryland.

Craig Bullis, PhD, is a professor of strategic leader development at the U.S. Army War College, where he is responsible for the War College's

Leadership Feedback Program (LFP). The LFP provides all War College students and other senior military leaders the opportunity to enhance their leadership self-awareness through an integrated program of behavioral and personality assessments, particularly by focusing on how these psychological factors affect health, fitness, and effectiveness. In 2002 Dr. Bullis joined the War College faculty upon his retirement from the Army. He has taught courses in strategic leadership, joint organization and processes, creative thinking, and systems leadership. Dr. Bullis earned his PhD in organizational behavior from Texas Tech University, and he has published work in several journals, including the *Journal of Applied Psychology*, the *Journal of Applied Behavioral Sciences*, and *Parameters*.

COL Lee DeRemer, U.S. Air Force, is the Director of Strategic Leadership at the U.S. Army War College and an instructor in the Department of Command, Leadership, and Management. He teaches the strategic leadership course and the joint processes and landpower development course, in addition to an elective course on leading and managing organizational change. An Air Force command pilot with 3,000 hours of flying time, he has commanded an Air Refueling Operations Group, an Expeditionary Operations Group, and an Air Refueling Squadron. He has served on the Joint Staff and the Air Staff and deployed to the Kingdom of Saudi Arabia four times between 1986 and 1994. COL DeRemer has an MS in national security strategy from the National War College, an MA in national security and strategic studies from the Naval War College, an MSA in public administration from Central Michigan University, and a BA in political science and philosophy from East Stroudsburg University.

COL Mark Eshelman, U.S. Army, is an instructor in the Department of Command, Leadership, and Management (DCLM) at the U.S. Army War College, where he teaches topics such as defense support of civil authorities. A career infantry officer with four operational deployments, he has a BS from the United States Military Academy and four master's degrees relating to military science from various colleges run by the Department of Defense.

Stephen Gerras, PhD, is a professor of behavioral sciences in the Department of Command, Leadership, and Management at the U.S. Army War College. COL Gerras served in the Army for more than 25 years, including commanding a light infantry company and a transportation battalion, teaching leadership at West Point, and serving as the Chief of Operations and Agreements for the Office of Defense Cooperation in Ankara, Turkey. He holds a BS from the United States Military Academy and an MS and PhD in industrial and organizational psychology from Penn State University.

COL Julie Manta, U.S. Army, is an instructor in the Department of Command, Leadership, and Management at the U.S. Army War College, where she teaches strategic leadership and government processes, as well as electives in human resources management and multicultural awareness. She has led several organizations in assignments as a military personnel officer in Korea, Germany, and the Balkans during humanitarian and peacekeeping operations. She has a BA in sociology from La Salle University, an MPA in public administration from Penn State University, and a master's in strategic studies from the U.S. Army War College.

COL James R. Oman, U.S. Army, is a career Army officer with more than 29 years of service. He served as the Department Chairman for the Department of Command, Leadership, and Management at the U.S. Army War College. COL Oman holds a BS from Bowling Green State University, an MA in management from Webster University, and a Master of Strategic

Studies degree from the U.S. Army War College. His last operational assignment was in Saudi Arabia, where he served from August 2001 through July 2002 as the commander, Army Forces Central Command—Saudi Arabia, and he was the first U.S. Army installation commander, Eskan Village, Riyadh, Saudi Arabia.

George E. Reed, PhD, is an associate professor of leadership studies at the University of San Diego. Before joining the faculty in 2007, he served for 27 years as an Army officer, including six years as the Director of Command and Leadership Studies at the U.S. Army War College. He teaches courses in leadership and organizational theory. Dr. Reed serves on the editorial board of the journal *Parameters* and is a reviewer for *The American Review of Public Administration*. He received his PhD from Saint Louis University in public policy analysis and administration.

COL George Woods, U.S. Army, is a professor in the Department of Command, Leadership, and Management at the U.S. Army War College. He currently teaches three core courses—strategic thinking, strategic leadership, and joint processes landpower development—and a negotiation elective. In his 27 years of service, COL Woods has served in a variety of assignments as an infantry officer, as a member of the Department of the Army staff, and as an instructor at the United States Military Academy. He earned a BS from the United States Military Academy, an MA in organizational psychology from Columbia University, an MMAS from the School of Advanced Military Studies at the Command and General Staff College, and an MA in national security studies from the U.S. Army War College. He is currently completing his doctoral requirements in public administration at Penn State University.

To our family members Amy and Carol Dixon,
Ferrin, Camber, and Brittia Grandstaff,
Olive and Wyly Jones, and Suzanna Strasburg

Contents

Editors' Preface

On February 21, 1906, the cornerstone for the U.S. Army War College was laid. In attendance were President Theodore Roosevelt, Secretary of War Elihu Root, several Supreme Court justices, and a host of foreign dignitaries. As Roosevelt entered the historic parade grounds, the flag was run up to the top of the flagstaff, and members of the Fourth Battery Light Artillery fired the traditional 21-gun salute. Simultaneously, more than 1,000 troops marched onto the field and saluted the commander in chief. The *New York Times* reporter covering the ceremonies captured the scene with one word: "momentous."

Roosevelt, known for his "progressive" and at times bellicose positions, stated that the War College should be a matter of pride for every American, as the United States was on its path to becoming a first-rate world power. "It is not open to decide whether or not we shall play [a major role in the world]," he thundered. "All we have to decide is whether we play it well or ill."[1] It is the War College, he continued, that would carry out the reforms and training to make the Army effective, efficient, and second to none.

It is the mission of the War College, but especially the Department of Command, Leadership, and Management, to help military leaders (typically lieutenant colonels and colonels) and their civilian equivalents transition from mid-level (operational) leaders and managers into the strategic realms of senior leadership. These officers are at the crossroads of their careers—a place, General George C. Marshall said in 1938, where they would "no longer rap out orders and make snap decisions, [but rather become] . . . experts in a whole new set of skills."[2] Graduates of the War College include some of the most esteemed names in 20th century military history, including John Pershing, Dwight Eisenhower, George Patton, Omar Bradley, Alexander Haig, and Norman Schwarzkopf.

Today bookstores are overflowing with titles on leadership of every conceivable sort. But the first institution of higher education to offer leadership education was the United States Military Academy at West Point, and much of the early research on leadership was funded by the U.S. government at the behest of President Dwight Eisenhower. The U.S. Army has led the way in leadership education. In the last few years in particular, there has been a great deal of interest in the Army's approach to leadership and leadership education.

This book offers an in-depth view of how the Army educates its senior officers to become strategic thinkers and leaders and presents lessons that can be applied to any situation. Just as graduates of the War College and other senior service colleges are expected to translate the goals of national policy into credible military objectives (ends), concepts (ways), and resources (means), it is our objective to provide readers with the ways, means, and ends to become better strategic thinkers and leaders.

This book is presented in four parts:

- ▸ Part I. A Culture of Leadership
- ▸ Part II. Strategic Thinking
- ▸ Part III. Strategic Leadership
- ▸ Part IV. Gettysburg: A Case Study in Strategic Leadership.

PART I. A CULTURE OF LEADERSHIP

The U.S. Army has developed an extensive culture of leadership development, which is discussed in Chapter 1. Key elements of the Army's leadership environment include a sequential and progressive network of schools and courses focusing on leadership, a shared framework and vocabulary for thinking about leadership, operational assignments designed to stretch and develop leadership capacity, a focus on individualized self-development, and a system of empowering others. A carefully constructed and sequenced leadership environment is central to the Army's successful approach to developing "Army Strong" leaders.

PART II. STRATEGIC THINKING

If most generals were asked the question, "What is the difference between a strategic leader and other types of leaders?" they would likely respond, "The type of thinking." Although most officers have been trained to think through problems at a tactical level, few know how to embrace the more nebulous world of strategic thought where things are tenuous and not susceptible to easy answers. Such thinking often has little to do with current crises, but focuses on understanding long-term processes in an all-encompassing context. In short, strategic thinkers deal with problems that are much wider in scope, more intertwined with other problems, laden with ethical dilemmas, and that sometimes must be managed rather than solved.

Strategic thinking includes different lenses and thought processes that are useful in any endeavor, but they are critical for senior leaders in a time of accelerating change that brings both threats and opportunities. These lenses and thought processes include critical thinking, systems thinking, thinking in historical time, and creative thinking.

The late Peter Drucker warned up-and-coming senior leaders to know themselves—their strengths, weaknesses, and values—or they would become obsolete. Like Drucker, Craig Bullis, PhD, the author of Chapter 2, argues that self-awareness is the key to organizational effectiveness. Discussing various assessment tools such as the Myers-Briggs personality instrument and the 360-degree assessment used as part of the Leadership Feedback Program at the War College, he demonstrates that insight into personal blind spots can lead to changes that will benefit both the leader and the institution. Without a sound personal assessment program, he asserts, no real leadership development can take place.

Chapter 3 discusses critical thinking—the purposeful, reflective, and careful evaluation of information as a way to improve judgment. Using a critical thinking model honed by the military, author Stephen Gerras, PhD, discusses how leaders learn to combat the egocentric and self-deluding tendencies leaders face when the stakes are high. Critical thinking requires leaders to constantly challenge their own point of view, their core assumptions, and their self-deluding inferences. Understanding thinking processes and biases helps senior leaders make better decisions, become skilled negotiators, and serve as more adept strategic leaders.

In Chapter 4, author George Reed, PhD, discusses why the U.S. Army places central importance on the ability to apply systems thinking to problems that arise in volatile, uncertain, complex, and ambiguous environments. Dr. Reed identifies the Army's approach to teaching systems thinking, which has been influenced by management scholars Russell Ackoff, Peter Senge, and Mary Jo Hatch, sociologists Robert Merton and James Q. Wilson, and research by the Institute for Defense Analysis. In addition to discussions about the military use of systems thinking, Dr. Reed discusses how a large bureaucracy like the Department of Defense uses systems thinking to contend with an environment that includes congressional committees, national media, and public budgetary constraints.

In Chapter 5, Mark Grandstaff, PhD, examines how strategic leaders use and misuse history. The first section complements Dr. Gerras's chapter on critical thinking with two case studies that demonstrate how making poor historical analogies can lead to poor strategic decision-making. The second section discusses how a senior leader's knowledge of history can help him or her understand complex situations. The chapter ends by explaining why it's essential that senior leaders understand the history of the organization they work for, so they don't make decisions that could have a damaging effect on the organization.

Most problems that strategic leaders face require novel approaches and creative thinking. In Chapter 6, author COL Charles Allen profiles great military leaders, including Napoleon, who mastered *coup d'oeil*—an intuitive and inspired situational awareness—to solve battlefield dilemmas. He contends that the military's use of standard operating procedures, regulations, and doctrine mitigate against creative solutions; in response, the War College uses personal assessments, creative exercises, group games, and other strategies to explore group strategies and processes.

PART III. STRATEGIC LEADERSHIP

Even though levels of leadership are often blurred in our complex culture, unique sets of knowledge, skills, and abilities are necessary for strategic leadership. In today's fast-paced society, strategic leaders need to scan the environment, anticipate change proactively, develop a vision of their organization's future, align the organization's culture with their vision, understand other cultures, and negotiate across a wide breadth of stakeholders. The Army War College introduces the concepts and skills required of leaders within the strategic environment by examining responsible command, leadership, and management practices.

In Chapter 7, authors COL James Oman and COL Mark Eshelman show how an organization's vision gives that organization its purpose, direction, energy, and identity. They methodically lay out a vision's characteristics and components, providing insights into how leaders can scan their environments, collect data, and make interpretations to create or maintain a dynamic vision for the organization. The chapter concludes with a discussion of how to evaluate future contingencies through scenario-based planning.

Why did the Army resist letting go of horses and mules after World War I, despite its awareness that the animals had become obsolete in the face of mechanized warfare? Why did the Navy continue to order new battleships despite its realization that aircraft carriers were the offensive weapon of the future? In Chapter 8, COL Charles Allen and Stephen Gerras attribute these decisions to culture. Drawing from the theories of Edward Schein and others, the authors posit that organizations have deeply embedded assumptions that form the core of their cultures and have an effect on decisions and behavior. The authors encourage leaders to examine fundamental artifacts, including rites, rituals, and stories, to determine cultural boundaries and facilitate cultural change as needed.

Chapter 9 addresses a long-standing strength of the Army—its diverse workforce—and highlights the complexity of managing the transition to a global environment. COL Julie Manta presents the framework developed by the Defense Equal Opportunity and Management Institute, which addresses multiple frames of identity, not just race and gender. These "secondary dimensions," which include geographic location, parental status, military experience, and religious beliefs, are often key drivers of personal identity and shape cultural belief systems. Using current thinking, creative pedagogy, and senior leader experience, the Army drills down in its three-stage approach toward understanding culture: cultural awareness, cultural knowledge, and cultural skills for senior leaders.

In Chapter 10, COL George Woods discusses the important role negotiation plays in strategic leadership. At the most basic level, for example, the Army's expeditionary imperative requires complex negotiations between it, the Navy, and the Air Force to develop a unified approach to war. And in an era where the Army participates in peacekeeping and nation-building, strategic leaders really have no choice but to become competent negotiators.

In Chapter 11, COL Lee DeRemer argues that it is not enough to lead change—leaders must manage change and create a culture that thrives on making positive changes. In a chapter that ties Parts II and III together,

COL DeRemer shows how a leader's self-awareness and ability to think strategically is central to embedding change mechanisms in an organization. A good strategic leader promotes a vision of change that people can support selflessly.

PART IV. GETTYSBURG: A CASE STUDY IN STRATEGIC LEADERSHIP

In Chapter 12, COL Mark Eshelman and COL James Oman provide a unique view of the Gettysburg battlefields. The authors describe War College class trips to the battlefields, where participants take a tour, debate historical decisions, and consider ways to apply the lessons of Gettysburg to their professional leadership experiences. The authors show how Gettysburg offers insights into strategic issues like visioning, decision-making, organizational and adversarial culture, and courage and creativity.

Finally, distinguished leadership scholar and political scientist James MacGregor Burns offers his own experience of strategic leadership. As a young Army soldier charged with establishing the Army history program during World War II, Burns learned that underlying the panoply of all strategic leadership strategies rests the enduring cornerstone of democratic values—the pursuit of happiness, justice, equality, freedom of speech and religion, life, and liberty itself.

* * *

We are indebted to Carolyne Wood and Don Norton for their excellent critique and for editing the book and to Myra Strauss and Courtney Chiaparas of Management Concepts for its skillful execution. Mark would also like to express his appreciation to Brigham Young University and the

Park City Library for their generous use of facilities and assistance. And of course, this book would not have been possible without our faculty colleagues at the Department of Command, Leadership, and Management at the U.S. Army War College.

Mark Grandstaff, PhD

Georgia Sorenson, PhD

September 2008

NOTES

1. *The New York Times*, 21 February 1906, 1.

2. Stephen Shambach, ed., *Strategic Leadership Primer*, 2nd ed. (Carlisle, PA: U.S. Army War College, 2004): 1.

PART I

A Culture of Leadership

CHAPTER 1

Creating a Culture of Leadership Development

George E. Reed, PhD

During the first weeks of Operation Iraqi Freedom, Sergeant First Class Paul R. Smith led an engineer unit as part of an infantry task force that was advancing toward the Baghdad airport. While constructing an enemy prisoner of war holding area, the unit was attacked by a force of over a hundred enemy fighters armed with automatic weapons and rocket-propelled grenades. Outnumbered and nearly surrounded, Sergeant Smith engaged the enemy with grenades, an antitank weapon, and small arms while directing the fire and movements of his soldiers. After several of his soldiers were injured, he realized that the enemy had the upper hand. Sergeant Smith then climbed into the hatch of a disabled armored vehicle and exposed himself to enemy fire in order to employ a .50 caliber machine gun in an attempt to delay the advance. He was successful in disrupting the enemy attack, but in the process he was mortally wounded.

His fellow soldiers honored him for his courageous leadership and for saving the lives of his men. Sergeant Smith's sister later recounted that he "had an incredible love for the troops under his command. . . . In the last letter that Paul Smith wrote from Iraq to our parents, he told them that now that he was a father himself, he realized just how much they had sacrificed to make his life a good life and he thanked them for that special effort. He spoke of being prepared to give—as he said—'all that I am, to ensure that all my boys make it home.' In that same letter, he told our parents how proud he was of the 'privilege to be given 25 of the finest Americans we call Soldiers to lead into war,' and he recognized their fears and his responsibilities for their welfare."[1] Congress celebrated his sacrifice by awarding him the nation's most revered medal—the Medal of Honor. In a touching ceremony at the White House, his wife and children received the medal in his stead.

One might well ask, "What do the actions of a senior noncommissioned officer, heroic as they are, have to do with strategic leadership or culture development in a large and complex organization?" The question reflects a common misunderstanding about levels of leadership. The actions of strategic leaders have a direct connection to, and impact on, those on the front line. Sergeant Smith's actions demonstrate that such efforts to imbue a warrior ethos and develop responsible leaders of character make a difference. Long before Sergeant Smith's unit took to the field, strategic leaders had created a culture of leadership development by providing a vision and example of what Army leaders should be, know, and do. They then defined requirements and allocated the financial resources for leadership schools and courses.

The public and private sectors outside the military are increasingly recognizing the value of strategic leadership as a means to obtain a competitive edge in a volatile and unpredictable environment. A 2004 Executive Development Trends survey identified the following top objectives for executive development in the next two to three years: (1) increasing bench strength, (2) accelerating the development of high-potentials, (3) communicating vision and strategy, (4) supporting change and transformation, and (5) developing individual leader capabilities.[2] Furthermore, in a 2005 survey, respondents were asked to identify gaps in the next generation's capabilities. Deficiencies most frequently cited included:

- Ability to create a vision and engage others so they feel ownership and passion about achieving it (58 percent)

- Understanding of the total enterprise, how the different parts work together to leverage their collective capabilities to serve customers/clients better than the competition (56 percent)

- Strategic thinking (55 percent)

- Cooperation and collaboration with other parts of the business to (1) optimize the operations of our business and (2) to leverage our collective capabilities in the marketplace to identify and serve customers/clients better than the competition

- Leadership (46 percent).[3]

The Army has taught these principles to its future leaders for a long time. While it is true that the Army is not a business in a conventional sense, as an enterprise it faces challenges that global business leaders would easily recognize. The Army is as a large and complex organization of 1.23 million members spread across 17 strategic business units operating in 120 countries. It operates with a budget of over $100 billion in fiscal year 2006, and it faces a high-risk, competitive, dangerous, and rapidly changing environment. Moreover, a recent Korn/Ferry report found that many former military members serve in the private sector as chief executive officers. This alone attests to the fact that leadership skills learned in the military enhance success in corporate life. Key military leadership traits that translate well to business leadership include learning how to work as part of a team; organizational skills, such as planning and effective use of resources; good communication skills; defining a goal and motivating others to follow it; a highly developed sense of ethics; and the ability to remain calm under pressure.[4]

WHAT IS A CULTURE OF LEADERSHIP?

A culture of leader development exists when supervisors agree that it is their duty to develop their subordinates to meet their full potential, and when organization members at all levels strive to achieve the next level of responsibility. There must be a commitment that development remain a priority, even in the midst of budgetary and operational pressures. Certain personnel policies and resource decisions, coupled with constant emphasis by senior leaders, should further reinforce this commitment.

Several policies and mechanisms in the Army combine to powerfully reinforce this type of culture:

- ► A shared framework and vocabulary for thinking and talking about leadership (leadership doctrine).

- ► A three-part model for leader development consisting of institutional training and education, operational assignments, and self-development.

- ► A sequential and progressive system of training and education through well-resourced institutional schools and courses (the system of professional military education).

- ► Assignment policies that maximize development by ensuring that all members progress through steadily increasing positions of responsibility.

- ► Funding for education and training that is centralized. Costs are transparent to the sending organization.

- ► Organizations that do not suffer extended personnel losses when sending personnel to schools and courses.

- ► Promotions and key assignments tied to successful completion of professional schools and courses.

- ► Leaders responsible for developing leaders. Leader development is not simply a human resources function.

- ► Personnel policies which require that to remain in the organization, members must be promoted within a specified period of time ("up or out").

THE ARMY'S LEADERSHIP FRAMEWORK

In the Army, clear lines of supervision are considered a virtue, while status, prestige, and power are largely distributed on the basis of rank and position. It should not be a surprise, then, that the Army leadership framework takes a stratified approach to the phenomenon (Figure 1-1). In other words, the Army leadership framework considers three levels of leadership: direct (or tactical level, which is focused at the team or unit level); organizational (focused on systems and processes); and strategic (global or regional perspective).[5]

These levels of leadership have strong face validity to anyone who has tried to make a transition from first-line supervisor to middle manager or from mid-level to executive leadership. What makes a person successful at one level will not ensure success at the next. There may even be skills and abilities that are highly rewarded at one level but that can be disastrous at other levels. As an example, quick decision-making with limited information, accompanied by technically competent and forceful execution, is a virtue at the tactical (or direct) level; at the strategic level, however, patience, negotiation, and consensus, combined with synthesis and integration skills, are absolutely necessary. This then sets an organizational imperative to prepare individuals for the demands of different levels and provides a framework for building a system of professional schools and courses.

FIGURE 1-1. Army leadership framework.

The Army also makes an extensive investment in the education and development of its leaders. Over a 20-year career, a typical Army officer might spend 4 years or more in schools and courses that sometimes include fully funded graduate studies in civilian universities. Although there are differences between officers, noncommissioned officers, and the civilian workforce, all have access to a system of professional development schools and courses. This is a massive investment when you consider the operational demands the Army faces during times of conflict. Some of the more extensive school programs, such as the U.S. Army War College, last for up to ten months, a period during which many of the "best and brightest" are unavailable for field assignments or missions.[6]

The Army, like all branches of the military, has a system of sequential schools and courses that are specifically designed to help leaders prepare for the next level of responsibility. Where there are known transition points, such as from enlisted soldier to noncommissioned officer, or from junior officer to field grade, there is a mandatory school to prepare them. These courses are not simply offered as options; they are prerequisites or "gateways" that must be completed before serving at the next level. They are considered rewards for effective performance and an essential preparation for promotion.

Education is thus tightly linked to a personnel system that handles promotions and selection for key assignments. Personnel policies serve as important drivers of organizational culture in the Army. Two are especially important: the "up or out" policy, which mandates that soldiers must either be promoted within a specified period of time or leave, and the lack of a mechanism to hire those from outside the organization into senior leadership positions. There are no career privates in the Army. Every soldier is preparing for promotion to the next level of responsibility. One either moves up the promotion ladder or is out of the Army. Given that one does not, under normal circumstances, qualify for retirement benefits until one has 20 years of service, there is a powerful motivation to make progress. Being passed over for promotion sends a clear message that one should look for another job.

When that policy is combined with the harsh realities of the battle-field, which demand that subordinates stand ready to assume the role of a wounded leader, the Army has compelling reasons for extending developmental opportunities to the lowest levels of the organization. Succession planning is therefore an inherent part of daily operations. Instead of focusing on educating and developing a few with the highest potential for leadership, the Army extends developmental opportunities to all soldiers. The Army is a closed system in terms of advancement. It does not hire executives from other walks of life, and this means that the generals of tomorrow are the lieutenants of today. Because it is impossible to determine with any accuracy which junior officers or noncommissioned officers will reach senior leadership, the institution must distribute leader development to all.

The system of professional military education works for another reason—two key processes and procedures, both of which are rarely observed outside the military: the Trainees, Holdees, and Students (TTHS) account and a policy of centralized funding for schools and courses. The TTHS account is a device that, in addition to other uses, provides a holding point for soldiers when they are undergoing entry-level training, attending long-term schools and courses, or moving from one post to another. It works something like this: Let's say a soldier is selected to attend a long-term developmental course. During the period of attendance, the soldier will be placed in the TTHS account and charted as a loss to his or her unit. This means that the personnel system will assign a replacement with roughly the equivalent grade and abilities in that person's place. Upon graduation, the schooled soldier will travel to an assignment appropriate to the newfound skills and abilities. This prevents organizations from suffering long periods with vacant positions. It also eliminates a powerful disincentive for sending high-potentials to schools and courses. Although the TTHS account is often targeted as a source of "overhead" and something to be minimized, it is rarely reduced in size, nor should it be. It is actually a mechanism that fuels a robust educational system that pays great dividends over time.

Centralized funding of educational programs also eliminates powerful disincentives that can confound leadership-development initiatives. In many organizations, when an employee is selected to attend even an in-house developmental course, the cost is assessed against the sending business unit. Put another way, if the marketing department wants to send an employee to a school or course, marketing must budget for that course and will be decremented for the cost of attendance as a measure of cost accounting. Although this may be a good way to capture costs for training and education, it also dissuades supervisors from sending employees, especially when budgets are tight. When costs are transparent to the sending organization and are centrally controlled, it sends the message that development is important as an organizational investment, not simply an operating cost that is to be controlled and minimized.

THE ARMY'S APPROACH TO LEADER DEVELOPMENT

The Army's approach to leader development can be seen as resting on three pillars (Figure 1-2): institutional training in the sequential and progressive network of professional schools and courses; operational assignments designed to stretch and develop leadership capacity "on the job"; and self-development, which is largely an individual responsibility.[7] In the Army, leadership is not simply a human resource function, although the Human Resources Command plays an important role in the processes of assignments and selection. Leaders are expected to coach, encourage, develop, and in some cases mentor other leaders. In the words of Department of the Army Pamphlet 350-58,

> As leader development unfolds in each of the three pillars, a continuing cycle of education and training, experience, assessment, feedback, and reinforcement and remediation occurs. . . . During this leader development process, the responsibility for a leader's complete development is mutually shared by the leaders of the Army education system, commanders and leaders in the field, and the leaders themselves.[8]

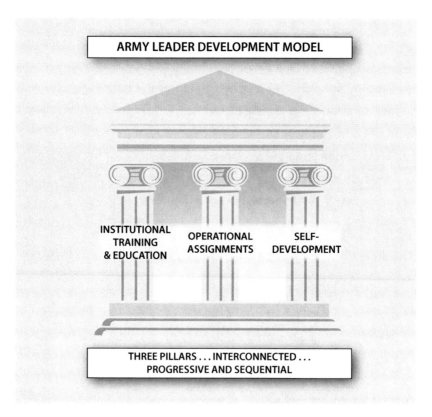

FIGURE 1-2. Army leader development model.[9]

The notion of pillars suggests that leader development would be incomplete or flawed without all three.

While institutional training and operational assignments are relatively obvious, self-development is worthy of some additional exploration. Self-development and reflection can be seen in an emphasis on professional reading and pursuit of civilian educational programs. The institution supports self-development through such measures as providing tuition assistance for civilian education, staffing military education centers with advisors, and providing resources designed to foster lifelong learning. As an example of senior leader emphasis on professional reading, in the preface to the Army Chief of Staff's reading list published by the Center of Military History, General Peter J. Schoomaker points out the importance of professional reading: "I challenge all leaders to make a focused, personal commitment to read, reflect, and learn about our profession and our world. Through the exercise of our minds, our Army will grow stronger."[10]

THE U.S. ARMY WAR COLLEGE AND THE EDUCATION OF STRATEGIC LEADERS

The U.S. Army War College represents the pinnacle educational experience for the professional Army officer. After about 18 to 20 years of exceptional service, the top performers are selected to engage in a developmental experience—a 10-month course designed to prepare them for even greater responsibility. Selection for attendance does not necessarily mean that these officers will become generals, but they will not be selected as general officers unless they successfully complete this level of education. A distinguished senior officer recently reminded the members of class that although they were most likely acutely aware of their many deficiencies and might consider themselves "just one of the guys or gals," they would soon be "running this thing [the Army]." He noted that their very presence at the Army War College indicated that they were very important to the success of the Department of Defense.[11]

It is at the Army War College that officers move from the study of tactics of battles and compliance with established procedures to the theory and art of war and strategy, international relations, global economics, and civil-military relations. The Army War College's faculty recognizes that it may well be more difficult to build an Army than to fight one, so emphasis is placed on the mechanisms of managing at the executive level. The core curriculum is designed to produce graduates who can:

- Distinguish the uniqueness of strategic-level leadership and apply competencies required by strategic leaders

- Use strategic thought processes to evaluate the national security challenges and opportunities facing the United States in the twenty-first century

- Evaluate the theory of war and strategy

- Evaluate Department of Defense, joint, interagency, intergovernmental, multinational, and nongovernmental processes and relationships, including Army contributions to the nation in peace and war

- Evaluate the role of the Army in joint, interagency, intergovernmental, and multinational operations

- Synthesize theater strategies, estimates, and campaign plans to employ military power in a unified, joint, multinational, and interagency environment

- Synthesize critical elements, enablers, and processes that define the strategic environment in peace and war

- Study and discuss the current and future state of the American military profession.[12]

After attendees complete the core curriculum, they select from a number of electives to round out their education. Some pursue newfound areas of interest, while others seek to develop areas that need some additional attention based on their experiences in the core curriculum.

The ten-month curriculum at the Army War College recognizes that, in the words of America's preeminent executive coach, Marshall Goldsmith, "What got you here won't get you there."[13] It is designed to expand perspectives and develop thought patterns that lead to a greater probability of success in the strategic environment. As an example, let's consider the opening block of instruction, "Fundamentals of Strategic Thinking." While recognizing that those selected to attend the College have been quite successful and have amassed a repertoire of effective leadership abilities, the course offers participants an opportunity to retune some cognitive approaches that are most suitable for a graduate-level educational program and for strategic-level responsibilities.

It is essentially a course that addresses not *what* to think but *how* to think. Specifically, it focuses on five cognitive domains of signature importance to senior-level leadership: critical thinking, creative thinking, systems thinking, ethical reasoning, and historical thinking. In the early part of the course, faculty and participants strive to create a supportive learning environment where assumptions can be challenged, dialogue supplants dogma, and all involved assume shared responsibility for learning. The faculty goes about facilitating this learning environment with great intent. They know that if they get the chemistry right in the early days, the class will reap the benefits throughout the year.

Most of the seminar members are used to working within a hierarchy. In the seminar; however, there are no such divisions in rank—all are equals.

The War College Seminar, a group of 15 to 17 students and 3 faculty members, is the prime learning community. The seminar studies and learns together throughout the year and forges deep connections that often last far beyond a military career. Although faculty members are usually colonels and most participants are lieutenant colonels or equivalent, the faculty insists that they be referred to by their first names. Faculty and students alike have the option of wearing business attire, which can help break down barriers of rank. Every effort is taken to ensure that ideas and dialogue are not sacrificed to status or position. This can be unsettling to some, but it is also necessary preparation for dealing with organizations outside the Department of Defense. Graduates of the War College are expected to work with interagency partners who are not necessarily impressed with military rank and position.

The first writing assignment provides an opportunity to assess participants' writing ability. When this assignment is combined with an objective evaluation that assesses writing mechanics, the faculty can identify those who would benefit from additional instruction. Because effective writing and speaking are of such extraordinary importance to senior leadership, they are a focus throughout the academic year. Although many officers believe they are good writers, they are often more comfortable with technical writing appropriate for e-mails, point papers, and PowerPoint presentations than the kind of expressive writing appropriate for inspiring others and communicating with outside audiences. All attendees are required to complete an extensive strategy research paper as a requisite to graduation. This project, similar in many ways to a thesis, is designed to address contemporary issues of importance to the profession, and unless the topics contain classified information, they are made available to the public through the Defense Technical Information Center.

All participants are expected to work with a faculty advisor to develop an individual learning plan. The plan, developed in the first weeks of the course, addresses both personal and professional goals and objectives. It is intended to guide the student through the many choices and options that arise during the year, including the selection of electives and complementary programs. Students also have the opportunity to take a battery of psychometric instruments that provide extensive information about their leadership skills and attributes. One such instrument—similar to a 360-degree assessment—provides them with an assessment of their leadership by superiors, peers, and subordinates. Skilled counselors and psychologists then provide detailed feedback to the participants. When the assessments are combined with the individual learning plan, the result is an opportunity for extensive growth and development.

Throughout the year, attendees are given the opportunity to participate in a host of extracurricular and complementary programs. The intramural sports program contributes to social bonding as much as to fitness, and many learning opportunities include family members. The Military Family Program is a source of pride at the Army War College because it provides resources and information useful to those in their early forties. It addresses such varied items as financial planning for retirement, preparing children for college admission, and caring for aging parents.

Furthermore, senior officers and government officials recognize that the Army War College class is an important audience. A host of lectures provide ample opportunity to engage speakers from the highest levels of government. President George W. Bush recently gave a policy speech at the College, and former Secretary of State Colin Powell commemorated a chair established in his honor. The College often invites speakers who provide alternative or critical viewpoints in an effort to expand perspectives and prepare attendees to deal with the varied opinions that are part of the rich tapestry of American society. During the last week of the academic year, guests invited from across the nation join the Army War College in an event known as the National Security Seminar. It is here that the guests, invited by students and faculty, interact with the class and with guest speakers. They get a taste of the College experience and provide a healthy seasoning to the final week of the course. Because most of them have no formal association with the military, they come to appreciate the complexities of the strategic environment and the intellect of the attendees.

One novel approach to leadership development at the Army War College is the Strategic Leader Staff Ride (see Chapter 12). In one sense it is a case study unlike any other. Students are paired with faculty members, and together they visit the Gettysburg National Military Park. There the focus is not so much on tactics or operational concepts as on the ideas that strategic leaders should keep in mind. These include how "winning or losing" affects public opinion and political resolve to carry on the fight. Although there is significant discussion of Pickett's Charge and the actions of the 20th Maine at Little Round Top, there are also important points about the volatility and uncertainty of situations in battle. Events on the battlefield provide an opportunity to discuss the impact of recruiting, retention, financial, and personnel systems. At Gettysburg, faculty members visually impress upon their students that strategic leadership is about understanding the big picture.

This unique experience is not reserved for students alone. The Strategic Leader Staff Ride proves to be a valuable opportunity for the faculty of the College to meet and exchange ideas with leaders in the private sector. Several times a year, groups from some of America's most successful and well-known companies visit the Army War College for an innovative two-to three-day program. With Army War College historians and leadership scholars, the guests visit Gettysburg, where they examine the events of the battlefield for immutable lessons. More than just a tour of the battlefield, the experience serves as a platform to address issues of leadership and management.

The guests then have the opportunity to dialogue with faculty members on a menu of topics, such as developing strategic leaders, strategy, and organizational change. Faculty members who participate in this program admit that while the program is part of the Army's strategic communications effort, it is also an opportunity to learn from those outside the military and a way to share best leadership practices in a rapidly changing world. Some groups use this event as an executive off-site where they make important decisions for their organizations. In a discussion with former General Electric Chief Executive Officer Jack Welch, one Army colonel said that Welch told him that he had changed a part of GE's business plan because of what he had learned on the Gettysburg staff ride.

In some respects the mechanisms that reinforce a culture of leadership development are fragile. The professional military education system is expensive in terms of both funds and personnel. The up-or-out policy and the need to place soldiers in developmental assignments ensures high personnel turbulence. Many short-term pressures could result in decisions that undermine the culture, and there has been no shortage of proposals to do just that. Some have proposed shortening training and education courses, or moving to distance education, in an effort to save time and money. The TTHS account is often targeted for reduction to put more boots on the ground, and opportunities for graduate-level schooling wax and wane. The fact that the institution has largely resisted such pressures, even during a time of conflict, illustrates how deeply the culture of leadership development extends.

Some of the mechanisms discussed above can be replicated in non-military organizations. Developing a leadership framework, centralizing funding for education and training, creating a TTHS-like personnel account, emphasizing self-development, and making leader development a primary responsibility of all leaders are not necessarily costly endeavors. Others, such as the up-or-out policy and the Army's extensive institutional school structure, may not be appropriate outside the military context. It is clear, however, that these factors combine in powerful ways that result in many dedicated, competent, and sometimes heroic leaders, like Sergeant Smith and Major David Rozelle.

Major Rozelle was commanding K Troop of the 3rd Squadron in the 3rd Armored Cavalry Regiment in Iraq when the vehicle he was riding in struck an antitank mine. A severe injury resulted in the amputation of his right leg below the knee. He struggled through a painful recovery with the expressed intention of rejoining his soldiers in Iraq. After he learned to use a prosthetic leg, he became the first amputee to return to duty in Iraq and complete a second combat tour. Today he serves as administrator for the Amputee Care Center at Walter Reed Army Medical Center in Washington, D.C., where he continues to inspire others. David Rozelle's story hits home with soldiers who unfailingly look up to his example with pride and admiration. There was no quit in him, and despite all that he suffered, he just had to return to his soldiers.[14] The telling of Major Rozelle's triumphant tale of servant leadership is also a culture-building mechanism. It reinforces an ethos of selfless service, which is the defining characteristic of the U.S. Army.

NOTES

1. For a full account of Sergeant First Class Paul Ray Smith's heroism, visit the website that commemorates Medal of Honor awardees at http://www.army.mil/ medalofhonor/smith (accessed 6 June 2007).

2. James F. Bolt, "Mapping the Future of Leadership Development," *The 2007 Pfeiffer Annual: Leadership Development*, James F. Bolt, ed. (Hoboken, NJ: John Wiley & Sons, 2007): 3–23.

3. Ibid., 10.

4. Tim Duffy and Dan Armstrong, *Military Experience and CEOs: Is There a Link?* (Los Angeles: Korn/Ferry International, 2006).

5. Department of the Army, "Field Manual 6-22—Army Leadership" (Washington, D.C.: Department of the Army, 2006): 3–6.

6. Despite the extensive manpower cost, the U.S. Army War College closed only once—during World War II—a decision viewed in retrospect as a mistake. See H.P. Ball, *Of Responsible Command: A History of the U.S. Army War College,* rev. ed. (Carlisle, PA: Alumni Association of the U.S. Army War College, 1994).

7. Department of the Army, "2005 Posture Statement," available online at http:// www.army.mil/aps/05/training.html (accessed 14 June 2007).

8. Department of the Army, "Pamphlet 350-58—The Enduring Legacy: Leader Development for America's Army" (Washington, D.C.: Department of the Army, 1994): 4.

9. Ibid.

10. Department of the Army, Center for Military History, "CMH Pub 105-5-1—The U.S. Army Chief of Staff's Professional Reading List," available online at http:// www.army.mil/cmh-pg/reference/CSAList/CSAReadingList.pdf (accessed 14 June 2007).

11. It is the convention of the U.S. Army War College to avoid attributing by name remarks made by guest speakers. The non-attribution policy encourages guests to speak freely and frankly without fear of being quoted outside the institution. It is therefore appropriate to reference such comments in somewhat vague terms, as in this case.

12. The U.S. Army War College institutional learning objectives are available online at http://www.carlisle.army.mil/usawc/daa/external_site/Objectives.shtml (accessed 1 August 2007).

13. Marshall Goldsmith and Mark Reiter, *What Got You Here Won't Get You There: How Successful People Become Even More Successful* (New York: Hyperion, 2007).

14. To read about Major Rozelle in his own words, see David Rozelle, *Back in Action: An American Soldier's Story of Courage, Faith and Fortitude* (Washington, DC: Regnery Publishing, 2005).

PART II

Strategic Thinking

2 Self-Awareness: Enhancing Strategic Leader Development

Craig Bullis, PhD

Make progress, my brothers; examine yourselves honestly again and again. . . . Do not be content with what you are. . . . Always add something more, keep moving forward, always make progress.

—St. Augustine, Sermon 169

Leader development programs that result in enhanced self-awareness can be one of an organization's most difficult and yet most rewarding efforts. The importance of this challenge is that leaders have significant effects on the competitive advantage of organizations.[1] Organizations that develop leaders are simply better than those that focus their emphasis elsewhere.[2] Optimizing strategic leadership development, therefore, provides the fundamental challenge for virtually all large-scale organizations in the modern world. In the U.S. Army, "growing adaptive leaders" is a major strategy of the Army's vision "to remain the preeminent landpower on Earth."[3] Research in nonmilitary organizations argues that a similar strategy can be advantageous in such firms.[4] Consequently, the development of leaders at all levels becomes the long-term priority of any organization that depends on competitive advantage for survival. Following St. Augustine's suggestion, this chapter argues for and describes processes to encourage leaders to "make progress" in their own development.

Leadership researchers have struggled for decades to identify a comprehensive list of behaviors that can be used for leader selection, development, and promotion.[5] Hundreds of lists have been produced. The continuous development of new lists, most of which overlap a great deal, suggests an interesting dilemma. It seems that the challenge for leaders and organizations is not to identify what good leaders do; the existence of such a number of overlapping lists is ample evidence that we understand the expectations of leaders. Rather, it seems that the real challenge is understanding why leaders do not do what they know they ought to do. One potential reason is simply that "They don't know what they don't know." This chapter, then, follows the logic suggested by researchers that an increase in self-awareness is a key prerequisite for effective leadership.[6]

Self-awareness is defined as the accurate and objective understanding of personal strengths and weaknesses. This personal information provides leaders knowledge in several important areas. As mentioned above, understanding oneself is a critical component for individual performance because an accurate self-awareness has been shown to be one of the fundamentals of effective leadership. Second, increased self-awareness presents a clear path to focus our leader development efforts. A multifaceted approach, especially when assessing leadership behavior, is necessary because research has supported the assertion that many senior leaders assess their personal leadership effectiveness differently than do their superiors, peers, and subordinates.[7] Finally, increased self-awareness (particularly of relative weaknesses in behavior) reinforces that leaders, at no matter what level in an organization, can be effective even with certain "developmental needs." The caveat, of course, is that leaders must be aware of potential blind spots, which have been shown to derail leaders who were otherwise very effective.[8] Accepting ourselves as "incomplete" might explicitly suggest circumstances in which we should surround ourselves with others who might have better abilities than us.[9] Information in this chapter should assist in understanding assessment processes and the challenges associated with leadership development.

METHODOLOGIES TO ENHANCE A STRATEGIC LEADER'S SELF-AWARENESS

I wanna talk about me. I wanna talk about I.
I wanna talk about number one, old my me my –
What I think, what I like, what I know, what I want, what I see.
I like talkin' 'bout you, you, you, you, usually.
But occasionally,
I wanna talk about me.

—TOBY KEITH, COUNTRY SINGER

Although organizations and researchers employ multiple methods to enhance self-awareness, this chapter focuses predominantly on the Army's use of leadership assessment measures: the use of surveys to gather data that provide participants important information about themselves. In categorizing these measures, this chapter uses a relatively straightforward methodology, which is to consider two broad measures—personality and behavior.

Personality Assessment

Understanding of one's own personality has unique importance for leaders who consistently operate in the strategic context because one's personality significantly affects behavior and can often drive an "automatic" behavioral response in times of increased stress. Examples of how personality manifests itself include what information one attends to, how quickly one makes decisions, how one interacts with others, or how conscientious one is about his or her responsibilities. Self-aware leaders understand those preferences and dispositions, which allows them to manage their own behavior and, by doing so, to become more effective.

At the U.S. Army War College, the core curriculum includes assessments intended to inform self-awareness, such as the Myers-Briggs Type Indicator (MBTI) and the Kirton Adaption/Innovation Inventory (KAI).[10] The MBTI is one of the most widely used personality measures in the world. It assesses personality preferences along four continuums: Introversion/Extroversion; Sensing/Intuition; Thinking/Feeling; and Judging/Perceiving. The results suggest the implications of those preferences for both work and life in general. The KAI, a complementary measure, provides feedback to students on their most comfortable method of implementing change within an organization by providing feedback on their creative style.

While these measures are relatively coarse-grained, discussing their results can be valuable, especially when one highlights the implications of the results for both individuals and the groups to which they belong. To enhance the broad information provided by the MBTI and the KAI, many organizations also provide more fine-grained assessments. In particular, Army War College students are offered the opportunity to participate in a much more detailed program, the Leadership Feedback Program (LFP).

The Army War College's Leadership Feedback Program provides all War College students the opportunity to enhance their leadership abilities by means of an integrated program of behavioral and personality assessments, with particular interest in how these psychological factors affect health, fitness, and effectiveness. This assessment obtains data from a behavioral assessment that focuses on strategic leadership responsibilities and integrates those results with a detailed personality measure, the NEO PI-R.[11] Following completion of the surveys, an experienced psychologist or behavioral science counselor reviews the results in a two-hour, one-on-one discussion with the individual student. These intensive efforts to integrate personality and behavior have been shown to increase participants' self-awareness, thereby providing the participants a clear picture of potential developmental growth to improve their strategic leadership.

Behavioral Assessment

Of course, we recognize that a leader's behavior is influenced by many organizational programs that are intended to develop technical, interpersonal, and conceptual skill sets. George Reed specifically addresses this issue in the preceding chapter as he makes the case for a culture of development in multiple domains: self-development, institutional training, and educational systems—as well as in on-the-job experiences. Often leaders consider these programs comprehensive, providing for ample leader development. In actual implementation, though, it seems that much of these formal programs focus predominantly on technical skill development with fewer formal efforts toward the facilitation of interpersonal and cognitive development.[12]

Throughout their careers, experienced senior leaders have been provided with a great deal of information that either confirms or questions the appropriateness of their behavior. Leaders watch others who are successful and attempt to shape their own behavior so that it is similar to that of their mentors. Continuing education courses teach leaders about their roles and functions in strategic-level positions. Professional reading can give leaders a glimpse into the complex nature of strategic problem-solving or other associated leadership tasks. Formal evaluation reports provide an assessment of one's performance compared with superiors' expectations.

All of these programs add value and can help to shape the appropriateness of behavior. However, they also have significant drawbacks as a comprehensive self-awareness and development program. The work environment and requisite leadership responsibilities can change so rapidly that what might have worked for former bosses does not work under a new one. Similarly, expectations of subordinates can differ because of generational differences.[13] Furthermore, some training courses can be so general that they lack an application component that specifically targets the leader's current situation. Translating information from the pages of a book into actual behavior can prove troublesome if the reader lacks basic skills or understanding of underlying causes of problems.

Evaluation reports, on the other hand, have a particularly strong impact on behavior because they not only determine a person's future in the organization but also are an important means of embedding an organizational culture.[14] These assessments, however, are often narrowly focused on technical skills—versus conceptual and interpersonal skills—because a superior's goal is often one of organizational performance over subordinate leader development. Finally, efficiency reports are a component of an *evaluation* process. Evaluation information can often be very different from information that is intended for *developmental* purposes, with developmental data often less inflated. In addition, efficiency reports are almost exclusively focused from the top down.

One of the recent advancements in leader development programs is behavioral assessments that include subordinate (and other) input. These are commonly referred to as 360-degree feedback programs, and they have emerged as one of the "best practices" associated with effective leader development programs in such respected companies as General Electric, Motorola, PepsiCo, and Johnson & Johnson.[15] A 360-degree leadership assessment is also a fundamental component of the Army War College's Leadership Feedback Program.

In general terms, an effective 360-degree leadership feedback program allows managers to compare their self-assessments with the assessments of their peers, superiors, and subordinates. Data are systematically collected from each of these groups, usually in the form of a written survey that asks about leadership behaviors that are important to both individual and organizational success. The results are then reported back to the targeted leader, who (often with some coaching) develops a plan for personal development. These 360-degree assessments, then, are *reflections* of the leader, as filtered through the *perceptions* of others. Understanding how behavior is perceived by these multiple stakeholders provides important information that the traditional top-down feedback programs cannot achieve.

THE PROCESS OF ENACTING INDIVIDUAL CHANGE THROUGH INCREASED SELF-AWARENESS

Increasing self-awareness begins with the recognition that leaders, while clearly successful in their leadership to date, can still improve their behavior. The next step is to change that behavior. Self-awareness and personal change are leadership principles that are easy to say and very hard to do. "Easy" because something has occurred that has caused the organization (and leader) to recognize that past performance will not effectively complete the future task. "Hard," however, because change, even at the individual level, is never an easy task. Kurt Lewin, one of the pioneers of social psychology, argued that personal development could be captured in three basic phases: (1) unfreeze the behavior that is currently practiced; (2) change the behaviors; and (3) refreeze the new pattern into that which is desired.[16] Only three steps—but often three very difficult steps.

Unfreezing Leadership Behavior

The most difficult step in this process is most often the unfreezing of the old behavior. In almost any circumstance, the prerequisite for change to occur is the recognition of a problem followed by a desire to make a change. But herein lies the challenge: Leaders may not see the problem.

A leading thinker in neuropsychology, Jack Feldman, presents several key reasons why it is difficult for humans to change.[17] One of those reasons is that the efficiency of our existing cognitive structures can actually limit our learning.

Human beings are cognitively efficient creatures. If the human mind needed to explicitly process everything it saw and did at the strategic level, it would be so busy thinking that nothing could ever be accomplished. What the brain does, then, is to make cognitive processing more efficient. Routines develop so that we generally know how to respond when we face a challenge: We can be quick to recognize a particular process failure, the unavailability of a planned critical resource, or the expectations of an external stakeholder who has arrived unexpectedly to "help." Leaders have often faced similar challenges in the past, and while the current situation might have a few nuances, what has worked for us in the past is often a satisfactory first attempt to solving the current crisis.[18]

In other words, as we learn, we develop "rules" that connect the context and associated behaviors. However, those rules can sometimes be developed in a simple, relatively unambiguous situation where cause-effect relationships are straightforward. In contrast, in the volatile, uncertain, complex, and ambiguous (VUCA) environment of the strategic leader, leader tasks are more "intuitive"—problems often lack clear definition, require subjective assessment and judgment, demand the consideration of multiple desirable (or uncomfortable) outcomes, and suggest immediate results that can provide equivocal feedback. The development of cognitive routines is necessary; they provide the basis for "experience," making individuals efficient, knowledgeable, and expert decisionmakers.

In essence, these are the mental models that reflect how we understand, interpret, and act on events.[19] Cognitive routines, however, can also make individuals stubborn, inflexible, and resistant to change. The "rules" we have developed can also be incomplete or even incorrect. The distinction between these two outcomes—expert decisionmaker or stubborn, incompetent boss—can be ascribed to the appropriate application of our experiences. Self-awareness, in essence, helps us to understand our cognitive preferences so that we can know better the "appropriateness" of our experiences for the current challenge.

An additional factor that Feldman argues impedes learning from experience is the nature of the feedback received. Feedback is often single-loop, in that we look at the outcome and compare the desired versus the obtained outcome. What might be more valuable, however, is what Feldman calls "process feedback,"[20] which closely resembles what others have called "double-loop learning."[21] Feldman posits that the challenge leaders face is to resist the outcome feedback and concentrate instead on the *processes* that result in the performance.

For example, a strategic leader who is concerned with the safety performance of a subordinate organization should resist simply looking at the numbers and instead look at the processes that generated the numbers. Are employees rightly trained and socialized so that the each understands safe procedures? Are internal transformation processes designed to reduce or eliminate unsafe conditions? Are leaders establishing a climate that results in a shared commitment to safety?

Fundamentally, Feldman suggests looking beyond both positive and negative outcomes and asking the detailed question, "Why did this outcome occur?" Of course, there is also a challenge in identifying cause-effect relationships at the strategic level because there is often a significant time delay between action by the leader and impact, a delay that further complicates the feedback process.

Finally, our cognitive processing is also susceptible to the errors that Stephen Gerras and Mark Grandstaff discuss in their chapters on critical thinking (Chapter 3) and the uses of history (Chapter 5), respectively. Those errors in attribution and analogical thinking can cause incorrect or incomplete learning from previous experience.

The effectiveness of strategic leaders depends on effective judgment, both about the organization and about themselves. Leaders have to recognize when new learning is necessary. Ultimately, the final impetus for change resides within each leader—you and me. When "disconfirming events are made salient," we have begun the important process of unfreezing our assessment of ourselves.[22]

Changing Leadership Behavior

If expanded roles and functions require new leader behaviors, why do leaders simply not change? Many theories exist to explain why leaders may reject information that suggests that they need to change. One reason is an individual's cognitive function—how the mind works and the cognitive routines that life's experiences have developed. This concept was discussed in detail above. A second potential reason is the socialization processes that teach the "right" way to think, act, and feel about problems faced by the organization and its leaders. One might also consider the fact that success breeds success: Past experiences (both successes and failures) help to direct learning for the future. Finally, impetus for change also depends on the validity of the processes used to identify the leader's "growth needs."

Socialization and expectation are power forces. The socialization process of the U.S. military, like that of many other large bureaucracies, is formally structured to produce a desired outcome. The education of military officers in particular encourages leader traits of decisiveness, tenacity, and endurance. Subordinate leaders demand and depend on their superior leader to set clearly defined limits on their behavior, intentionally focusing responsibility for subordinate leaders to clearly defined tasks. Training tasks and mission sets are nested from the highest to the lowest levels in the military so that every squad, team, and even soldier, sailor, pilot, and marine can envision the relationship between his or her task and an important element of national security. These are necessary restrictions that help to focus individuals and units on appropriate and necessary skills.

Necessarily, these same socialization and nesting processes also have the effect of "training" leaders in the "right" way to do things. The potential problem, of course, is that the challenges at the tactical and operational levels can be significantly different from those at the strategic level. Leaders at the strategic level cannot necessarily depend on a "superior" to set clearly defined boundaries or to provide all the desired resources to perform the assigned tasks. As discussed earlier, strategic leadership is about effectively managing paradox and tradeoffs.[23] Most developmental processes have not necessarily focused on or rewarded those skills. Consequently, leaders may develop strategies that are counterproductive to institutional success.

Success breeds success? Or practice makes permanent. It is always hard to argue with success. Military and civilian leaders who are selected for Senior Service College schooling are by many measures successful individuals. They have led or acted as principal advisors to leaders of organizations of potentially thousands of people; have effectively managed multimillion-dollar budgets; have been responsible for the maintenance and operation of millions of dollars' worth of equipment; and have been provincial governors and advisors to national leaders.

The experiences of such leaders incline them to believe that *practice makes perfect*. On the other hand, practice also makes *permanent*. Some developing strategic leaders are hesitant to expand their repertoire of leadership skills for a variety of reasons. Some argue that individuals are concerned about competing commitments to their role as a successful leader.[24] It might also be that "the best predictor of future behavior is past behavior"—people know and are comfortable with the styles that have made them successful in the past. Leaders possessing these types of approaches resist change or encouragement of self-awareness.

These examples of logic work well in a static environment where the future can be accurately and perfectly gauged by the past. This assumption, however, is invalid, and such logic fails in a constantly changing world. As discussed earlier, the foreseeable future can be characterized by uncertainty, ambiguity, and complexity beyond what the leaders have experienced before. Researchers who study trends in their attempts to describe the future often argue that a critical difference between the past and the future is one of *speed* of operations—things simply happen faster in the current environment—and that speed is predicted to increase even more in the future.[25] Information is disseminated faster, and standard methods of operating grow outdated quickly. Consequently, effectively preparing a leader for a new skill set requires at least an understanding of the leader's current skill set, along with a discussion of the implications of the leader's current styles for the impending challenges.[26]

Feedback and change. In their seminal work on feedback processes in organizations, Ilgen, Fisher, and Taylor explore the complex relationship between feedback and behavioral change.[27] They argue that the acceptance of or resistance to feedback varies, much like all communications, based on the nature of the source of feedback, the message itself, and the characteristics of the recipient.

From a source perspective, people act on feedback from others if the source of the feedback is attributed to be credible, possessing both expertise in the subject and trustworthiness. Alternatively, if the source of feedback information is limited in either category, the effectiveness of the feedback suffers. For example, many military exercises include "senior mentors"— former general officers who succeeded at the highest ranks within the military—to provide feedback to the current senior leaders on their performance. Feedback provided by such individuals has the credibility that motivates recipients to attend to it.

The nature of the skill to be developed might also be a factor that influences one's responsiveness to feedback. At the strategic level, the lack of specificity of leadership responsibilities and the subjective nature of the measures associated with those responsibilities make feedback somewhat problematic. Technical, interpersonal, and cognitive skill sets present specific concerns. Generally, the most objectively measured of these skills are the technical skills because there are professionally accepted "right" and "wrong" ways of accomplishing technical tasks according to established procedures. Feedback in these tasks can motivate a senior leader to act, primarily because it is specific, timely, and often provided by a credible senior mentor.

However, feedback on interpersonal skills can be more problematic. The lack of an established standard of performance can lead to the argument that one type of behavior is as effective as another, but just a *different style*. Because of different leadership styles, feedback that motivates change in interpersonal behavior must come from two sources. The first should be a credible, trustworthy person who has power over the individual (a senior mentor, as discussed earlier). These people often possess significant personal influence over the subordinate leader, and consequently their feedback is more likely to be acted upon.

The second source is the self. Self-assessment provides feedback to an individual and highlights aspects of personality or behavior that may prove inconsistent with how the individual wants to be perceived. The disparity between actual perception and how an individual desires to be perceived can be a catalyst for change. Valid 360-degree behavioral assessments, combined with detailed personality assessments, provide the information to generate this dissonance.

In terms of the message itself, feedback is often ignored when it lacks specificity. Although general feedback ("You're doing a good job") can be received as praise or reinforcement, the lack of precise data renders such information relatively useless as a means of feedback. Likewise, broad negative comments ("You're not worth a plug nickel") often fail to effect a change in behavior.

Although a review of these aspects of resistance to change can appear daunting, research is clear that each hurdle can be overcome. Hughes and Beatty from the Center for Creative Leadership argue that an effective leader feedback program facilitates leader development not only by focusing on behaviors but also by influencing individual motivation to improve behavior.[28] That increased motivation facilitates individual change and adaptability. The reason for this motivation is that the results of such assessment processes often focus on not only what is done but also how it is done. Consequently, the feedback provided to the leader can be seen as an accurate reflection of how that leader is perceived by those he or she works with on a daily basis.

Refreezing Leadership Behavior

The final factor that affects the appropriateness of a strategic leader's behavior is his or her individual motivation to refreeze behavior. The organizational culture and climate factors also play an important role in reinforcing the desired actions. In other words, refreezing is accomplished through the strategic leader's establishment of an organizational climate and culture that reinforce the desired behavior. An overview of culture is included in Chapter 11 later in this text. However, it is important for leaders to recognize that socialization processes that teach "approved" behaviors to new members must reflect the types of behaviors most desired to achieve individual and organizational goals.

This chapter was written to provide a renewed understanding of the importance of self-awareness and also to describe the individual and organizational processes that facilitate better self-understanding. Organizations that invest resources toward the implementation of these processes for the development of leaders at all levels will be those that flourish in the future. Developing all skill sets, particularly interpersonal skills, is essential to becoming an effective strategic leader. The prerequisite for a leader's improvement is establishing a baseline—a means by which a leader can focus his or her improvement so that he or she can obtain the maximum benefit. An important first step in that development process is taking advantage of programs that provide an accurate self-awareness.

NOTES

1. David V. Day and Robert G. Lord, "Executive Leadership and Organizational Performance: Suggestions for a New Theory and Methodology," *Journal of Management* (1988): 453–464.

2. Jim Collins, *Good to Great: Why Some Companies Make the Leap...and Others Don't* (New York: Harper Collins, 2001).

3. Department of the Army, "2007 Army Posture Statement," available online at http://www.army.mil/aps/07/execSummary.html (accessed 11 May 2007).

4. Noel Tichy, *The Leadership Engine: How Winning Companies Build Leaders at Every Level* (New York: Harper Collins, 2002).

5. Bernard M. Bass, *Bass and Stogdill's Handbook of Leadership*, 3rd ed. (New York: Free Press, 1990).

6. Allan H. Church, "Managerial Self-Awareness in High-Performing Individuals in Organizations," *Journal of Applied Psychology* (1997): 281–292. See also Cynthia D. McCauley and Russ S. Moxley, "Developmental 360: How Feedback Can Make Managers More Effective," *Career Development International* (1996): 15–19.

7.   Craig T. Chappelow, "360-Degree Feedback," *The Center for Creative Leadership Handbook of Leadership Development*, Cynthia D. McCauley, Russ S. Moxley, and Ellen Van Velsor, eds. (San Francisco: Jossey-Bass, 1998): 29–65.

8.   Morgan W. McCall and Michael M. Lombardo, "Technical Report No. 21—Off the Track: Why and How Successful Executives Get Derailed" (Greensboro, NC: Center for Creative Leadership, 1983). See also Sydney Finkelstein, *Why Smart Executives Fail* (New York: Portfolio, 2004).

9.   Deborah Ancona, Thomas W. Malone, Wanda J. Orlikowski, and Peter M. Senge, "In Praise of the Incomplete Leader," *Harvard Business Review* (February 2007): 92–100.

10.   "Myers-Briggs Type Indicator (Form M)" (Palo Alto, CA: Consulting Psychologists Press); Michael J. Kirton, "Adaption-Innovation in the Context of Diversity and Change" (New York: Routledge, 2003); "KAI Response Sheet" (Berkhamstead, UK: Occupational Research Centre).

11.   Robert R. McCrae and Paul T. Costa, "Validation of the Five-Factor Model of Personality across Instruments and Observers," *Journal of Personality and Social Psychology* (1987): 81–90.

12.   George E. Reed, "Toxic Leadership," *Military Review* (July/August 2004): 67–71.

13.   Leonard Wong, *Generations Apart: Xers and Boomers in the Officer Corps* (Carlisle, PA: U.S. Army War College, 2000).

14.   Edgar H. Schein, *Organizational Culture and Leadership*, 2nd ed. (San Francisco: Jossey-Bass, 1992).

15.   David V. Day, "Technical Report No. 1141—Leadership Development: A Review of Industry Best Practices" (Alexandria, VA: U.S. Army Research Institute for the Behavioral and Social Sciences, 1999).

16.   Kurt Lewin, "Frontiers in Group Dynamics: Concept, Method, and Reality in Social Science, Social Equilibria, and Social Change," Human Relations (1947): 5–41.

17.   Jack Feldman, "On the Difficulty of Learning from Experience," *The Thinking Organization: Dynamics of Organizational Social Cognition*, Henry P. Sims and Dennis A. Gioia, eds. (San Francisco: Jossey-Bass, 1986): 263–292.

18.   For a good review of automatic versus controlled cognitive processing, see Robert G. Lord and Karen J. Maher, "Alternative Information Processing Models and Their Implications for Theory, Research, and Practice," *Academy of Management Review* (1990): 9–28.

19.   Peter M. Senge, *The Fifth Discipline: The Art and Practice of the Learning Organization* (New York: Currency and Doubleday, 1990).

20.   Feldman, 270.

21. Double-loop learning is not focusing on whether a particular outcome is achieved; rather, it means questioning whether the objective/goal was appropriate in the first place. See Chris Argyris and David Schön, *Theory in Practice: Increasing Professional Effectiveness* (San Francisco: Jossey-Bass, 1974).

22. Feldman, 273.

23. Robert E. Quinn, *Beyond Rational Management: Mastering the Paradoxes and Competing Demands of High Performance* (San Francisco: Jossey-Bass, 1988).

24. Robert Kegan and Lisa Laskow Lahey, "The Real Reason People Won't Change," *Harvard Business Review* (November 2001): 85–92.

25. John Smart, "How to Be a Tech Futurist," a presentation given at the World Future Society Conference, Chicago, Illinois, July 2005.

26. Marshall Goldsmith and Mark Reiter, *What Got You Here Won't Get You There: How Successful People Become Even More Successful* (New York: Hyperion, 2007).

27. Daniel R. Ilgen, Cynthia D. Fisher, and M. Susan Taylor, "Consequences of Individual Feedback on Behavior in Organizations," *Journal of Applied Psychology* (1979): 349–371.

28. Richard L. Hughes and Katherine M. Beatty, *Becoming a Strategic Leader: Your Role in Your Organization's Enduring Success* (San Francisco: Jossey-Bass, 2005).

Thinking Critically about Critical Thinking

Stephen Gerras, PhD

Technological advances alone do not constitute change. The most dramatic advances in military operations over history have been borne of ideas—ideas about warfighting, organization and doctrine. The Army's most critical asset will not be technology; it will be critical thinking.[1]

—AUSA TORCHBEARER NATIONAL SECURITY REPORT, MARCH 2005

In the post-Cold War security environment, many senior leaders in the Army and throughout the Department of Defense have asserted a need to develop better critical thinking skills.[2] The requirement for better critical thinkers stems from a realization that the complexity, uncertainty, and ambiguity of the current environment mandates a need to refrain from Cold War thinking methodologies and assumptions.

One of the main impediments to understanding and using critical thinking, both inside and outside the military, centers on a lack of a common definition. No one discipline owns the construct. Most of the material about critical thinking derives from philosophy, education, and psychology.[3] There are, however, competing schools of thought on what critical thinking is and how to best develop it.

Some Army leaders mistakenly refer to the *critical* in critical thinking as mere fault-finding. Fault-finding is not what critical thinking entails. The word *critical* refers to the purposeful, reflective, and careful evaluation of information as a way to improve one's judgment. As senior leaders, whether we are evaluating the information from a PowerPoint presentation at the Pentagon, reading a newspaper article, or participating in a discussion with an Iraqi mayor, we are critically thinking. Consequently, one of the most important things that a strategic leader must learn is not simply how to think critically, but how to do it well.

Critical thinking is purposeful, directed thought. It is not easy, because it requires explicit mental energy. The great majority of the decisions and issues we face throughout the day do not require critical thinking. The route we drive to work, what clothes we wear to a party, and what book we read on Saturday are examples of decisions or concerns that do not normally require critical thinking and can be made in an "automatic" mode of cognitive thought.

An example of an automatic mode of cognitive thought is the routine of driving down the interstate at 70 miles per hour to a familiar destination. At some point the driver may recognize that he or she is not quite sure where he or she is or does not actually remember driving the last five miles; it is probably because the mind has switched to an automatic processing mode. This is a common experience. How does the brain permit this mode of thought while operating a 5,000-pound vehicle moving 70 miles per hour and within several feet of large tractor trailers moving equally fast? The explanation is that over time, driving even at a high rate of speed becomes an "automatic" routine. To conserve mental energy, the brain tends to reduce focus, especially with seemingly routine activities. Unfortunately, most decisionmakers make judgments on significant issues using an automatic mode as opposed to taking the time and investing the energy needed for a more controlled thought process.[4]

Exercising controlled thought involves the deliberate use of elements of critical thinking. Examples of when critical thinking is probably called for include assessing a PowerPoint presentation on courses of action for an upcoming military operation, preparing to meet with an Iraqi governor to discuss joint security issues, and proposing to your future spouse. Knowing when to reign back on automatic processing in order to conduct a conscious assessment of the parameters of the situation is more an art than a science. A good rule of thumb is *if you are in doubt as to whether to use critical thinking about an issue, you probably ought to apply critical thinking.* The main point is that most routine decisions made on a day-to-day basis do not involve critical thinking; however, once familiar with the concepts and terminology of critical thinking, you are in the position to ask yourself whether the issue being considered warrants the application of critical thinking methodology.

A CRITICAL THINKING MODEL

Picture an armored brigade commander recently deployed to Iraq. His predecessor informs him that in his area of operations (AO) over the past two months, the number of civilians killed from an improvised explosive device (IED) or vehicle-borne improvised explosive device (VBIED) is twice the average of any sector in the country. He advises that his brigade has increased its vigilance and number of patrols in susceptible areas, but due to unit redeployment challenges, it has not really improved the situation. The new brigade commander directs his staff to present some options for reducing the number of civilian deaths. As the brigade commander thinks about how to reduce civilian deaths, he will be much more effective if he reasons within the framework of some critical thinking model. In classes at the U.S. Army War College, the critical thinking model portrayed in Figure 3-1 provides such a framework.[5]

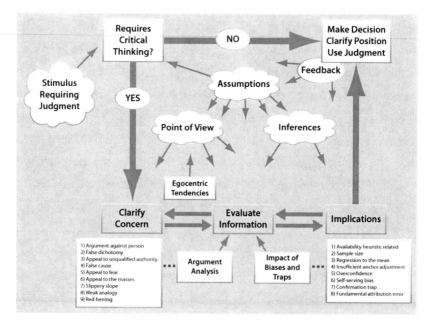

FIGURE 3-1. A critical thinking model.

The clouds in the center of the model labeled *point of view, assumptions,* and *inferences* are meant to demonstrate that this is generally a nonlinear model. *Assumptions,* for instance, will affect whether you perceive an issue to be worthy of critical thinking, and your *point of view* will affect how you define the boundaries of the issues. Although there are arrows going from *clarify concern* to *evaluate information* (implying linearity), there is also a reciprocal arrow going in the reverse direction to suggest that as you are evaluating information, you may end up redefining the concern. If, for example, you are seeking to *clarify concern* regarding some inappropriate behavior by your teenage son or daughter, the *evaluation of information* may indicate that the real issue has more to do with the nature of the relationship between you and your child than the actual behavior prompting the initial concern. The nonlinear nature of the model will be more evident as you read about its main components: to clarify concern, evaluate information, consider points of view, identify assumptions, make sound inferences, and consider implications.

Clarify Concern

The critical thinking process begins with an individual perceiving some stimulus. Often we respond to the stimulus by defaulting to our known view of the world, which is an "automatic" response. In many of these cases, the automatic mode is appropriate, and the perceiver should proceed to make a decision, use judgment, etc. However, if the topic is complex, it has important implications, or there is a chance that strong personal views on the issue might lead to biased reasoning, thinking critically about the issue is imperative.

A critical element, and often the first step, in critical thinking methodology is to **clarify concern**. This is not as straightforward as it seems. The concern or issue needs to be identified and clarified up front, yet consistently revisited as other elements of the model are considered. The term *concern* is preferred over the term *problem* because a critical thinker should be proactive as well as reactive. In many cases, the critical thinker will encounter information that causes him or her to identify related or subsequent issues that should be addressed. A critical thinker ensures that he or she has considered all the complexities of the problem at hand and focused his or her mental energy appropriately. An assessment needs to determine whether the concern has unidentified root causes or unaddressed subcomponents.

A critical thinker should ensure that the concern or issue is not framed in a way that limits the types of questions that can be asked. In the case of the new brigade commander in Iraq, a cursory attempt at concern clarification would probably conclude that the concern is that the average number of civilians killed over the last two months is much higher than that anywhere else in the country. If the question is limited to simply whether the number of civilians killed over the last month is higher than that in other places in the country, you will get one answer: *Yes, in my sector the number of civilians killed was higher than anywhere else in the country.*

You can imagine the variety of "solutions" that might come from that conclusion. A new brigade commander fresh from the Army War College and taught how to think critically would ask different questions: *What is the source of the data? Are there other motivations for the people presenting the data that may be improperly framing the issue? Is there a more systemic issue or problem that has caused this increase in deaths that needs to be addressed before we focus on the IED/VBIED attacks?*

At a War College lecture, a general officer who had recently returned from Iraq described a situation where it was imperative for him to identify the root causes of attacks in his area of operation. He and his staff, working through a critical thinking process, began to ask a variety of questions, finely honing in on the right ones. The general and his staff eventually concluded that there was a strong inverse correlation between functioning civil infrastructure, such as electrical power, sewer, and water service, and the number of enemy attacks in that sector. As a result, the unit focused more on improving civil infrastructure and less on the use of military force. For complex questions like the one facing the general, one should limit the scope of a problem to be addressed—or at least be very deliberate in framing the questions asked.

Evaluate Information

Now let's return to that new brigade commander concerned about the increased attacks in his area. Once he has clarified the real concern, the brigade commander begins to focus on other elements of the critical thinking model. In this hypothetical, the brigade commander, while *evaluating information*, might see a new pattern emerging in the data. In fact, it becomes clear that although the average number of deaths has increased in the last two months, the statistic is driven by only two significant attacks where VBIEDs exploded near civilian buses. In fact, the actual number of attacks decreased significantly. Such an evaluation of information might lead to a reframing of the question from *How can we reduce the average number of civilian deaths in the AO?* to *How can we reduce the number of VBIED attacks in populated areas* or *How can we protect the civilian population from terrorist attack?* These are three different questions, and each has an unique answer.

Consider Points of View

Another element of the critical thinking model is *considering points of view*. We all have points of view or frames of reference. The key is to be aware of them and recognize how they may bias our thinking. We want to develop a frame of reference that is evenhanded and open to other points of view.[6] In fact, it may become absolutely essential that we examine a problem from a variety of points of view. Good critical thinkers, however, do their best to recognize their own point of view and to consider, understand, and even empathize with other views.

Empathy is not a characteristic of soft leaders; rather, it is a characteristic of smart, thoughtful, and reflective leaders. The more the battalion commander can put himself in the shoes of an Iraqi town mayor, the greater the likelihood that his decisions will be successful from not only a U.S. standpoint but an Iraqi perspective as well. This congruence will enable long-term solutions and build the respect and trust that are absolutely critical in the contemporary operating environment. Good strategic leadership is predicated upon the ability to shift one's perspective and reflect on another's point of view. Perhaps then the battalion commander might better understand why both our allies and our foes, in light of their cultural backgrounds and points of view, seem to take such rigid stances when negotiating.[7]

As we attempt to empathize with the viewpoints of others, our own self-awareness becomes increasingly important. Leaders need to be self-aware of *egocentric tendencies*, which are probably the most significant barrier to effective critical thinking.[8] Military officers, for instance, are typically very successful individuals who have a wide range of interests. From academics to sports, leadership jobs to hobbies, a typical officer has in most cases been handpicked for military commissioning and advancement based on a track record of success. Therefore, typical military leaders have exceptional confidence in who they are and in the validity, accuracy, and correctness of their views. This enhanced confidence only increases as rank and responsibility increase because senior leaders are continuously rewarded for their judgment and decision-making.

Unfortunately, this constant positive reinforcement in the form of promotion and selection for key billets encourages an absolutist frame of
reference within a narrow point of view. Many college students, for example, think that they have figured out how the world works, and they are
exceedingly confident that their view is correct. This type of egocentric
leaning tends to insulate leaders' thinking processes and often presents a
significant obstacle to their empathizing with and considering the viewpoint of others.

A critical thinker must be aware of several egocentric tendencies. *Egocentric memory* is a natural tendency to forget information that does
not support one's line of thinking. *Egocentric myopia* refers to thinking
within an overly narrow point of view. *Egocentric righteousness* describes
a tendency to feel superior based on the belief that one has actually figured
out how the world works. *Egocentric blindness* is the natural tendency not
to notice facts and evidence that contradict what one believes or values.[9]
Fortunately, just as egocentrism can prevent us from appreciating the
underlying thinking processes that guide our behavior, critical thinking,
especially in the form of appreciating multiple points of view, can help us
learn to explicitly recognize that our point of view is often incomplete and
sometimes blatantly self-serving and wrong.[10]

As critical thinkers assess the point of view of someone presenting
information to them, they not only need to be aware of their egocentric
tendencies and attempt to empathize with the various other relevant points
of view, but they also need to apply some measures of critical reasoning to
the assessment. As an example, when you as a senior officer are presented
with recommendations for a court-martial by a subordinate unit, it is probably smart to evaluate who the recommender is: ask yourself what biases
he or she brings to the issue (based on past statements or previous recom-

mendations), whether there are any factors that might interfere with the accuracy of this person's judgment, and whether there is evidence from any other source that corroborates this person's statements or recommendations.[11] This assessment protocol would apply to any information source, whether that source is face-to-face communication, written text, or the public media.

Identify Assumptions

A third component of the critical thinking model is to *identify assumptions*. This is a concept that should be very familiar to a military officer. An assumption is something that is taken for granted.[12] Within the scope of critical thinking, however, the concept of an assumption is somewhat different from that which we use to provide boundaries in the military decision-making process. As critical thinkers, we need to be aware of the beliefs we hold to be true, which have been formed from what we have previously learned and no longer question.[13] We typically process information based on assumptions about the way the world works and operate below the level of consciousness. These are sometimes referred to as mental models or schemas.

The brigade commander in Iraq makes inferences, forms opinions, and makes decisions that are largely rooted in his assumptions about cause-effect relationships with respect to the way the world works. He probably has assumptions about the way people should interact, what a good leader looks like, how a typical town should appear (in terms of organization and cleanliness), and how responsible an individual is for what happens in his or her life. All of these assumptions (and many more) will affect his judgment with respect to possible courses of action for dealing with increased civilian casualties.

The arrows in the critical thinking model show that various assumptions influence all aspects of the model. Indeed, our point of view, our inferences, and whether we decide a problem is worthy of critical thinking all affect how we pose questions, seek solutions, and select answers. Truly, the more in touch an individual is with his or her assumptions, the more effective a critical thinker he or she will be.

If the brigade commander, for example, assumes that the primary cause of most of the problems in Iraq is a lack of willingness by the populace to effect a solution, he will evaluate the efficacy of courses of action with this assumption in mind. He might not support any course of action that relies on the Iraqis. Whether this is an accurate assumption is, in fact, irrelevant. What matters is that the brigade commander implicitly draws upon his assumptions as part of the critical thinking process. More important, the brigade commander needs to create a command climate where subordinates feel they can surface and question assumptions they believe are relevant to the concern at hand.

Peter Senge, a War College lecturer, wrote in *The Fifth Discipline* about the importance of dialogue, as opposed to discussion, in a learning organization. He posits, "In dialogue, a group explores complex difficult issues from many points of view. Individuals suspend their assumptions but they communicate their assumptions freely."[14] To suspend assumptions, leaders must first be aware of them. This reflective self-inquiry, in relation to a specific concern, is extremely important in the critical thinking process, as is the creation of a climate in which individuals feel free to communicate their assumptions and to question others.

Make Sound Inferences

Another component of the critical thinking model that needs to be considered is to *make sound inferences*. Critical thinkers need to be skilled at making sound inferences and at identifying when they and others are making inferences. An inference is a step of the mind or an intellectual leap of faith by which one concludes that something is true because something else is true or seems to be true.[15] Whereas an assumption is something we take for granted, an inference is an intellectual act in which we conclude something based on the facts and evidence of a situation. If a soldier sees an Iraqi man approaching with his hands hidden behind his back, he may infer that the man is hiding a weapon and intends to do him harm. This inference is based on the assumption that Iraqi men who hide their arms when approaching are very likely dangerous and quite probably insurgents or terrorists.

Critical thinkers strive to become adept at making sound inferences.[16] Ask yourself, *What are the key inferences made in this situation?* Then ask yourself if the inferences are justified, logical, and follow from the evidence. Remembering the earlier components of the critical thinking model, obviously inferences are heavily influenced by the point of view and assumptions we bring to the issue. This explains why two officers viewing the same PowerPoint slide may come to completely different conclusions in terms of what the data mean or represent.

An interesting exercise we do at the Army War College to make this relationship more salient is to provide students brief information and then ask them to identify their inferences and underlying assumptions. This exercise never fails to show that people make very different inferences from the same stimulus, and, as would be imagined, these inferences are based on very diverse assumptions. Once these assumptions are identified, they, along with the inferences, can be questioned, examined, and discussed.

In terms of our brigade commander in Iraq, it is easy to see the importance of inferences. If an Iraqi informant tells the brigade interpreter that the local police captain is aligned with the terrorists, the brigade commander might infer that this information is useless and therefore direct that no action be taken on the intelligence. In this case the commander's underlying assumption that informants are untrustworthy and typically lie affects his inference and subsequent directive. The brigade operations officer—or brigade S-3—however, may have a different assumption about the efficacy of informant intelligence and might think the correct course of action will involve bringing in the police captain or at least putting him under observation.

From a critical thinking perspective, both the commander and the S-3 should be aware that each is making an inference based on an underlying assumption. They should question their underlying assumptions and ensure that other equally valid considerations have been entertained before drawing inferences from the available information.

Consider Implications

The last component of the critical thinking model is to **consider implications**. Critical thinkers need to understand the short-term consequences of accepting initial inferences or resisting opposing perspectives. They obviously also have to appreciate the long-term consequences of the information they accept and the decisions they make, including the second- and third-order effects. Critical thinkers ask themselves, "What if my assumptions are incorrect? What if the variables I think are defined are actually uncertain or quite different from what I think? What things haven't I considered that I need to consider?" Many of these questions will be ignored or minimized if the egocentric tendencies discussed earlier override sound judgment.

As part of considering implications, the critical thinker needs to analyze the impact of a decision on all relevant stakeholders. A *stakeholder* is a person, group, or unit that has a share or an interest in a particular activity or possible decision.[17] For example, the brigade commander trying to reduce civilian deaths may, after going through the components of the critical thinking model, come to a decision that he needs to increase his information operations campaign through the local mosque and tell the populace that the increase in attacks is due to bad guys from outside the sector coming into the sector.

Assuming the brigade commander made this decision while cognizant of his own viewpoint and assumptions, and assuming that it was based on sound information and inferences, he now needs to consider the implications of this decision. What if the imam at the mosque is not as trustworthy as he thinks? What if the populace knows that the attacks are actually coming from terrorists who live in the area, not outside operatives—will the brigade commander lose credibility? What if the populace starts to overwhelm his intelligence assets with reports of purported bad guys? Does he have the force structure to do something about it? Who are the stakeholders in this case? The brigade commander needs to assess his course of action along many lines, including the impact on his troops, adjacent units, the local populace, Iraqi military and police forces, and higher headquarters.

HEURISTICS

Decisionmakers often rely on simplifying strategies or "general rules of thumb" called *heuristics*, which are a mechanism for coping with decision-making in volatile, uncertain, complex, and ambiguous (VUCA) environments. Critical thinkers need to appreciate not only the framework for assessing their own thinking, but also the heuristics that they and others rely upon when making decisions. The concept of heuristics relates strongly to the automatic mode of cognitive thought described earlier.

Heuristics as an aid to decision-making are not bad; in fact, if we did not use heuristics, we would probably be paralyzed with inaction. As an example, you might have a heuristic for which coat to wear to class each day. Your heuristic might be, "If there's frost on the car, I wear the parka." Without this heuristic shortcut, you would have to check the thermometer and compare it to a chart that prescribed the correct coat to wear under certain temperature conditions.

Heuristics help leaders to make good decisions rapidly a significant proportion of the time. Unfortunately, however, heuristics also can lead decisionmakers into making systematically biased mistakes. Cognitive bias occurs when an individual inappropriately applies a heuristic when making a decision.[18] As critical thinkers, we need to be aware of cognitive biases to more effectively evaluate information. Critical thinkers need to assess whether the premises of the argument—theirs or someone else's—are true or false and whether they might lead to a fallacious argument or a wrong decision. Identifying unacceptable, irrelevant, and insufficient premises gives an advantage to critical thinkers in evaluating arguments for fallaciousness.

There are three general heuristics: (1) the availability heuristic, (2) the representativeness heuristic, and (3) the anchoring and adjustment heuristic.[19] Each is briefly elaborated below.

Availability Heuristics

The availability heuristic acknowledges that people typically assess the likelihood of an event by the ease with which examples of that event can be brought to mind. Typically, people recall events that are recent, vivid, or recurrent. This heuristic works well in most instances; however, a critical thinker needs to be aware of the biases that result from an expeditious process.

For example, a division commander doing Officer Efficiency Reports (OERs) on two equally capable battalion commanders might be inclined to give the battalion commander who challenged him at the last Unit Status Report (USR) a lower rating. The recentness and vividness of the challenge might cause the division commander to overlook the impressive accomplishments of this particular battalion commander and accord a rating that is actually inconsistent with the officer's performance. This would be, in effect, a poor decision.

Recall our brigade commander in Iraq. Imagine that on the morning prior to his staff brief on possible courses of action to deal with the terrorist threat, he has a conversation with a brigade commander from a sister division. In that discussion, the other brigade commander mentions that the only successful way he has been able to deal with terrorist attacks is to increase his information operations campaign by providing accurate information on terrorist attacks through the local mosque. The brigade commander most likely will be tainted by the comments of the sister brigade commander because they will remain at the forefront of his thoughts. This may or may not lead to a good decision. It's important for the brigade commander to understand this tendency to process information within the context of like situations easily recalled from memory. The environment and circumstances in his brigade sector may not be at all conducive to the same solution used in the sister brigade. Critical thinking and self-reflection can help prevent this error.

At the strategic level, it is easy to posit the influence of the availability heuristic in the early years of American involvement in Vietnam. Decisionmakers had recent and vivid impressions of the failure of appeasement in World War II and the success of Korea to serve as a bases for imagining likely scenarios if the United States did, or did not, get involved in Vietnam. With respect to decision-making and Iraq, it could be argued that Americans inappropriately applied the relatively peaceful conclusion to the Cold War and apparent ease of democratic change in the Eastern Bloc countries to the Middle East, where democratic change will be anything but easy. This can be explained, at least in part, by the availability heuristic.

Representativeness Heuristics

The representativeness heuristic focuses on the tendency for people to make judgments regarding an individual, object, or event by assessing how much the item of interest is representative. Several biases emanate from this heuristic; two of the most prevalent are problems with the sample size and regression to the mean.

Sample size bias occurs when decisionmakers improperly generalize the reliability of sample information. An example of this tendency is illustrated here: The First Battalion had three attempted suicides last month. There are

300 soldiers in the battalion. The one-percent attempted suicide rate in this battalion for this month is four times the Army average and ten times the national average over a one-month period. The division commander concludes that there is clearly a problem in the First Battalion. Unfortunately, this reasoning is all too common, and most likely incorrect. A 300-soldier unit over a one-month period is too small a unit and too short a time period to draw a meaningful conclusion that there is actually a problem.

In the Abu Ghraib incident, many would argue that Congress, the international community, and some of the American people unfairly generalized the behavior of a few soldiers to the entire American Army. From another angle, we have all seen the commander's inquiry saying that the reason for the poor decision-making by the soldiers involved in the incident was a lack of training. The net result was that six months later, the entire Army was subjected to long training days on the subject, despite the fact that the actual incident was limited to a very small group of violators. Critical thinking, indeed.

Let's return once again to the story of our hypothetical brigade commander. This time, one of his battalion commanders briefs him on the success that his company commanders had using a Raven unmanned aerial vehicle (UAV) the preceding day. Three of the enemy were killed with no residual casualties. Now that is good news to the brigade commander. He might look at the situation and then recommend this solution to the other battalions when, in fact, this success is based on one event. If two battalions had said they had tried this technique and that it had worked 15 or 20 times in the past couple of weeks, the sample size would have been large enough to conclude that this was possibly a long-term viable solution. Certainly this bias does not mean that we should not try new techniques even if we have a small sample size; rather, it highlights the significant risks that a critical thinker needs to be aware of when generalizing a small sample to an entire population or environment.

Another important bias related to the representativeness heuristic is *regression to the mean*. This bias is based on research that extreme high or low scores tend to be followed by more average scores. Therefore, when predicting future performance, decisionmakers often assume poor performers will stay poor (i.e., they are representative of poor performers) and strong performers will stay strong. Unfortunately (or fortunately), extremely low or high performance is typically followed by a performance level closer to average. This is why the sports teams that make the cover of *Sports Illustrated* tend to lose and the mutual fund that was the strongest performer last year is probably not the one to buy this year.

An awareness of regression to the mean for our brigade commander in Iraq would hopefully cause him to investigate to determine *why* there has been an increase in attacks. If there is no apparent cause for the increase, a critical thinker might be a little more patient before reprioritizing resources to address a problem that will level out in the near future and may in fact not be the most pressing issue faced by the unit at the current time.

Applying regression to the mean at the strategic level enables a better assessment of Operation Iraqi Freedom casualty data. In the first ten days of April 2006, there were 30 combat deaths. The media highlighted that this number already exceeded the combat deaths from March 2006, implying an increase in the intensity of the war. A critical thinker, however, would note that the March 2006 casualty numbers were the lowest in two years; hence, regression to the mean would probably be a better explanation for the April numbers than was assuming the intensity of the war had increased significantly.

Anchoring and Adjustment Heuristics

There are certainly other types of biases. For instance, biases derived from anchoring and adjustment include *insufficient anchor adjustment* and *overconfidence*. In terms of anchoring, research has shown that decisionmakers develop estimates by starting from an initial anchor, based on whatever information is provided, and adjusting from there to yield a final answer.[20] Military personnel often fall victim to this bias.

For a host of reasons, probably closely associated with constant personnel turnover and a lack of knowledge about a specific job due to constant permanent change of station (PCS) moves, military personnel base their estimates on last year's numbers. Whether we are talking about a unit's budget, how long a war will take, or how many casualties we will have, we use previous numbers and experience as an anchor and adjust accordingly, rather than using current information to develop a value.

A practical application of ways to use this bias to one's advantage can be seen in negotiations. It is usually good to initiate the first offer in a negotiation if you have reasonable belief that you understand the bargaining zone. The opening offer will serve as the anchor and will most likely create a range for possible negotiation that will be more advantageous to you.

In our Iraq scenario, the brigade S-3 might tell the commander that the previous brigade conducted 15 patrols a day in the southern sector. Fifteen patrols will thus become an anchor. The courses of action for dealing with the terrorist situation might, therefore, include a recommendation to increase the number of patrols to 20 a day. A critical thinker, however, will realize that the 20/day recommendation is based on the anchor of 15 from the previous unit. He would then ask, "Why 20? Why not 60 or why not 4?" to force his staff to reassess the numbers of troops necessary to complete the task again.

Overconfidence describes a bias in which individuals tend to overestimate the infallibility of their judgments when answering difficult questions. As an example, when you are receiving a briefing from a subordinate and you ask him or her to estimate the probability of an event's occurring, keep in the back of your mind that this probability is inflated. If the subordinate says, "Sir, we have a 90 percent probability of eliminating all the enemy in the city," a critical thinker will remember this bias and assume that a more realistic estimate would be substantially lower. The Army's "can do" culture tends to reinforce a subordinate's overinflated estimates as proxy measures of confidence in the command—and they might be completely wrong, or right.

The *confirmation trap* describes a condition in which people tend to seek confirmatory information for what they think is true and either fail to search for—or discard—inconsistent and disconfirming evidence. This bias highlights the need for subordinates to provide candid feedback to their superiors and, more importantly, for superiors to encourage their subordinates to give them all the news, good or bad. Failure to make a concerted effort to be absolutely candid typically leads to a situation in which the boss looks for information that supports his or her decision, while discounting information, no matter how valid and important, that challenges that decision.

As critical thinkers evaluating an issue, we need to appreciate this bias and know that it is a natural tendency that needs to be overcome, no matter how painful it is to the ego. (This bias is clearly related to egocentric tendencies such as egocentric memory and blindness.) At the strategic level, the

Bay of Pigs decision by the Kennedy Administration is a poster child for the confirmation trap. Similarly, in 2004 it was not hard to find a Sunday morning talk show pundit arguing that President Bush and Prime Minister Blair placed more weight on evidence that supported their position than on that which challenged it (i.e., Hans Blix's view). One may try to keep an open mind, but once committed, it becomes very hard to assess all the evidence impartially.

If our Iraq brigade commander believes that the increase in attacks is due to guidance from the local imam, he (and probably his direct reports) will have a tendency to search for information that supports this perspective. He will also be inclined to discount valuable information that might lead to another cause.

The *fundamental attribution error* describes a phenomenon in which people tend to have a default assumption that what a person does is based more on what "type" of person he is than on the social and environmental forces at work in that situation. This default assumption causes leaders to sometimes attribute erroneous explanations for behavior to a person when the situation or environment provides a better explanation. When a soldier comes to work late, our first thought is that the individual does not care or is incompetent. In fact, the soldier could have a justifiable reason for being late. At the strategic level, an example of this would be concluding that the critical negotiation failed because General Jones blew it, as opposed to attributing the failure to the large range of environmental conditions that were more likely to have caused the failure.

Similarly, we are more likely to attribute our successes to internal factors and our failures to external factors. This is the *self-serving bias*. When we ask our child why he did poorly on a test, he responds that "the teacher asked questions that weren't in the book." If we ask why he received an "A," he may say it is "because I'm smart." Similarly, a person not selected for promotion is more likely to say, "The system is broken" than "I'm just an average performer."

In his book *Good to Great*, author Jim Collins looks at the factors that allow good companies to turn into great companies.[21] He asserts that leaders of companies that do not make the list of great companies tend to "look out the window for something or someone outside themselves to blame for poor results, but would preen in front of the mirror and credit themselves when things went well."[22] Critical thinkers must accept the responsibility for successes and failures. Blaming others or events for failures makes it impossible to find good solutions.

IDENTIFYING FALLACIOUS ARGUMENTS

In addition to developing an understanding of biases and heuristics as a means to improve his or her ability to evaluate information critically, a strong critical thinker also assesses the soundness of the arguments presented. When we make an argument, we offer reasons as to why others should accept our view(s) or judgment. These reasons are called premises (or evidence), and the assertion that they allegedly support is called the conclusion.[23] A sound argument meets the following conditions:

1. The premises are acceptable and consistent.

2. The premises are relevant to the conclusion and provide sufficient support for the conclusion.

3. Missing components have been considered and are judged to be consistent with the conclusion.[24]

If the premises are dubious or do not warrant the conclusion, our argument is fallacious.[25] In accord with the critical thinking model, as we *evaluate the information* presented, we need to keep in mind our tendency to let biases influence our decision-making. We also need to be aware of the traditional types of fallacious reasoning that are often used, sometimes intentionally and sometimes out of ignorance, to try to convince us to support an argument.

Fallacies are very common, and they are typically convincing. Recently, for example, in a TV documentary about alternative medicine, a U.S. senator defended his congressional bill to exclude vitamins and herbal medicines from USDA review by saying, "At least 100 million Americans use vitamins and other supplements every day and they can't all be wrong [appeal to the masses]; I know many senators, who also use these products [appeal to unqualified authority]; this is just another case of the liberal left trying to intrude on the daily life of the average American [arguments against the person]."

The average viewer probably thought these arguments made sense, but as critical thinkers, we need to assess arguments, especially important and relevant arguments, to identify fallacious reasoning. Bad judgments prompted by fallacious reasoning that draws upon invalid and questionable evidence are the enemy of critical thinkers.

Unfortunately, logically fallacious arguments can be psychologically compelling. Many Army War College students, because they have never really learned the difference between a good argument and a fallacious one, are often persuaded to accept and believe things that are not logically supported. As a critical thinker evaluates information, he or she needs to ask: Are the premises acceptable? Are they relevant? Are they sufficient? If the answer to any of these questions is no, the argument is not logically compelling.

Fallacious reasoning can take several forms, including arguments against a person, false dichotomies, appeals to unqualified authority, false causes, appeals to fear, appeals to the masses, slippery slopes, weak analogies, and red herring.

Arguments against a Person

When someone tries to attack the individual presenting an argument and not the argument itself, he or she is guilty of this fallacy. A common example of this is the denigration of a position with the statement "That guy is just a left-wing liberal." Instead of assessing the argument or position based on the premises and conclusion, the argument is ignored and the arguer is attacked. Our new brigade commander in Iraq during a battle update briefing might discard some important intelligence because the briefer highlighted the negative aspects of the intelligence source over the content of the intelligence. Awareness of this fallacy should cause critical thinkers to constantly be aware of their own biases and prejudices to ensure that they do not fall victim to a seemingly convincing argument that is, in reality, based on an unsupported attack on a person or group advancing the information.

False Dichotomies

When someone presents a complex situation in black-and-white terms— i.e., they present only two alternatives when many exist—he or she is committing the fallacy of a false dichotomy. Military officers often present information this way. "Sir, we can either commit the $10 million to force protection or start preparing our response to *60 Minutes* when our troops get blown up." This illustrates a false dichotomy. In this case, there is a wide range of other alternatives (commit $3 million, for instance) that are not presented in the argument.

As we work to develop more innovative and creative leaders, the ability to identify false dichotomies becomes even more important. Rather than reducing complex issues to a choice between two extreme positions, critically thinking leaders need to use their creative abilities to identify the wide range of possible alternatives actually available. Our brigade commander might be briefed, "Sir, we either provide the security for the protest Sunday or pre-place evacuation vehicles for the guaranteed terrorist attack." In reality, there is a large continuum of courses of action, including having the United States provide outer-ring security while the Iraqis provide local security.

Appeals to Unqualified Authority

This fallacy occurs when the authority we use to support our premises is the wrong authority for the matter at hand. In the hierarchical and rank-centric military, this is an especially salient fallacy. Although a command sergeant major or a general officer is knowledgeable about many things, in many cases neither one may be an expert on some particular issue.

Many active-duty military are frustrated when 24-hour news channels, for instance, feature a retired Army general discussing the efficacy of the air campaign in Kosovo or a long-retired Special Forces major assessing the problems with the current ground campaign in Fallujah being fought by the Marines. Unfortunately, the American public at large does not understand military rank structures, nor do they understand the tenuous link that a retired Special Forces major has with what is actually going on anywhere in Iraq. The net result is that many people are misled by appeals to unqualified authorities and hence are convinced of the validity of what is, in fact, a fallacious argument.

False Causes

In this common fallacy, someone argues that because two events occurred together and one followed the other closely in time, the first event caused the second event. Night follows day, but that does not mean that day "caused" night. Similarly, just because attacks in an Iraqi city decreased the day after a new president was elected in the United States, one should not infer that the U.S. presidential election caused the decrease in attacks. The two events are probably completely exclusive.

There are many reasons why one event may follow another yet bear no causal relationship. We have all seen a case where a new leader comes into the unit, and the unit does much better or much worse on a measurable evaluation (e.g., gunnery, command inspection). We almost always assume the positive or negative change is due to the new leader, when in fact it could be due to a wide range of other explanations, such as lower-level key personnel changes, new equipment, or even regression toward the mean or its opposite.

In a complex and stressful environment like Iraq, leaders are especially vulnerable to the false-cause fallacy. Soldiers are being wounded and killed; everyone wants to find a cause for the attacks in order to eliminate it. Critical thinkers ensure that presented causes of bad events are, in fact, causally related.

Appeals to Fear

This fallacy involves using an implicit or explicit threat of harm to advance one's position. A fear appeal is effective because it psychologically impedes the listener from acknowledging a missing premise that, if acknowledged, would be seen to be false or at least questionable.[26] An example of this fallacy would be for a prosecutor at a court-martial to argue that the defendant needs to be convicted because if he is not put in jail, the spouse of the juror might be the next victim. In reality, what the defendant might do in the future is irrelevant in determining his guilt at the court-martial.

Another example would be for a company commander to argue to the brigade commander by saying, "If we don't detain and question every young male in the southeast corner of the town, you can count on deadly IED attacks along the main supply route every day." In this case, the company commander is distracting the brigade commander from the weak and questionable premise that every young male is planting IEDs by focusing attention on the fear of losing more soldiers to IEDs.

Appeals to the Masses

This fallacy focuses on an assertion that if something is good for everyone else, it must be good for me. Advertisements try to convince us that "everyone" is seeing a new movie, trying a new taco, or wearing a new pair of jeans, and therefore we should, too. In a military context, we often hear a comment like, "Sir, all the other TRADOC [Training and Doctrine Command] posts have already gone to this system." Unfortunately, popularity is not always a reliable indication of sensibility or value.[27]

Slippery Slopes

The fallacy of the slippery slope occurs when the conclusion of an argument rests upon an alleged chain reaction and there is not sufficient reason to conclude that the chain reaction will actually take place. For example, during the early months after the "don't ask, don't tell" policy was established, it was not uncommon to hear military officers argue for resistance to this policy because acceptance would lead to gay military personnel getting married, having children, and taking housing away from traditional heterosexual couples on-post. In reality, there was no support for this conclusion.

Similarly, many Americans argue against the National Security Agency's policy of listening to phone conversations placed by potential terrorists overseas. The argument is that by allowing this policy, the NSA will be encouraged to eventually listen to the phone calls of all American citizens. The alleged chain reaction in this case has not been clearly supported and should not be used as a premise to oppose the NSA policy.

Weak Analogies

Using analogies is an effective way to communicate concepts, especially complex ones. An analogy puts one situation next to another to point out a similarity. Quite often these analogies are strong and useful in illustrating a valid point. The fallacy of a weak analogy is committed when the analogy is not strong enough to support the conclusion.[28]

For example, several recent editorials posited that the United States should deal with the Iranian nuclear threat just like we dealt with the Cuban Missile Crisis (i.e., out-of-the-box thinking as opposed to offensive military force or traditional diplomacy). They argued that the Iranian nuclear issue is similar to the Cuban Missile Crisis and therefore warrants a similar response. Although the United States was in both cases concerned about nuclear proliferation in a rival country, the dissimilarities are too vast (e.g., peer competitor sponsorship in the case of Cuba, impact of radical Islam in Iran) to argue that the techniques for dealing with Iran should replicate what we did with Cuba. Therefore, the conclusion that we should deal with Iran in 2006 much like we did with Cuba in 1962 appears to be an example of a weak analogy fallacy.

As an additional example, many pundits in late 2003 argued that U.S. forces in Iraq should mirror the British tendency to discard battle gear when dealing with Iraqis as the proper way to engage the population and create stronger community ties. Unfortunately, these pundits did not understand, or intentionally ignored, the fact that the Shiite populations in Basra (where the British were operating) were significantly different, in terms of the threat they posed, from the Sunnis in the Sunni triangle (where U.S. forces were operating). These pundits were guilty of a weak analogy fallacy.

Red Herring

The red herring fallacy diverts the attention of a reader or listener with flashy, eye-catching information that is generally not relevant to the topic at hand.[29] For example, in recent months it has not been uncommon for Army leaders to respond to questions about lowering standards for new enlistees and recruitment challenges by responding that current reenlistment rates are higher than ever, especially for units returning from Iraq. These Army leaders do not really address the issue of recruiting, but instead, they subtly change the focus of the conversation to retention.

Similarly, interviewees opposed to Operation Iraqi Freedom often change the focus from whether democracy is good for Iraq or whether U.S. forces have made life better for Iraqis by highlighting the number of the battle amputees and combat deaths. In this case, they are moving the focus away from a discussion on the merits of U.S. policy by inserting an emotional issue guaranteed to distract and redirect the listener's attention.

The bottom line is that a critical thinker considers all these things in a deliberate and conscious manner. All leaders, but especially senior leaders, must continuously ask themselves, "Is this something I need to think about critically? How are my egocentric tendencies and point of view affecting the way I look at this? What is the point of view of the person presenting the information? What are my assumptions? Are we making the correct inferences based on the data provided? Are there other data we need to consider and can access? Is the information true, or at least plausible? Are the conclusions warranted by the evidence? Are biases and traps affecting our judgment? Have I considered all the implications?" The more we can introduce these terms into our thought processes, the more we will make better decisions, become more skilled negotiators, and become more adept strategic leaders.

NOTES

1. Association of the United States Army, *Torchbearer National Security Report* (Arlington, VA: Institute of Land Warfare, Association of the United States Army, March 2005): 21.

2. Ibid.

3. Susan C. Fischer and V. Alan Spiker, *Critical Thinking Training for Army Officers,* vol. 1 (Alexandria, VA: U.S. Army Research Institute for the Behavioral and Social Sciences, May 2004): 3.

4. For a good discussion on automatic versus controlled processing, see Robert G. Lord and Karen J. Maher, "Cognitive Theory in Industrial and Organizational Psychology," *Handbook of Industrial and Organizational Psychology*, Marvin D. Dunnette and Leaetta M. Hough, eds. (Palo Alto, CA: Consulting Psychologists Press, 1991).

5. This model is derived from the elements of reasoning in Richard Paul and Linda Elder, *Critical Thinking: Tools for Taking Charge of Your Learning and Your Life* (Upper Saddle River, NJ: Prentice Hall, 2001): 50.

6. Ibid., 98.

7. Bruce J. Avolio, *Leadership Development in Balance* (Mahway, NJ: Lawrence Erlbaum Associates, 2005): 77.

8. Paul and Elder, 214.

9. Ibid., 234.

10. Ibid., 233.

11. Anne Thomson, *Critical Reasoning: A Practical Introduction*, 2nd ed. (New York: Routledge, 2002): 44.

12. Ibid., 26.

13. Paul and Elder, 70.

14. Peter M. Senge, *The Fifth Discipline: The Art and Practice of the Learning Organization* (New York: Currency and Doubleday, 1990): 241.

15. Paul and Elder, 70.

16. Ibid., 102.

17. Thomas L. Wheelen and J. David Hunger, *Strategic Management and Business Policy*, 3rd ed. (Reading, MA: Addison-Wesley Publishing Company, 1989): 89–90.

18. Max H. Bazerman, *Judgment in Managerial Decision Making* (Hoboken, NJ: John Wiley & Sons, 2002): 6–7.

19. Ibid.

20. Ibid., 27.

21. Jim Collins, *Good to Great: Why Some Companies Make the Leap... and Others Don't* (New York: Harper Collins, 2001).

22. Ibid., 35.

23. Theodore Schick, Jr., and Lewis Vaughn, *How to Think about Weird Things— Critical Thinking for a New Age,* 3rd ed. (New York: McGraw Hill, 2002): 298.

24. Diane F. Halpern, *Thought and Knowledge: An Introduction to Critical Thinking*, 4th ed. (Mahway, NJ: Lawrence Erlbaum Associates, 2003): 203.

25. Schick and Vaughn, 298.

26. Patrick Hurley, *Critical Thinking: Excerpts from Patrick Hurley, A Concise Introduction to Logic*, 8th ed. (Belmont, CA: Wadsworth/Thomson Learning, 2004): 115.

27. Schick and Vaughn, 302.

28. Hurley, 139.

29. Hurley, 125.

4 Systems Thinking and Senior Leadership

George E. Reed, PhD

For every problem there is a solution that is simple, neat—and wrong. This maxim has been attributed at various times to Mark Twain, H.L. Mencken and Peter Drucker as a wake-up call to managers who mistakenly think that making a change in just one part of a complex problem will cure the ails of an entire system. Everyday management thinking too often looks for straightforward cause and effect relationships in problem solving that ignore the effect on, and feedback from, the entire system.[1]

—Ron Zemke, "Systems Thinking"

The U.S. Army War College suggests that senior leadership often takes place in an environment that is volatile, uncertain, complex, and ambiguous. Problems in this arena are rarely simple and clear-cut. If they were, they would likely have already been solved by someone else. If not well considered (and sometimes even when they are), today's solutions become tomorrow's problems. Inherent in the concept of strategic leadership is the notion that this environment requires different ways of thinking about problems and organizations. The Army War College curriculum stresses concepts of *systems thinking* and suggests that systems thinking is a framework that should be understood and applied by strategic leaders.

It is insufficient and often counterproductive for strategic leaders to merely be good cogs in the machine. Strategic leaders must also be able to discern when a venerated system or process has outlived its usefulness or when it is operating as originally designed but against the overall purpose for which the organization was established. Sometimes we forget that systems are created by people based on an idea about what should happen at a given point in time. Although times and circumstances may change, systems tend to endure. We seem to be better at creating new systems than changing or eliminating existing ones.

Systems also influence the behavior of people in organizations. Sociologist Robert K. Merton coined the term *goal displacement* to describe what happens when complying with bureaucratic processes becomes the objective instead of focusing on organizational goals and values.[2] When this happens, systems take on a life of their own and seem to be immune to common sense. Thoughtless application of rules and procedures can stifle innovation, hamper adaptivity, and dash creativity. Wholesale disregard of rules and procedures, however, can be equally disastrous.

When members of an organization feel as though they must constantly fight the system or beat it by circumventing established rules and procedures, the result can be cynicism or a poor ethical climate. Senior leaders, because of their experience and position, are invested with the authority to intervene and correct or abandon malfunctioning systems. At the very least, they can advocate for change in a way that those with less positional authority cannot. Strategic leaders should therefore be alert to systems driving human behavior that are inimical to organizational effectiveness. It is arguable that military organizations placing a premium on standardization and tradition are predisposed to goal displacement.

THE PROCEDURAL ORGANIZATION

Sociologist James Q. Wilson notes that the Army in peacetime can be rightly described as a "procedural organization."[3] In such an organization, adherence to established doctrine, rules, and operating procedures serves as a substitute for the Army's ultimate test of effectiveness—battlefield victory. Since war is normally not a constant state for the military, the substitute metric, compliance with established procedures, consumes a fair amount of the attention of leaders at all levels. The drive to procedural compliance occurs despite the fact that there may be little evidence that such compliance will translate to mission accomplishment. An example at the organizational level may illustrate the point.

After an annual general inspection, an infantry battalion commander in a mechanized division was informed that his unit was determined to be "red" (major deficiencies noted) in the area of communications. The signal corps expert from the Inspector General's office (IG) explained that the unsatisfactory rating was due to a combination of deficiencies, including poor documentation of completed maintenance and minor errors observed in the installation of radio equipment. Using a formula devised by the IG, the minor deficiencies added up to a percentage of errors deemed to equate to an unsatisfactory rating. The commander accepted the deficiencies but then asked a key question: "If I went to combat tomorrow, would my unit be able to communicate?"

"Yes," the briefer admitted.

"Then why am I red in commo?"

After a lengthy re-explanation of the formula for determining the red, yellow, and green assessments, the commander continued to press the issue, questioning the validity of an inspection result that did not correlate with combat readiness. The actions of the battalion commander were noticed by the division commander, who directed a reexamination of the inspection criteria for the entire division. The inspection system was changed, in part because a subordinate commander had the temerity to question conventional wisdom. In effect, he was questioning whether the system was accomplishing the goal for which it was originally intended. In this case the division commander recognized the issue his subordinate raised and used his positional authority to direct a change.

During wartime, feedback in terms of effectiveness is both immediate and definitive. Tactical units must quickly adapt to the environment as a matter of survival. This explains, in part, why it is so difficult for doctrine, techniques, tactics, and procedures published by the functional Army to keep up with the experiences of units in the field. In peacetime the procedural flow is largely top down from the functional Army to the field, whereas war tends to reverse the direction. When at war, units in the field provide information about what works to the functional Army, which attempts to capture the best practices and authoritatively document them in an effort to aid other units and synchronize efforts. Thus, the rational decision-making process predicated upon a best-practices approach may serve a leader well at the tactical level of operations, but in a strategic environment, where dealing with political issues is vital, such a rational approach may prove woefully inadequate.

As Field Manual 22-100 notes, "Strategic leaders must concern them-selves with the total environment in which the Army functions; their decisions take into account such things as congressional hearings, Army budgetary constraints, new systems . . . just to name a few."[4] We need senior leaders who can see both the parts and the big picture; to this end some of the concepts of systems thinking are useful.

UNDERSTANDING SYSTEMS THINKING

The Department of Defense can be viewed as a large and complex social system that has many interrelated parts. As with any system of this type, when changes are made to one part of the system, many other parts are ef-fected in a cascading and often unpredictable manner. Thus, organizational decisions are fraught with second- and third-order effects that result in unintended consequences. Fire-and-forget approaches are rarely adequate and are sometimes downright harmful. Extensive planning combined with even the best of intentions does not guarantee success. Better prediction is not the answer, nor is it possible. There are so many interactions in complex systems that no individual can be expected to forecast the impact of even small changes that are amplified over time.

In her book *Organization Theory: Modern, Symbolic, and Postmodern Perspectives*, Mary Jo Hatch provides an introduction to general systems theory that is useful in thinking about organizations.[5] She makes a point worthy of repeating: the use of lower-level models is problematic when applied to higher-level systems. Thus, the language of simple machines creates blind spots when used as a metaphor for human or social systems; human systems are infinitely more complex and dynamic. In other words, it can be counterproductive to treat a complex dynamic social system like a simple machine. Yet machine-age references are all around us. Our primary schools are largely still set up in a factory model, we speak of units running like "well-oiled machines," and we "leverage" change as if organizations were mechanistic.

Noted management scholar Russell Ackoff puts it another way. He asserts that we are in the process of leaving the machine age, which had roots in the Renaissance and came into favor through the industrialization of society.[6] In that era the machine metaphor became the predominant way of looking at organizations. The universe was envisioned by thinkers, such as Isaac Newton, as having the characteristics of a big clock. The workings of the clock could be understood through the process of analysis and the analytical method. At the time, analysis involved taking apart something of interest, trying to understand the behavior of its parts, and then assembling the understanding of the parts into an understanding of the whole. Ackoff explains, "One simple relationship—*cause and effect*—was sufficient to explain all relationships."[7]

Machine-age thinking remains with us today, but there are alternatives. Ackoff believes that we are entering the systems age as we seek answers to complex problems not answered by the machine-age approach. By the 1950s, the narrative of systems took hold. Systems, like the human body, have parts, and the parts affect the performance of the whole. All the parts are interdependent. The liver affects the brain, heart, kidneys, etc., and vice versa. You can study the parts singly, but because of the interactions, it doesn't make much practical sense to stop there. Understanding of the system cannot depend on analysis alone. The key pathway to understanding is therefore synthesis. Thus the systems approach is to:

1. *Identify a system.* After all, not all things are systems. Some systems are simple and predictable, whereas others are complex and dynamic. Most human social systems are the latter.

2. *Explain the behavior or properties of the whole system.* This focus on the whole is the process of synthesis. Ackoff says that analysis looks *into* things while synthesis looks *out* of things.

3. *Explain the behavior or properties of the thing to be explained in terms of the role(s) or function(s) within the whole.*[8]

The key difference here is that the focus remains on the system as a whole, and the analysis (as in step three above) is always in terms of the overall purpose of the system. This form of inquiry never loses sight of the ultimate goal of the system. Applying Ackoff's approach to a military example might help clarify what is admittedly abstract at first glance.

APPLYING SYSTEMS THINKING

A machine-age thinker confronted with the need to explain an army would begin by disassembling it until he or she reached its elements, e.g., from army to corps, to divisions, to brigades, to battalions, to platoons, to companies, to squads, to teams, and then to soldiers. Then the thinker would examine and define each subcomponent of the army—its soldiers, teams, etc. Finally, he or she would aggregate these into a definition of team, squad, and so on, eventually concluding with a definition of an army.

A systems thinker confronted with the same task would begin by identifying a system containing the army; for example, the defense establishment. Then such a thinker would define the objectives and functions of the defense establishment, doing so with respect to the still-larger social system that contains it. Finally, he or she would explain or define the army in terms of its roles and functions in the defense establishment.[9]

As an example of how a systems thinking approach can be applied to a contemporary defense issue at a strategic level, consider the Institute for Defense Analyses (IDA) report entitled *Transforming DoD Management: The Systems Approach.*[10] The authors of this study suggested an alternative approach to service-based readiness reporting—one that considers the entire defense transportation system.

One section of the report suggests that knowing the status of equipment, training, and manning of Army transportation units is helpful but insufficient to determine the readiness of a system that includes elements such as airfields, road networks, ships, and ports. The defense transportation system includes elements of all services and even some commercial entities. It only makes sense, therefore, to assess the readiness of these elements as part of a larger system that has an identifiable purpose—to move troops and equipment to the right place at the right time. In this example you can clearly see the approach recommended by Ackoff.

THE PROBLEM OF "BUSY-NESS"

Few would disagree, in principle, that senior leaders must see not only the parts but also the big picture. So why don't we do more of it? One reason is that we are so darn busy! Immersed in the myriad details of daily existence, it is easy to lose sight of the bigger picture. While it may be important to orient on strategic goals and objectives, the urgent often displaces the important. Fighting off the alligators inevitably takes precedence over draining the swamp.

The problem of "busy-ness" can be compounded by senior leaders who are overscheduled and uneducated in systems thinking. It seems as though contemporary military officers work excessive hours as a matter of pride. A cursory examination of the calendar of most contemporary officers, especially flag officers, will indicate an abusive pace.

Consider as an alternative the example of one of America's greatest soldier-statesmen, General George C. Marshall. Even at the height of World War II, General Marshall typically rode a horse in the morning for exercise, came home for lunch and a visit with his wife, went to bed early, and regularly took retreats to rejuvenate. To what extent are such pauses for reflection and renewal valued today? Simple cause-and-effect thinking combined with a culture of busy-ness can result in decisionmakers who rapid-fire short-term solutions to long-term problems.

A common symptom of this phenomenon is evident in senior leaders who unrealistically demand simplicity and certainty in a complex and uncertain environment. The drive for simplicity can lead to the need for excessive assumptions. Few strategic-level issues can be understood, much less solved, in a two-page point paper or a PowerPoint slide. We might also ask whether speed in decision-making and decisiveness, so valued at the tactical level, works to the detriment of good decisions at the strategic level. Absent some discipline and techniques to do otherwise, it is very hard to find time for reflection and deliberative decision-making.

> Most people expect learning just to happen without taking the time for thought and reflection, which true learning requires. In the past, with slower communication systems, we often had a few weeks to ponder and rethink a decision. Today we're accustomed to e-mails, faxes, overnight letters, and cell phones, and have come to believe that an immediate response is more important than a thoughtful one.[11]

RECOGNIZING INTERRELATIONSHIPS AND PATTERNS

Peter Senge submits that systems thinking provides just the type of discipline and tool set needed to encourage seeing "interrelationships rather than things, for seeing patterns of change rather than static snapshots.[12] Senge argues that this shift of mind is necessary to deal with the complexities of dynamic social systems.

Senge suggests that we think in terms of feedback loops as a substitute for simple cause-and-effect relationships. Imagine a farmer who determines that an insect infestation is eating his crop. The conventional approach is to apply a pesticide designed to kill the insect.[13] Our example at this point depicts the lowest level of the thinking hierarchy—reaction. In response to the appearance of insects, the farmer applies a pesticide because he assumes that what worked in the past will work in this instance. As additional insects appear, the farmer applies more of the pesticide. While the farmer's goal is to produce a crop, his activity is increasingly consumed by recurring applications of the chemical. He is surely busy, but he may not necessarily be productive.

A systems thinker might step back from the problem, take a broader view, and consider what is happening over time. For example, the systems thinker might think about whether any patterns appear over weeks or months and attempt to depict what is actually occurring. Recognizing the pattern of a system over time is a higher-order level of thinking. The systems thinker might notice that insect infestation did decrease after applying pesticide, but only for a short time. The insects that were eating the crop were actually controlling a second species of insect. Eliminating the first species resulted in a growth explosion in the second that caused even more damage than the first. The obvious solution caused unintended consequences that worsened the situation.

An accomplished systems thinker would model the above example using a series of feedback and reinforcing loops. The specifics of the modeling technique are less important at this point than the observation that systems thinking tends to see things in terms of loops and patterns, aided by constant assessment of what *is* happening rather than flow charts and reliance on what *should be* happening. At the highest level of thinking, the farmer would try to identify root causes or possible points of intervention suggested by these observations.

In *Why Smart Executives Fail,* Sydney Finkelstein examined more than 50 of the world's most notorious business failures.[14] His analysis indicated that in almost every case the failures were not attributable to stupidity or lack of attention. On the contrary, many of the leaders of well-known corporations such as Samsung, General Motors, WorldCom, and Enron were exceptionally bright, energetic, and deeply involved in the operation of their businesses. Up to the point of massive corporate failure, they were all extremely successful, and in almost every case, some members of the organization had vainly raised objections to the course that eventually proved disastrous.

Instead, in most instances the executives failed to see or accept what was actually happening. In some cases they were blinded by their own prior successes, and in other cases they inexplicably held tenaciously to a vision despite plenty of evidence that the chosen strategic direction was ill-advised. The systems thinker's pragmatic focus on determining what is actually happening serves as a preventative to self-delusional wishful thinking. Wishful thinking is no substitute for a realistic appraisal. In the language of systems thinking, the executives were trapped by their own faulty mental models.

Consider the advantages of a systems thinking approach when preparing for counterinsurgency operations and other complex military contingencies. The destruction of enemy forces is an important consideration to be sure, but it is only one factor of many. Combat operations against insurgent groups may pale in comparison to establishing other civil services that bring legitimacy to a newly established government. In some circumstances, excessive focus on combat operations and kinetic solutions could actually work to the detriment of long-term mission success.

The continuous assessment process that is characteristic of systems thinking is essential in a volatile environment that is changing rapidly. It takes time and good habits of critical reflection to engage in this kind of learning.

As an exercise in systems thinking, consider the factors that led to the abuse of detainees in U.S. custody documented at the now-infamous Abu Ghraib prison in Iraq. We know a great deal about this unfortunate incident because of publicly available reports like the *The Independent Panel to Review DoD Detention Operations*, commonly referred to as the Schlesinger Report.[15] Most military officers were quick to cite weak leadership and the lack of effective training as central causes of the debacle. Strategic leaders should, however, be suspicious of one-sentence explanations for the failure of complex human systems.

While we can accept that the chain of command failed to aggressively enforce ethical standards at Abu Ghraib and some bad apples lost their moral compasses, numerous other factors also contributed to the debacle.

The Schlesinger Report suggested a number of contributing variables in a chain that began with a disjointed mobilization long before arrival in Iraq. Some of the other noteworthy contributing factors were an inadequate staff-to-inmate ratio; an assignment of a unit trained to perform an enemy prisoner of war mission to the technically demanding and unfamiliar job of running a maximum-custody prison; poor morale; a convoluted chain of command; pressure to produce intelligence; procedural confusion; and the morally disorienting impact of being under frequent attack in the center of a burgeoning insurgency. Each contributing factor identified suggests a potential point of intervention to take corrective action and prevent recurrence.

A systemic approach to preventing failure is more likely to result in effective long-term solutions. Imagine for a moment that the incidents of abuse at Abu Ghraib were chalked up merely to ineffective leadership and miscreant behavior by some thugs on the night shift. After relieving the chain of command for cause and prosecuting the abusers, the members of the replacement chain of command might have found themselves in an equally untenable situation. While inspired leadership can make a difference under the worst of conditions, we might ask just how heroic we expect our leaders to be on a regular basis. When a system is so obviously stacked against our leaders, there is a moral imperative to change the system.

A SYSTEMS THINKING FRAMEWORK

In *The Fifth Discipline*, Peter Senge suggests 11 laws of systems thinking that are worthy of consideration as a summary to the points made in this chapter.[16] We often use this framework when discussing systemic approaches at the Army War College.

Today's problems come from yesterday's solutions. "Fire and forget" solutions may be well intentioned, but they may also fail to consider second- and third-order consequences. Sometimes solutions merely shift the problem from one part of a system to another. What worked one time may not work the next. It is necessary to launch intended solutions, but it is not okay to assume that the solution will have the intended effect on the system. It is hard to predict how complex, dynamic systems will react to interventions; therefore, attention should be paid to carefully observing system reactions.

The harder you push, the harder the system pushes back. Senge calls this *compensating feedback*, which occurs when an intervention prompts a response from within the system that offsets the benefits of the intervention.[17] Understanding the source of the opposition and system dynamics that drive the resistance can help avoid the leadership exhaustion that results from just pushing harder.

The cure can be worse than the disease. As with the case of the farmer who repeatedly applied pesticides, Senge writes, "the easy or familiar solution is not only ineffective, sometimes it is addictive and dangerous."[18] One-sentence solutions to complex problems at the strategic level are rarely a good idea.

Faster is slower. Complex social systems tend to respond at their own optimal rate. The impatience of the leader to make a difference is understandable, but sometimes it takes wisdom and patience to have an impact at the strategic level.

Cause and effect are not closely related in time and space. Strategic leaders must think in terms of longer time horizons than those at the direct and organizational levels of leadership. There are often significant time delays between an action and an observable reaction. It may take time for small but important changes to amplify through a system over time, but this should not discourage leaders from taking actions that could make a difference.

Small changes can produce big results, but the areas of highest impact are often the least obvious. "Obvious solutions don't work—at best they improve matters in the short run, only to make things worse in the long run,"[19] says Senge. It is important to think about the forces at play in human systems, including the subtle network of incentives and disincentives that motivate change or resistance to change.

You can have your cake and eat it too—but not at once. Sometimes seemingly either/or choices can both be achieved, provided a longer time horizon is considered. Many dichotomies are false when viewed from this perspective. As an example, consider the classic tradeoff between military personnel costs and equipment modernization. One may require priority at a given point in time, but under certain circumstances both may be emphasized over the long run.

Dividing an elephant in half does not produce two small elephants. This is a call for seeing things as a whole instead of as a collection of parts. Senge uses the Sufi example of three blind men describing an elephant to make this point.[20] The first touched the hide and described it as a rug; the second felt the trunk and thought it like a pipe; and the third, holding the leg, related it as a pillar. Our organizational boundaries can keep us from seeing important interactions. As with our defense transportation readiness example, some things make sense only when thought of as a whole— through synthesis in addition to analysis.

There is no blame. Humans seem to be almost hard-wired to blame someone when things don't go as anticipated. The search for blame drains organizational energy and promotes defensive reactions that hamper efforts to find facts important to preventing recurrence. Systems thinking accepts the fact that many factors interacting over time contribute to failures. While accountability goes hand in hand with good leadership, singling out scapegoats is no substitute for identifying and correcting systemic factors that drive human behavior in unproductive ways.

Systems thinking is not a panacea for senior-level leaders. There is no checklist to work through that will guarantee that someone is thinking in a way that will capture the big picture or identify root causes of difficult problems. Some concepts and approaches embedded in the systems thinking literature, however, can be very helpful when considering why a situation seems to be immune to intervention, or why a problem thought to be solved has returned with a vengeance. Thinking about systems and their dynamics can suggest alternative approaches and can be helpful by attuning senior leaders to important aspects of organizational behavior.

NOTES

1. Ron Zemke, "Systems Thinking," *Training* 38.2 (February 2001): 40.

2. See Robert K. Merton, *Social Theory and Social Structure* (New York: Free Press, 1968) for his discussion on "goal displacement."

3. James Q. Wilson, *Bureaucracy: What Government Agencies Do and Why They Do It* (New York: Basic Books, 2000).

4. Department of the Army, "FM 22-100—Army Leadership" (Washington, D.C.: Department of the Army, 1999): 10–12.

5. Mary Jo Hatch, *Organization Theory: Modern, Symbolic, and Postmodern Perspective* (New York: Oxford University Press, 2006).

6. Russell Ackoff, *Ackoff's Best: His Classic Writings on Management* (Hoboken, NJ: John Wiley & Sons, 1999): 6.

7. Ibid., 10.

8. Ibid., 17.

9. Russell Ackoff uses the example of a university in the same way that I use the example of the Army. The example in this paragraph is modified from the work contained in pages 17 and 18 of *Ackoff's Best*.

10. John C. F. Tillson et al., "Document D-2886—Transforming DoD Management: The Systems Approach" (Alexandria, VA: Institute for Defense Analyses, 2003).

11. Peter M. Senge, "The Fifth Discipline: A Shift of Mind," *Classics of Organization Theory*, Jay M. Shafritz and J. Steven Ott, eds. (Belmont, CA: Wadsworth, 2001): 451.

12. Steven Robbins, "Organizational Learning Is No Accident," *Harvard Business School Working Knowledge* (May 19, 2003).

13. This example is adapted from Daniel Aronson, "An Introduction to Systems Thinking" (1996), which is available on the *Thinking Page* website at http://www.thinking.net/Systems_Thinking/OverviewSTarticle.pdf (accessed 4 February 2004).

14. Sydney Finkelstein, *Why Smart Executives Fail and What You Can Learn from Their Mistakes* (New York: Portfolio, 2004).

15. James R. Schlesinger, *The Independent Panel to Review DoD Detention Operations* (Arlington, VA: Department of Defense, 2004).

16. Senge, 57–67.

17. Ibid., 58.

18. Ibid., 61.

19. Ibid., 63.

20. Ibid., 66–67.

Strategic Leaders and the Uses of History

Mark Grandstaff, PhD

Having taught at two war colleges, I have observed a trend among many field-grade officers to see the study of history as irrelevant.[1] Why? Many undoubtedly find themselves too focused on immediate concerns to properly learn how to "use" history. Others do not like to read traditional history, finding the prose turgid, the results dubious, and the arguments exhausting.[2] Some simply do not like the academic approach. Professors typically ask more questions than they answer, seemingly enter into long debates over trifles, and perhaps worst of all, encourage students to shatter preconceptions. Other officers argue that technology, i.e., superior weapons and new intelligence-gathering methods, has made the study of history "a thing of the past."[3] For them it is about the future and finding the right technology—the right "silver bullet"—to handle the situation. It is about "forward-thinking" and "transformation."

And is it any wonder? For most of their careers, military officers and many business practitioners are trained to think about lessons learned and often meet with subordinates to discuss such lessons to discern best practices that can be used later when faced with a similar problem.[4] There is something to be said about not "reinventing the wheel." Yet lessons learned and best practices can (and often do) stifle original thinking because they usually substitute linearity for multicausal thinking.

Now War College students are asked to put such a cut-and-dried mentality aside in order to replace it with a new approach: Senior leaders should learn "how to think, not what to think." They are taught that, at the strategic level of leadership, officers rarely find the "right" or "best" answers because most of the problems faced by senior leaders are multifaceted and complicated. In fact, because of the complexity, the best thing that might be said of problem situations for strategic leaders is that they can be managed rather than solved.

Today's world calls for strategic leaders to understand that history is far from irrelevant. It is something to use and leverage. The study of history can help leaders understand the nature of change and the consequences of being trapped in a parochial worldview. It provides leaders with a series of questions that, if properly developed and applied, will help them make good decisions by ferreting out what is important from what is not.

I have selected three specific areas where the knowledge of history and the historical process is absolutely vital to the strategic leader. The first section of the chapter focuses on how faulty historical analogies can lead to poor strategy and decision-making and offers advice on how to avoid them. The second section demonstrates how history is central to maintaining an institution's culture and making sense out of a volatile, uncertain, complex, and ambiguous world. The final section presents three important concepts that, if followed, will enable a strategic leader to "think historically."

STRATEGY AND CHOICE

One of the important ideas that the Army War College faculty attempts to instill in strategic leaders is that high-level strategy comes down to one thing—choice. Simply, the essence of an institution's strategy is what it chooses to do and not to do. The quality of the thinking that goes into such choices, as Giovanni Gavetti and Jan Rivkin put it in the April 2005 *Harvard Business Review*, is the key driver of the quality and success of an institution's strategy. Most of the time, they added, leaders are so immersed in the specifics of strategies—the ideas, the numbers, the plans—that they do not step back and examine how they think about strategic choices.[5] Herein lies the rub: Leaders often grasp at the first strategic analogy that comes along and stick with it. The bottom line is this: A senior leader must be aware of what historical assumptions and analogies he or she is making when thinking about strategy.

A historical analogy can set the stage for faulty presumptions that lead to poor strategic choices. For example, in one experiment, a Stanford psychologist told two groups of international conflict majors that they were to solve a hypothetical case study of a small democratic nation threatened by a neighboring totalitarian state. They were to consider themselves members of the U.S. State Department tasked with suggesting a course of action to their bosses.

The background to the case was changed slightly for each group. The first group was told that the President was from New York (the same state as Franklin Roosevelt) and that oppressed peoples were living in boxcars. On top of this, the briefing for the case study was held in Winston Churchill Hall. The other group of students was told that the President was from Texas (like Lyndon Johnson) and that the refugees were fleeing in small boats. In this case, the briefing was given in Dean Rusk Hall.

To solve the problem, the first group applied lessons of World War II, and the second group applied lessons of Vietnam.[6] There were no logical reasons to choose either historical period to make sense of the situation they were given. But because the experiment presented superficial likenesses, the students thoroughly embraced the strategic analogies without asking why. It appears that once a presumption or historical analogy has been made, it is extremely difficult to change.

CASE STUDY: THE KOREAN WAR DILEMMA

An example of poor presumptions and historical analysis can be found in President Harry S. Truman and his aides' analogical process when assessing North Korea's breach of the 38th parallel in the early summer of 1950. I choose this example for two reasons. First, scholars have examined the decision-making process in some detail. Second, it is likely the type of thinking process that strategic leaders would perform.[7]

In 1948 Truman and the State Department agreed that the United States should focus on defending areas in the Pacific that had a "strategic purpose." Korea, they agreed, was not one of them. Secretary of State Dean Acheson made this policy known publicly in 1949.[8] Less than a year later, on June 24, 1950, one of his aides notified President Truman that the North Koreans had just invaded South Korea. Truman, however, did not look at the North's invasion as an incursion into an area of little interest to the United States. Rather, for him it was possibly the beginning of World War III. The lessons of the 1930s told him that he must stop aggression because appeasement only begets more aggression. Truman's remarks shortly after hearing of the invasion demonstrated such a resolve: "By God," Truman said, "I am going to hit them hard."[9]

What had changed in little more than a year—from Korea having "no strategic purpose" to the president's being willing to go to war over a breach of the 38th parallel? The decision "to hit them hard" apparently rested in the president's and his cabinet's beliefs about the past, their view of the Communists, and the current domestic situation.

President Truman's linking pre–World War II analogies to the Korean conflict is well documented. For example, he wrote in his memoirs that after being briefed on the invasion, he reflected on the past couple of decades. "I remembered," he wrote,

> how each time that democracies failed to act it had encouraged the aggressors to keep going ahead. Communism was acting in Korea just as Hitler, Mussolini and the Japanese had acted. . . . I felt certain that if South Korea was allowed to fall Communist leaders would be emboldened to override nations closer to our own shores. If the Communists were permitted to force their way into the Republic of Korea without opposition from the free world, no small nation would have the courage to resist threats and aggression by stronger Communist neighbors . . . it would mean a third world war, just as similar incidents had brought on the second world war. It was also clear to me that the foundations and principles of the United Nations were at stake unless this unprovoked attack on Korea could be stopped.[10]

Juxtaposing Adolf Hitler and the Nazi Party with Josef Stalin and the Communist Party, he further reasoned that "should the Communists force their way into the Republic of Korea without opposition from the free world, no small nation would have the courage to resist threats of aggression by its stronger Communist neighbors."[11] Thus, he concluded, if the Soviet-backed North Koreans were allowed to go unchallenged, it would mean a third world war, just as similar incidents had brought on the Second World War. In other words, you could not appease the Communists as British Prime Minister Neville Chamberlain did the Nazis at Munich in 1938. In the minds of the President and his aides, appeasement meant weakness and would only embolden the Communists to attempt to control all of Asia.

Truman also reflected on the failure of the League of Nations to stem Nazi advances during the 1920s and 1930s. The institution had no power to enforce its proclamations. Moreover, despite its being the brainchild of American President Woodrow Wilson after World War I, America had not become part of the League. Thus, as some scholars have pointed out, the United States was at least partially to blame for the onset of World War II because it did little to stop Hitler. Now in the wake of World War II, the United States pushed for a new United Nations in which it could play a major role. The North Korean invasion of the South would be the first test of this new institution, and Truman strongly desired that the United Nations make a bold statement about its ability to enforce collective security.

Some important realities also affected Truman's thinking. A year before the invasion of Korea, the Soviets had tested their first atomic bomb. With this development, European leaders became worried about the United States' willingness to protect them. Would America really risk its own destruction simply to prevent theirs? Truman's own doctrine further complicated the matter. Proclaimed by the President in 1947, it committed the United States "to help free peoples to maintain their free institutions and their national integrity against aggressive movements that seek to impose upon them totalitarian regimes."[12] When Truman first announced the doctrine, it meant monetary help to Greece and Turkey. Yet in the wake of the 1948 Berlin airlift, the so-called fall of China in 1949, and the successful detonation of a Soviet atomic bomb, monetary aid began to transform into a commitment to military aid as well. A country known for avoiding "entangling alliances" was by the early 1950s a member of several treaties, the largest of which would be the North Atlantic Treaty Organization (NATO), a military alliance between the United States and Western Europe.

Furthermore, the National Security Council had prepared a document known as NSC 68, which explained the relationship between the United States and the Soviet Union in strong ideological terms. Written in early April of 1950, it couched the situation between the United States and the USSR as an almost apocalyptic battle of good versus evil—a war for the survival of Western civilization. These factors and the assumptions that undergirded them placed Truman and his aides in the position to believe that the United States was the only entity that could stop evil from enveloping the world.[13]

To recap, Truman viewed North Korea's invasion of the South as a move by the Soviets to dominate all of Asia. He compared North Korea's actions to the events of the 1930s, which he said included the Manchurian incident of 1931–1932, when Japan seized Manchuria from China; Italy's aggression against Ethiopia in 1935; and Hitler's forcible annexation of Austria in 1938. He also thought the Munich conference of 1938 had led to "appeasement," and he recalled the feelings of guilt when, as a senator, he had supported American isolationism. The decision seemed clear to use force under the banner of the United Nations to push the North Koreans back over the 38th parallel. This would demonstrate that the United States and United Nations would not appease "aggressors." There would be no return to the 1930s; it was a lesson learned well.

Selecting Objectives

But what would be the objective of an intervention? Richard Neustadt and Ernest May, in their book, *Thinking in Time: The Uses of History for Decision Makers*, argue that Truman and his aides should have thought more about defining the short- and long-term objectives by focusing on what was possible in the 1950s, not the 1930s. In other words, get the facts straight before relying on personal or historical experience to help shape a decision, remembering that history is not the "past." To do this, they suggest that the following steps would help strategic leaders "get the objectives right."

First, separate that which is known from what is unclear, and then separate the known and unclear from what is presumed. (Indeed, you may not have a problem at all—we are only presuming that one exists.) This is not an easy task. There is so much information out there. How do we select the information most pertinent to our decision? First (and this is important), narrow the data by specifying exactly why a decision needs to be made.

Second, identify the decision's potential objectives. According to Neustadt and May, "understanding why a decision must be made helps to define what the potential or possible objectives of the action are. . . . [One must know] the significant items [that] are known, unclear, and presumed, . . . which make the situation different now from what it was before, when it did not require attention."[14]

So let's look at Korea and the Truman administration in late June 1950—particularly the administration's examination of the specific problem and the analogies that shaped their thinking—in more detail. Using the Neustadt and May processes of defining problems and examining analogies, we will begin by defining what was known, unknown, and presumed.[15]

What Was Known

▶ North Korea had crossed the 38th parallel and attacked South Korea. The South Korean army was in retreat.

▶ There were tensions between the Soviets and the free world over the two Germanys. Middle Asia, especially Taiwan and French Indochina, were vulnerable to Chinese attack now that the Communists had taken control of the largest part of the Chinese mainland.

▶ Domestically, congressional elections were about four months away; there were problems with converting industry back to a peacetime footing following World War II; Democrats, including the president, were down in the polls; Republican senator Joseph McCarthy was accusing many in the State Department of being "Communists," and the domestic "red scare" was gaining some momentum. There were accusations that the Democrats, specifically the Truman administration, had "lost China" and continued to be "soft on Communism."

What Was Unknown

▶ What would happen to South Korea if the United States or the United Nations did not intervene?

▶ How would the Chinese react if the United States and the United Nations came close to or breached their borders? For that matter, how would the Soviets respond to the fact that a new "second front" had opened? Would they see it as an opportunity to move farther into Europe?

▶ Domestically, it was unclear what political conditions might prevail at election time. Did people really believe that the Democrats were responsible for "the loss of China" or that there were Communists in the State Department or in the Truman administration? Would American citizens support Truman's domestic recovery plans, including issues like health insurance and other Fair Deal programs?

What Was Presumed

▶ Was it the Soviets who had directed the North Koreans to attack South Korea?

▶ Did the South Koreans actually care for their current government and political leadership? Perhaps if allowed to vote, many would choose to unify under Communist leadership. Was this not self-determination, or was it Communist coercion?

▶ Was Communism monolithic? Did all Communists, including "Red China," take direction from the Soviets?

▶ Given that the United States had more atomic weapons than the Soviets, would the latter actually start a war in the face of such superiority?

▶ Was it true that if America did not enter Korea, it would look like weakness to the Russians and the Europeans? Would the new United Nations appear impotent? What about NATO? Was its reputation also at stake?

▶ Domestically, according to the polls, the choice to intervene in Korea would be popular at first; however, such support wanes quickly. But if Truman and the Democratic Party failed to respond to North Korea's invasion and South Korea became unified under a Communist banner, would there be strong political fallout?

▶ Would there be another global war should the United States defend South Korea?

Examining Analogies

Once the *presumed* is differentiated from what is *known* and *unknown*, it is a good time to examine the significant analogies. As the reader will recall, much of President Truman's and his aides' thinking focused on analogies from the 1930s, i.e., appeasement, Munich, isolationism, and the Second World War. Those analogies, in terms of their *likenesses* and *differences*, must be tested against what is actually known, unknown, and presumed.

Likenesses

▶ Aggression was taking place (as in Ethiopia and Manchuria in the 1930s).

▶ Korea requested help, as had Austria, Ethiopia, and Czechoslovakia.

▶ There were mechanisms in place that should have brought military aid to Korea by the United Nations and to Austria, Ethiopia, and Czechoslovakia by the Treaty of Versailles, the Locarno Treaty, the League of Nations, and the Treaty of Trianton.

▶ In the 1950s, as well as in the 1930s, there were aggressive dictatorships and ill-prepared and unwilling democracies.

Differences

▶ The two Koreas were not separate nations. The 38th parallel had been established after the war. No major power had crossed the border, as had happened in Manchuria, Ethiopia, the Rhineland, or Austria and Czechoslovakia in the 1930s.

▶ Since 1945, it appeared, the United Nations had successfully maintained the peace. Remember, Truman had agreed with the State Department that Korea held little, if any, strategic interest to the United States. Moreover, when the United Nations ordered in 1946 that the Soviets withdraw from Iran and Azerbaijan, they complied. The United States had also been successful in bringing food to the East Berliners in the 1948 Berlin airlift, and American leaders had entered into a treaty with Europe that established a military pact to ward off Soviet aggression. Thus, unlike the 1930s, there was significant power in Western Europe to repel or at least slow Soviet aggression. This had been untrue when the Italians attacked Ethiopia and the Germans raced into Austria and Czechoslovakia during the 1930s.

▶ Truman had made it clear that the United States was committed to aid any state threatened by totalitarian aggression (Truman Doctrine).

▶ Domestically, there was little, if any, support for American isolationism, let alone support for appeasement as in the 1930s.

▶ Militarily, nuclear weapons now existed, and the United States had already used them against an enemy.

Lessons from Korea

Although Truman did not overtly use such a process as Neudstadt and May suggest, he came to the only decision possible given his presumptions and the 1930s analogies: he must intervene. Here is where such a decision, without testing the analogies, can have second- and third-order effects. What was the objective? You could use force to punish the "aggressors," seek retribution, or simply restore the status quo antebellum. Truman chose to reestablish the status quo. Yet, although the objective seemed clear, given the analogies Truman and his confidants used, it soon became obscured. It morphed almost imperceptibly from status quo antebellum to one of "rollback." Indeed, shortly after the North Koreans breached the border, various ambassadors and congressional representatives began to talk about Korea in terms of reunification. Unfortunately, the president never corrected them. Even he began to readjust his thinking toward re-unification despite voicing his desire to reestablish the border.[16]

Accordingly, the president and his aides agreed that if such a rollback had taken place in the 1930s, World War II might never have happened. The analogy that led to an intervention now also governed the idea of rollback. Dean Acheson first suggested the "new" analogy of rollback during the Greek crisis in 1947. It was called the "rotten apple theory"—the idea that the rotten apple of Communism could ruin the rest of the barrel. This rest of the barrel included Europe and Asia.

One of the major programs designed to keep the Communists out of Europe and prevent them from contaminating the other apples was the Marshall Plan. There was no such program for Asia, with the exception of Japan. Consequently, it was believed that weak nations like Korea were far more susceptible to contamination than any in the West. Ultimately, this analogy would devolve into the "domino theory," the unquestioned belief that any Communist movement in Asia could eventually lead to co-opting the Far East.[17]

The bottom line was that the original objective of reestablishing the border was imperceptibly replaced by the analogy of rolling back Communism and reunifying Korea. When the United States crossed the 38th parallel, U.S. decisionmakers learned a sad fact: The Soviets did not intervene, but Communist China did. Unfortunately for the president, what he thought would be a short conflict turned into a nightmare, lasting until 1953 and costing millions of dollars and thousands of American lives. Politically, "the Korean crisis" proved disastrous for the Democrats, and Truman chose not to seek a second term. In 1952 the Republicans gained control of Congress and the White House.

President Truman's decision-making process demonstrated an over-reliance on lessons learned without a serious effort to understand the story—getting the facts, examining them, questioning presumptions, and testing the analogies. His use of history, both his reading of it and his personal experience, biased his decision to enter Korea and even more so his decision to accept a rollback analogy.

It should be clear by now that strategy is about making judicious choices and that more often than not, strategy is a product of analogical reasoning rather than deduction. Both deductive thinking and trial and error play important roles in strategy, but each is effective only in certain circumstances. Deduction typically requires a plethora of data and is more powerful in information-rich settings. Trial and error is an effective way to make strategic decisions in settings that are so complex and ambiguous that any rational thinking effort will fail.

Nevertheless, it is the analogical thinking process that is the most prevalent among strategy makers because they often deal with close choices—between the vast amounts of experience that senior leaders have, their knowledge of history and lessons learned, and the need for new strategies to spark creative answers. As we have seen, however, it is easy for strategic leaders to reason poorly through analogies because they seldom think about how to use them well. The best strategic thinkers use deduction and trial and error to test and improve analogies.[18] More analogies and new questions will ensue and, after a time, the "fog of war" may be somewhat lifted.

CASE STUDY: THE DECISION TO FIGHT AND OCCUPY IRAQ

The next case demonstrates the danger of focusing on the superficial. Often it is difficult to understand the complexities and depth of a given problem, especially when they are unknown. The ambiguity of the problem often causes people to concentrate on the surface similarities and fail to recognize a distinction between what is obvious and what is ambiguous. Moreover, senior leaders often seek out evidence that proves their analogy legitimate and ignore evidence to the contrary. One can see these problems borne out in an article that Undersecretary of Defense Paul Wolfowitz wrote for the *Philadelphia Inquirer*.

In February 2003 Wolfowitz believed, as did many others, that a war with Iraq would end Saddam Hussein's tyrannical regime. He went further in his optimistic prediction than many, however, when he wrote that "[Saddam's] demise will open opportunities for governments and institutions to emerge in the Muslim world that are respectful of fundamental human dignity and freedom." He added that he thought the occupation would be short and would change Iraq into a free and democratic nation. When one person brought up the difficulties we had with the occupation of Germany and Japan, the Undersecretary of Defense brushed the point aside: "If you are looking for a historical analogy, it's probably closer to post-liberation France [after World War II] than anything else."[19]

In the same month, a member of a Washington think tank, Pascale Siegal, confronted Wolfowitz about the Iraq-France analogy. For Mr. Siegal, Iraq was no post-liberation France. He listed the flaws he had found in Wolfowitz's thinking. Here is his dissection of the analogy:

▸ In World War II, France was occupied by its archenemy, Nazi Germany. Saddam Hussein, however unloved he might be, is homegrown in Iraq.

▸ By 1944 the French populace was virtually united in its desire for liberation from the Nazis and for the overthrow of the Vichy regime. It is unclear whether [the various factions within the] Iraqis will consider Americans as liberators or as occupiers.

▸ France had a long democratic and capitalist economic tradition on which to build. Iraq has never been a democratic state and has rarely been an open market economy.

▸ French forces played a significant role as part of the forces fighting to liberate France, through both the resistance and the Free French forces under de Gaulle. Such contributions by Iraqis are at best a remote possibility.

▸ De Gaulle was the recognized and acknowledged leader of the Free French forces, with a legitimacy across all segments of the French population. He had authority over essentially all resistance forces (including those led by the Communist Party). No similar charismatic legitimate Iraqi leader allied with the West exists inside or outside Iraq.

▸ Liberated France had a huge structure (after some cleansing of collaborators) of bureaucrats on which to base a functioning government (from schools to courthouses to trash collection). Does this mass of competency exist in Iraq?

▸ Last, and not least, in 1944–1945, the United States was part of a true international coalition—the Allies—that was supported by virtually all citizens in the alliance states and had clearly shared objectives in the defeat of the Axis powers (even if holding differing views of the post-war world). In 2003 no such popularly supported "coalition of the willing" truly exists.[20]

Whether you agree or disagree with Siegel's analysis is not important. What is important to remember is that experience and history (and not necessarily the past) underpin analogies, and these can greatly simplify a complex issue. Selecting a superficial analogy may promote a "false sense of confidence" and a belief that hard thinking has taken place, when what really has taken place is the justification for a risky endeavor that could place a nation's or institution's reputation and credibility in jeopardy. Even worse, it could cost lives.

In summary, many strategic leaders naturally connect present events with "handy" historical analogies in an almost instantaneous moment of recognition. Rarely do they examine the details of the analogy itself. In short, soft thinking using poor historical analogies often results in poor strategic choices.[21] George Santayana, the Spanish poet, wrote in 1905, "Those who cannot remember the past are doomed to repeat it." I have found this advice not quite accurate. Only the mind run by hard-and-fast historical assumptions and poor analogies repeats itself again and again.

LEADERSHIP AND CHANGE: KEEPING WHAT'S IMPORTANT TO THE INSTITUTION

The second aspect of learning how to think historically is understanding that some aspects of an institution or culture must be preserved for it to remain viable. Certain things change with time, but strategic leaders must determine what remains for a society or institution to make sense of the ambiguities and uncertainties its members face.

Truman, Kennedy, and Preventive Strikes

An example of strategic leaders making such choices can be found in Harry S. Truman's and John F. Kennedy's belief that "America never strikes first." For Truman, the idea of a preventive strike first came up in the late 1940s when it was discovered that the Soviets were constructing their own atomic bomb. Some, like Major General Orville Anderson, the first commandant of the Air War College, promoted the idea of a preventive nuclear strike against the factories in the Urals to stop the Soviets from later using atomic weapons to destroy "western civilization." His outburst sent ripples through the White House and ended up on the front page of the *New York Times*, especially when the Soviet ambassador told the United Nations that the U.S. Air Force was preparing to strike the Soviet Union.[22]

Truman took immediate action: He called the Joint Chiefs and had Anderson fired. Truman, in a speech to the nation, made it clear that as a country we do not practice surprise preventive attacks such as when the Japanese attacked the American base at Pearl Harbor.[23] He would later write in his diary,

> [Some have] said that we ought to fight a "preventive war." I have always been opposed even to the thought of such a war. There is

nothing more foolish than to think that war can be stopped by war. You don't "prevent" anything by war except peace.[24]

He later used the same argument during the Korea crisis when some advocated a first strike against the Chinese. Truman, understanding the crucial cultural beliefs and rituals that make America a nation, chose to continue the precedent begun at Concord and Lexington: Americans do not plan sneak attacks or shoot first—even if we have evidence that potential enemies are building weapons of mass destruction.

President John F. Kennedy came to a similar conclusion about the decision to order a first strike. As you may remember, on October 15, 1962, reconnaissance aircraft discovered nine short-range nuclear missile sites being constructed in Cuba. Missiles launched from the sites could strike much of the eastern part of the United States. Eventually, Cuba could become a basing site for bombers and middle-range nuclear missiles that could hit anywhere in the Western Hemisphere. President Kennedy and his aides determined that these deployments were a grave threat to the national security of the United States and its position in the region. President Kennedy assembled an executive committee of cabinet members and others, called "ExComm," to come up with a solution to the crisis.

When some in ExComm argued for a surprise preventive strike against the Cuban missile bases, Kennedy said that the United States would never commit such an act, for it would be considered immoral by the American public and would alienate allies. Robert Kennedy put it succinctly when discussing the preventive option: It was something that America would simply never do; it went against all "we stood for," he said in one ExComm meeting. It would be a "Pearl Harbor in reverse," as Ambassador George Ball put it.[25]

Ultimately, ExComm members found a solution other than a preventive strike. On October 22, the President announced publicly that there were missiles in Cuba and that he had authorized a blockade (quarantine) of the island. After another tense week, Kennedy announced on October 28 that Premier Nikita Khrushchev had agreed to dismantle the missiles and return them to Russia. Privately, Kennedy had promised the Soviet leader that he would not invade Russia and that the United States would remove the missiles it had placed in Turkey. America's reputation as a moral bene-factor to the world was preserved. Both Truman and Kennedy understood what must remain from the past and what could change. The belief of these two men that a first strike was an inviolable tenet of the American way of life was something they saw as worth preserving even to the detriment of national security. This was a strategic choice predicated upon the two presidents' understanding of what it means to be an American.

Bringing the Best Forward: General George C. Marshall and the Army Tradition

Here is another example of what strategic leaders should think about when determining what to change and what not to change when making decisions that may affect institutional culture. General of the Army George C. Marshall was placed in such a decision-making position during World War II. In 1943 he began looking at the future of the Army and reflecting on the American past, the nation's future, and the Army's culture. It was a transformational period. He was charting unknown waters—whether it be in creating a 15 million-person army or in planning for the occupation of conquered territories. After thinking about the latter for some time, he appointed Major General John Hildring to head up the occupational planning and administration. The conversation between these two men demonstrates Marshall's ability as a strategic leader to "hold fast" to American and Army values while at the same time navigating the unknown. "Hildring," Marshall instructed,

> I'm turning over to you a sacred trust and I want you to bear that in mind every day and every hour you preside over this military government and civil affairs venture. Our people sometimes say that soldiers are stupid. I must admit that at times we are. Sometimes our people think we are extravagant with the public money, that we squander it, spend it recklessly. I don't agree that we do. We are in the business where it's difficult always to administer your affairs as a businessman would administer his affairs in a company, and good judgment sometimes requires us to build a tank that turns out not to be what we want, and we scrap that and build another one, . . . but even though people say we are extravagant, that in itself isn't too disastrous. . . .
>
> But we have a great asset and that is that our people, our countrymen, do not distrust us and do not fear us. Our countrymen, our fellow citizens, are not afraid of us. They don't harbor any ideas that we intend to alter the government of the country or the nature of this government in any way. This is a sacred trust that I turned over to you today. . . . I don't want you to do anything, and I don't want to permit the enormous core of military governors that you are in the process of training, and are sure going to dispatch all over the world, to damage this high regard in which the professional soldiers in the Army are held by our people, and it could happen, it could happen, Hildring, if you don't understand what you are about . . . this reputation we have is of enormous importance, not only to the Army but to the country. This is my principal charge to you, this is the one thing that I never want you to forget in the dust of battle and when the pressure will be on you. . . .[26]

What was important to keep in regards to the institution? Marshall as Chief of Staff made it clear: "[The] things that you are about."[27] He understood the Army's mission, its past, and the historical role it had played in

American life. He told Hildring that there were important core beliefs that set the Army apart as an institution and the United States as a nation. He further deemed the keeping of these core beliefs a "sacred trust." What were those beliefs?

- ▶ America is a constitutional government that firmly believes in freedom of self-rule and inalienable rights.

- ▶ The Army is the protector of such freedoms at home and now abroad.

- ▶ The Army has a sacred trust given by its fellow citizens to remain subject to legally constituted authority.

- ▶ The Army's greatest asset is the American people.

- ▶ The Army is a business that is often unlike those run by executives. Sometimes the Army must "scrap" one product because the situation has changed.

- ▶ Our fellow citizens do not fear us, nor do we have designs to overthrow the government in any way.

- ▶ The soldier is always a citizen first, and a soldier second.

- ▶ Senior leaders are the conscience of the institution.

Thinking from a strategic perspective, Marshall underscored his message by telling Hildring that the Army's leadership could jeopardize the nation's trust and tarnish the Army's image if they don't understand their history, culture, and relationship to American society. Simply put, you must know yourself and your institution, and the study of history will help you do this. An examination of the history of an institution will demonstrate clearly its core beliefs—some things that are unwritten but are deeply woven into its society and culture.

THINKING HISTORICALLY

I have stressed in this chapter some of the key issues that a senior leader must remember when using history to make strategic choices.[28] The most important, I believe, are in the areas of analogies and preconditioning. In addition, many decisionmakers forget about what impact the decision may have in the long term (i.e., second-, third-, and fourth-order effects); hence the use of history as a foundation for bringing the important aspects of the past into the future.

There is one more set of ideas that I want to leave with you. History as written by historians is not the "past"; rather, in academe, it is a discipline in which its practitioners attempt to quell their biases, search the documents and artifacts, and make interpretations about the past. Some historians use different methods and approaches. Moreover, rarely would you find us coming to similar conclusions. But we would all agree that the study of history is about understanding context, causality, and complexity.

History Provides Context

If only those who have a cursory understanding make the decisions, they will make poor analogies that lead to poor strategic choices, culminating in a flawed strategy. We saw this with Truman and Wolfowitz. Even Kennedy's concern about a "Reverse Pearl Harbor" was an analogy misapplied strategically, but given his assumptions about America's mores, it was the correct strategic moral assumption.

History Demonstrates Multicausality

One must remember that an event is predicated upon a multitude of factors that are not linear. A senior leader must become self-aware of his or her own black-and-white thinking. He or she must go through the analogical process to differentiate what is unclear, unknown, and presumed. Only a thorough examination of the historical presumptions will help the strategist understand which decision to make—and what effects might result.

History Is Complex

It is more than names, dates, and descriptions of battles or biographies of great leaders. The historical process is about analytical rigor. We have seen that poor analogies go hand in hand with "soft thinking." As discussed elsewhere in this book, one of the significant competencies a senior leader must provide is a need to make sense out of disorder. Our need to find order in the face of volatility and ambiguity often forces us to make decisions based upon myths of a golden past that obscure our understanding of how past worlds operated and thus blind us to what is taking place socially, politically, and culturally in our nation or others.

Practitioners—whether in the military or business—often dismiss the study of history as irrelevant. After all, they deal with "real-world" problems, which demand "real-time" answers. There is often angst among some who feel uncomfortable when their ideas and assumptions are called into question or their ordered world is demolished, especially when they find that the study of history does not lead to finality but rather opens doors for new questions and new ways of thinking. "History," as one former Army officer observed, "forces leaders to recognize unpalatable truths...[and] compels them to think dispassionately about potential opponents—their nature, worldviews, aims and options."[29]

Today there is no place for the uninformed leader or the "soft-thinking" strategist. Too much is at stake. We must learn to read scholarly history critically. Learn to question assumptions and analogies, for they are all rooted in past experience and "history." In the pantheon of great American military leaders, the best were able to marry the roles of a soldier and a scholar. Sir William Francis Butler once warned that the "nation that makes a great distinction between its scholars and its warriors will have its thinking done by cowards and its fighting done by fools." True strategic leaders can marry both roles—warrior and thinker. In a time of "transformation," it is a must.

NOTES

1. For an example of the view that history is irrelevant, see Antulio J. Echevarria II, "The Trouble with History," *Parameters* (Summer 2005): 78–90. For recent publications that provide a contrast to this view, see *Past as Prologue: The Importance of History in the Military Profession*, William Murray and Richard Sinnreich, eds. (West Nyack, NY: Cambridge University Press, 2006); and Conrad Crane's review of the Murray and Sinnreich book in *Parameters* (Autumn 2007): 111–113.

2. For an excellent discourse on the problems with history lessons and discovering the past, see Michael Howard's "The Lessons of History," *The History Teacher* 15.4 (August 1982): 489–501.

3. Murray and Sinnreich, 27.

4. This process is also used upon the completion of a training or operational event and leads to creating some form of an after-action report (AAR). These AARs are used to reinforce and share lessons learned, to improve future performance.

5. Giovanni Gavetti and Jan Rivkin, "How Strategists Really Think," *Harvard Business Review* 83.4 (April 2005): 54–63.

6. Gavetti and Rivkin, 58–59.

7. See Richard Neustadt and Ernest May, *Thinking in Time* (New York: Free Press, 1986). A more recent and extensive work that examines the impact of World War II analogies on American decisionmakers can be found in Yuen Foong Khong, *Analogies at War: Korea, Munich, and the Vietnam Decision of 1965* (Princeton, NJ: Princeton University Press, 1992), especially Chapters 1, 2, and 5. Dated, but useful, resources include Ernest R. May, *Lessons of the Past: The Use and Misuse of History in American Foreign Policy* (Oxford: Oxford University Press, 1973), Chapters 2 and 3; and Richard Neustadt, "Uses of History in Public Policy," *The History Teacher* 15.4 (August 1992): 503–507. Other works that are important to this analysis include Gordon Paige, *The Korean Decision* (New York: The Free Press, 1968); Bruce Cummings, "Korean-American Relations," *New Frontiers in American-East Asian Relations*, Warren I. Cohen, ed. (New York: Columbia University Press, 1983): 237–282; Robert J. Donovan, *Tumultuous Years: The Presidency of Harry S. Truman, 1949–53* (New York: W.W. Norton, 1982): 187–248; and William W. Stueck, Jr., *The Road to Confrontation: American Policy Toward China and Korea, 1947–1950* (Chapel Hill: University of North Carolina Press, 1981).

8. Richard Haynes, *The Awesome Power: Harry S. Truman as Commander in Chief* (Baton Rouge: LSU Press, 1973): 163.

9. Margaret Truman, *Harry S. Truman* (New York: William Morrow, 1973): 455.

10. Harry S. Truman, *Memoirs*, vol. 2 (Garden City, NY: Doubleday & Co., 1955–1956): 333.

11. Ibid.

12. Harry S. Truman, "President Harry S. Truman's Address before a Joint Session of Congress, March 12, 1947." The Avalon Project at the Yale Law School. Available online at http://avalon.law.yale.edu/20th_century/trudoc.asp (accessed 6 November 2008).

13. David McCullough, *Truman* (New York: Simon and Schuster, 1992): 771–773.

14. Neustadt and May, 38–39.

15. Neustadt and May, 39–40, 42.

16. Marc Tractenberg, "Making Grand Strategy: The Early Cold War Experiences in Retrospect," *SAIS Review* 19.1 (Winter-Spring 1999): 33–40.

17. Robert Beisner, *Dean Acheson: A Life in the Cold War* (New York: Oxford University Press, 2006): Chapter 7.

18. Gavetti and Rivkin, 63.

19. Pascale Cobelles Siegel, "Thoughtless in Time?" (Silver City, NM, and Washington, D.C.: Foreign Policy in Focus, February 18, 2003). By September 2003, analogies compared Iraq to America in 1787 and to the wars in Korea, Vietnam, and Algeria. In 2005 President George W. Bush compared the events in Iraq to the co-

lonial American quest for a president and constitution. See Fred Kaplan, "1787 vs. Bagdad 2005," *Slate* (August 19, 2005): 1; and Tom Englehardt, "Iraq Analogies," *TomDispatch* (September 29, 2003). For a comprehensive list of Iraq analogies, see "Iraq Analogies," presented online by George Mason University's History News Network at http://hnn.us/articles/4695.html (accessed 6 November 2008).

20. Siegel, 1–2.

21. Otis Graham, "Using and Misusing History," *The Long Term View* (Spring 1988).

22. Mark Grandstaff, "Standing Before the Bar of Christ: Major General Orville A. Anderson, Preventive War and the Origins of the United States Air War College, 1945–1951," an unpublished manuscript in author's possession.

23. Harry S. Truman, 359.

24. Harry S. Truman, 383.

25. Dominic Tierney, "Pearl Harbor in Reverse: Moral Analogies in the Cuban Missile Crisis," *Journal of Cold War Studies* 9.3 (Summer 1997): 49–77.

26. Forrest C. Pogue, *George C. Marshall: Organizer of Victory* (New York: The Viking Press, 1973): 458–459.

27. Ibid.

28. See Thomas Andrews and Flannery Burke, "What Does It Mean to Think Historically," *Perspectives* (January 2007), available online at http://www.historians.org/perspectives/issues/2007/0701/0701tea2.cfm (accessed 6 November 2008).

29. Murray and Sinnreich, 4.

Creative Thinking for Individuals and Teams

6

COL Charles D. Allen, U.S. Army

The United States' national security and contemporary operating environments have been characterized by the U.S. Army War College *Strategic Leadership Primer* and other Department of Defense (DoD) documents as volatile, uncertain, complex, and ambiguous (VUCA).[1] Operating effectively in this context requires leaders to manage the multiple demands of such an environment by enhancing their strategic thinking. In the first core course in the Army War College curriculum, "Strategic Thinking," we study five important thinking domains: creative thinking, critical thinking, historical thinking, ethical reasoning, and systems thinking. An underlying assumption is that providing students with the fundamentals of *how* to think, not *what* to think, is essential for leaders at the strategic level.

Learning how to think is no small task, especially in highly technical professions operating in VUCA environments. Our senior leadership must be skilled in developing and applying creative strategies to circumstances about which they have limited current knowledge or understanding. For that reason, we expect students to apply creative and critical thinking skills to the myriad scenarios that they will face throughout the academic year, both individually and in groups.

Using an initial short presentation of concepts that addresses individual creativity and group dynamics, the faculty seeks to increase awareness of how individual preferences and creative styles may help or hinder contributions to group efforts. We review functions that are characteristic of effective groups and processes that support group creativity and innovation. The goal is to enhance learning and increase the effectiveness of future leaders as strategic thinkers during the academic year and beyond.

To that end, the development of organizational culture that fosters creativity and innovation is also addressed. Throughout the Army War College curriculum, we operate under the premise that individual attributes and skills that students possess have served them well in past assignments and will also be valuable in the future. But we caution students to remember that they are now at the position where those skills may be insufficient. The attainment of new skills and competencies, specifically in individual creativity and maintaining a creative climate, are required for success at the senior levels of our institutions.

In teaching the creative thinking curriculum, we subscribe to the following basic assumptions:

▶ Creativity is absolutely essential for effective individuals and organizations.

▶ Everyone is creative.

> ► Everyone is motivated to become more creative in response to changing conditions.

> ► There are processes that can improve individual and group creativity.

A commonly used definition of *creativity* is the ability to produce novel ideas that are valued by others. While great works of art and music are frequently attributed to creative genius, creative expression clearly extends beyond the fine arts. Psychologist Abraham Maslow found creative people in all endeavors—in cooking, gardening, raising a family, or working in community associations.[2] He found a relationship between creativity and self-actualization, not necessarily between creativity and greatness.

Creativity involves intuition and inspires innovation. At its most basic, *innovation* can be defined as taking an idea and introducing something new. Management guru Peter Drucker saw innovation significantly reshaping three major arenas: incorporating cutting-edge technology; revolutionizing the way business is conducted; and, more tangibly, developing and providing new products or services.[3] The great American inventor Thomas Edison was an innovator who brought to reality many ideas that were adopted by the American populace and the world. Edison's imagination gave impetus to his creative energies to experiment and invent the light bulb, phonograph, and nearly 1,100 other items for which he received patents. As an exemplar of Drucker's view of innovation, Edison was very effective in adopting technology and equally prolific in developing new and useful products.

The process of intuition is frequently discussed within the context of creative problem-solving and decision-making. Duane Ireland and Michael Hitt define *intuition* as "thoughts, conclusions, or choices produced largely or in part through subconscious mental processes."[4] Intuitive problem-solving is either attributed to a gut feeling or deep expertise that facilitates problem recognition and the development of a corresponding solution.

Leadership at all levels is involved with tackling existing problems and anticipating those problems that may emerge to pose a threat to the organization and the attainment of its goals. Rarely are those problems identical; most issues facing strategic leaders require novel approaches. Consequently, solutions to tough problems require creativity and innovation from the members of the organization if it is to adapt and thrive in a competitive landscape.

Historian Mark Stoler recounts that in 1945 General George C. Marshall was faced with the prospect of a post-war Europe.[5] Marshall foresaw that a "world of suffering people" without food and shelter and under desperate economic conditions could lead to another global catastrophe. His intuition was undoubtedly developed during his study of post-World War I Germany. Marshall demonstrated creativity in breaking from the traditional American pattern of thought, "leaving Europe to the Europeans" after the war. Through a combination of intuition based on his past experience and the willingness to imagine a novel alternative future for post-war Europe, Marshall produced a true innovation that was demonstrated in 1947 with the announcement of the European Recovery Program, more famously known as the Marshall Plan. His creativity and innovative efforts served the nation well during two major conflicts in his service as the senior Army officer (Chief of Staff) during World War II and as secretary of state during the Korean War—positions that developed and defined his strategic leadership.

Columbia Business School professor Bill Duggan writes of another great military leader in his book *Napoleon's Glance*.[6] Duggan attributes

Napoleon's military success to his ability to look at situations that Prussian military philosopher Carl von Clausewitz termed *"coup d'oeil"*—"a stroke of the eye"— or, in military terms, intuition-inspired "situational awareness." Napoleon, through in-depth studies of campaigns conducted by historic generals like Alexander the Great of ancient Greece and Prussia's Frederick the Great, developed an intuitive feel for tactical battles and military campaigns. Although some claim that he did not develop innovations in warfare, Napoleon was able to employ tactics that had been successful in past campaigns in new combinations on the European battlefields. Thus his *coup d'oeil* served as the foundation of his creative genius for war.

Thinking creatively is central to fostering what Peter Senge calls a *learning organization*, one that "is continually expanding its capacity to create its future."[7] The greater challenge for leaders that extends beyond individual problem-solving is the development of organizations that have the ability to adapt to accelerated change and an unpredictable future. Characteristic of such an organization is its ability to shape and interact successfully with the external environment. Because of the need to provide new and effective approaches to challenges, creativity is required of individuals, groups, and organizations at the tactical, operational, and strategic levels.

Creative thinking can also help leaders address the friction that occurs when external environments and organizations interact. The external environment influences the organization, and it is that interaction that necessitates creative action. In stable environments, problems may be well defined and resolved by using rote methods. However, in complex environments, repeating established patterns of behavior might be not only ineffective but also potentially disastrous. Therefore, changes in behaviors, attitudes, and processes at the respective levels of individuals, groups, and organizations are necessary to explore new ideas in response to new challenges, contexts, and situations.

If creativity is the ability to develop new ideas and concepts that are effective in resolving situations at hand, it is also much more than merely "problem-solving." Creativity is as much about *finding* problems as it is about problem-*solving*. Particularly at the strategic level, we must be sensitive to how we even *define* problems because very often the specificity or breadth of the problem statement will constrain the development of viable solutions. The terms *novelty*, *quality*, and *appropriateness* are commonly used in definitions of creativity. Creative solutions may be modifications of previously accepted methods or a synthesis of disparate concepts that successfully address the circumstances. Moreover, the solutions must be deemed practical enough to be implemented and, hence, seen as appropriate by others.

BARRIERS TO CREATIVITY

If we assume that creativity is highly desired by individuals and organizations, then why does it seem to be such a rare commodity? We use the work of Roger Von Oech to help identify attitudes that serve as barriers to creativity, which he calls "mental locks."[8] These attitudes are mostly developed through social interaction with others and the requirements to fill the "role" we have been assigned. To fulfill our need to belong or to be accepted, we may choose not to be different, so practicality and conformity take precedence. As adults, we marvel at the creativity exhibited by children, but within our education system we often stress "rational," linear, and standardized approaches that provide rules for everything. We emphasize that problem-solving is serious business and thus requires somber efforts. We seek to minimize deviations and error by following set procedures in the quest for the "right" answer. Wrong or just-good-enough solutions are viewed with disdain in the pursuit of the optimum. Dan Pink asserts that this predominantly left-brain thinking (rational, systemic, and relying on predictable patterns), characteristic of the United States in the twentieth century, will no longer be sufficient for this new century.[9] We also have become victims of our own achievements as individuals and within organizations, so we default to ways of thinking and acting that have made us successful in the past.

Some who have studied military innovation suggest that the culture of the U.S. military does not reflect a true learning organization.[10] The military's use of standard operating procedures (SOPs), regulations, and doctrine are designed to provide control over how people and organizations behave without tolerating departures from the "tried and true." Military training programs often follow very structured programs of instruction (POIs) to teach specific knowledge and competencies that are predominately focused on what to think and how to react to situations.

Other observers further assert that the Army personnel selection and promotion process results in senior leaders who are limited in their ability to think or act "out of the box." Consider the fact that most Army War College students have a Myers-Briggs Type Indicator (MBTI) profile of STJ—sensing, thinking, judging. This is in contrast with the profile type NTP—intuitive, thinking, perceiving, where creative individuals tend to be more intuitive ("N") rather than sensory ("S"), more thinking ("T") rather than feeling ("F"), and more perceiving ("P") rather than judging ("J").[11] Although the MBTI type profile is not predictive in all situations, it does inform how people (including senior Army leaders) *prefer* to act in stressful conditions. The following sections of this chapter address the three factors that affect creativity—the individual, the process, and the group climate.

INDIVIDUAL PREFERENCES AND CREATIVE STYLE

Creative thinking is a cognitive process that supports divergent and convergent aspects of problem-solving and decision-making. Thinking creatively provides a means to identify that a problem exists by looking at the situation from different perspectives, and therefore it helps with problem definition. It also gives rise to the generation of multiple alternatives and a range of options in this divergent component. Through the application of critical thinking, the alternatives are then analyzed and judged for effectiveness and appropriateness in solving the problem. The convergence on the problem solution results in a decision for implementation.

Research on creativity has revealed many attributes and competencies that are recurrent in creative individuals and innovative organizations. Psychologist Diane Halpern, in her book *Thought and Knowledge*, presents the following as key elements of creative thinking:[12]

- ▶ Stretching and rejecting paradigms

- ▶ Problem finding

- ▶ Selecting relevant information

- ▶ Generation, exploration, and evaluation

- ▶ Insight and incubation

- ▶ Analogical thinking (lateral versus vertical).

To provide an illustration of our stated assumptions and the key elements of creativity, we engage Army War College students in a thought exercise whereby a simple task is presented as part of the lesson. One such exercise is to provide each student with a standard sheet of paper, a paper clip, and a length of tape. The task instructions are to develop a system to project the paper the farthest possible distance down a hallway. The students are given ten minutes to complete the task and may not ask any questions of the instructor. At the end of the allotted time, students demonstrate their systems. A typical solution is creating a ball of paper around the paper clip, using the tape on the outside, and throwing it like a baseball. Another common solution is folding the paper into a traditional paper airplane with the paper clip attached with tape. Although both of these methods are effective ways to project the items, some students derive more innovative and curious systems that greatly exceed the projection distances of the "in-the-box" solutions.

In one case, a student used his camera phone to take a picture of the items and then sent the digital image to his spouse, who was arriving at a distant airport. Another innovative solution resulted when the students decided among themselves to collaborate. The resulting system consisted of the 17 students forming a human chain around the hallway and passing the paper, clip, and tape ball in a continuous circle that could theoretically could be projected an infinite distance. The latter of these solutions demonstrated the creativity of an individual that was fostered by teamwork. After the completion of such an exercise, the seminar conducts an after action review to explore how the students as individuals interpreted and went about the task. Other exercises are just as effective in demonstrating the individual barriers to creativity. Engaging in these somewhat simple and even silly exercises allows the students to overcome their mental blocks and gives them the opportunity to apply creative thinking strategies. It also demonstrates firsthand that creativity can be learned and applied when a supportive environment is established.

The exercises also reveal the personal factors related to creativity that are posited by Teresa Amabile in *Creativity in Context*.[13] Amabile presents a model composed of task motivation, domain-relevant skills, and creativity-relevant processes. Army War College students are typically highly motivated to complete a task, whether based on the competitive nature of the individual or just a desire to fulfill the expectation of the instructor. Whether the rewards are intrinsic or extrinsic, students are very engaged in the task and seek to present a quality product within the designated parameters

The breadth of knowledge and domain-relevant skills are also important factors in the type of solution presented. The more innovative solutions seem to be extracted from other domains. Such was the case with the camera phone, where the student used existing technology in stretching the paradigm of a system and expanding the concept of projection. The ambiguity of the instructions and the inability to ask questions could be frustrating for some, but for others it opened the door to new possibilities. Students who chose to work together used the ambiguity (no one said it had to be an individual effort) to their advantage and used their knowledge of simple geometry to develop a solution that involved all members of the group. Under these conditions, there was an opportunity to be somewhat foolish, have fun, and take risks in a nonthreatening environment.

Throughout their careers, U.S. military officers undergo a number of assessments that are intended to increase self-awareness and identify areas of strength as well as areas for improvement. Our students have the opportunity to participate in the Army War College's comprehensive Leader Feedback Program (LFP), where they are administered a series of personality and behavioral assessments in a number of areas that we feel are important for success at the levels of senior leadership. Participants receive individual counseling later through the Leader Feedback Program as part of the College's complementary academic programs.

Three assessment tools are particularly important for self-awareness and are related to creativity. Many students may already be familiar with the MBTI from prior experiences. Students also take the Kirton Adaption-Innovation (KAI) instrument early in the year, along with the Team Roles assessment, as part of the Leader Feedback Program. The first two of these tools measure personality preferences or styles; the third assesses behavioral implications of personality.

The MBTI has four factors that help describe an individual's creative style: (1) where you draw your energy, (2) how you gather information about the world, (3) how you prefer to make decisions, and (4) how you organize your life.[14] The Army War College offers a very informative and entertaining lecture by a noted MBTI expert that illustrates the profile types, but more important, provides insights on how individuals approach creativity. The typical Army War College student with an ESTJ or ISTJ profile (as previously mentioned, many War College students fall within these two profiles) may claim to be not that creative, but rather an *efficient* problem solver.

Kroeger et al. have presented the Z Problem-Solving Model, which suggests that individuals in groups can use their multiple profiles to effectively solve problems.[15] Here, we present a modified version (Figure 6-1). The *Sensors* of the group look at facts and details. The *Intuitives* can employ their imaginations to brainstorm various alternatives. The *Thinkers* excel at objective analysis and consideration of consequences. The *Feelers* can evaluate with their unique insight how the proposed solution may affect others. In the end, all of these preferences bring a unique and valuable perspective to the creative problem-solving process.

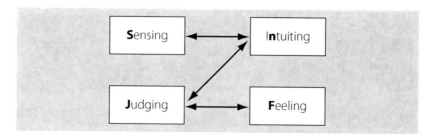

FIGURE 6-1. Modified Z problem-solving model.

A second assessment tool, the KAI, examines the manner in which creativity is expressed. While it is not a measure of how creative a person is, it does indicate preference for a particular creative style. Kirton, through substantial research, identified a continuum of focus for individual creativity and discovered differences in creative style based upon occupation (Figure 6-2).[16] On one end is the development of options based on adaptation of existing information and ideas using established processes and rules. On the other end is the generation of original and novel ideas.

FIGURE 6-2. Kirton continuum of focus.

Adaptors tend to focus on the "tried and true" to arrive at efficient solutions to problems. Their approach tends to be more evolutionary, where the options are less disruptive, easier to accept, and thus easier to implement, and where ideas are refinements of existing paradigms. *Innovators*, however, are those who come up with novel ideas that can often be counter to the prevailing culture because they challenge the status quo. Their approaches to problems tend to result in solutions that may require more time and resources to implement because of their revolutionary perspective. The *Innovators* build new paradigms, much to the discomfort of others who find reassurance in familiar procedures and rules.

Although people often work effectively outside their preferences, it is easy to imagine that preferences, whether measured by MBTI or KAI, have implications for how individuals approach creativity. *Introverts* may have a hard time brainstorming and presenting their ideas in a group setting. *Sensing Judgers* may focus on collecting data from reliable sources, quickly discounting nontraditional approaches, and then making lists of solution sets. Kirton's *Innovators* may look for other perspectives, tend to start with a blank sheet of paper, and redefine the problem. In any case, there are strengths for each profile and areas for improvement that can enhance creativity.

INDIVIDUAL AND TEAM ROLES

To overcome some of the barriers to creativity that individuals naturally possess, Von Oech presents four roles—*Explorer, Artist, Judge,* and *Warrior*—essential for developing, selecting, and implementing creative solutions to problems.[17] Individuals must consciously assume these roles as appropriate and address the obstacles of personal preferences. The *Explorer* is a seeker of information from several sources, always on the lookout for something new and interesting. It is this role that collects information, asks questions, and is always on the prowl. The *Artist* is the creator who is able to piece together existing ideas in new combinations or to generate new ideas. The *Artist* is the experimenter who is willing to try out concepts, willing to fail, and willing to try again in order to learn from the experience. The *Judge* applies analysis and evaluation to the ideas in order to decide which problem solution to pursue. This is a role for which many of us have been trained and to which we quickly move—gather the data, assess, decide quickly, then act—is our model of a military leader.

The challenge for successful strategic leaders is to devote time to the specific consideration of the first two roles—Explorer and Artist—which have the greatest value in defining the problem and generating options. The *Warrior* is the implementer of the creative solution. Through perseverance, passion, and the influence of others, the *Warrior* is able to follow a plan through to its fruition and to adapt its execution to achieve the goal. This role is the one that military members are the most comfortable with; the focus is directed toward accomplishing the mission and overcoming any and all obstacles. To be an effective and creative problem solver, however, the mantles of each of these four roles should be worn.

Other authors present various categories of roles in support of creative thinking that use similar concepts. Noted creativity scholar Edward DeBono described six thinking hats as a method for addressing and creatively solving problems.[18] He suggested that the use of parallel thinking represented by the hats provides a disciplined approach to addressing problems and results in more effective solutions. Tom Kelley and John Littman's study of the leading innovation company IDEO observed ten "faces," or roles that its members perform, that have led to the phenomenal success of that company.[19]

It is beyond the scope of this chapter to provide a detailed description of the symbols used by DeBono, Kelley, and Littman; however, in each case the roles, hats, or faces provide a framework for examining a situation from a variety of viewpoints. The use of such a framework can foster collaboration among individuals, increase the productivity of groups, and increase creativity and innovation within organizations.

One of the instruments of the Leader Feedback Program requires Army War College students to describe how they have functioned in the past within a team or group setting using Meredith Belbin's eight team roles or functions for effective team performance.[20] These roles are as follows:

- ▶ Generate and provide new ideas (innovative, with a vision for the future, creative).

- ▶ Serve as a catalyst for group action (inquisitive, extroverted, likes to build on the ideas of others).

- ▶ Be practical (reliable and conservative, a realist that gets work done).

- ▶ Be the driving force (dominant, authoritative, decisive, driving toward objectives).

- ▶ Be supportive of group members (sympathetic, considerate, draws upon the best from others).

- ▶ Consult with others (even-tempered team players).

- ▶ Be a critical judge (calm critic, a source of quality control).

- ▶ Be a detail type (meticulous, orderly, possibly compulsive).

You have probably noticed that some of the attributes from the MBTI and the KAI are used to describe the contribution of individuals to team efforts. Kirton's *Innovator* is important for providing new ideas for the team to consider, while the *Adaptor* attempts to modify existing processes to solve novel problems. The MBTI *Extrovert* provides the spark that serves as the catalyst for team action. Von Oech's *Warrior* is decisive and pushes the team to accomplish its goals. The MBTI *Feeler* is aware of the importance of interpersonal relationships and can help Von Oech's *Judge* in selecting a solution by considering more than strictly objective and quantifiable information. The point is that individual preferences affect the roles that we prefer within groups, so we should be aware of the potential impact. Awareness also informs us that we may have to assume certain roles, even though they may be out of our comfort zone, to support team creativity and performance.

PROCESSES FOR GROUP CREATIVITY

Research by Simon Taggar identified specific individual factors that are important in determining group creativity.[21] The premise is that individuals—with their personality preferences and unique abilities—can behave in a manner that contributes to the creativity of the group when the appropriate team processes are in place. Three main categories seem to influence group creativity: task motivation, creativity-relevant processes, and team creativity-relevant processes.

The two areas of ***task motivation*** are the commitment of individual members to the team and the focus of the members on the task at hand. Motivated members accept the goals and norms of the team and direct their energies to accomplishing the task. Hence, this adds to the performance of a creative team.

Certain processes at the individual level reflect the behavior of group members and are relevant to generating creative ideas. Taggar referred to these as *creativity-relevant processes*. They are:

- Individual preparation
- Openness to new ideas and the synthesis of the ideas of the team
- Establishing personal goals
- Developing a strategy to achieve the team goals
- Active participation by individual members of the team.

As we saw in Belbin's team roles, individual behaviors must align with the required functions for effective group performance.

There are also several processes that are important for generating ideas and solving problems. Taggar designated these as *team creativity-relevant processes*, in which the interactions among the team's members support the application of individual creative resources and result in creative group performance:

- Team citizenship
- Performance management
- Effective communication
- Involving others
- Providing feedback
- Conflict management.

The main processes for effective and innovative groups involve communication of goals and expected behaviors, coordination of the activities and contributions of members, and the handling of conflict.

Consider the following: In a problem-solving team, there are two fundamental challenges, managing the team and solving the problem. If leaders fail to understand the individual and team processes involved, they will never get past focusing efforts on the team dynamics.

Understanding and managing the team is a prerequisite for the team's ability to effectively solve problems. There must be a process to allow for effective communication that allows for other members to contribute ideas, to listen to the ideas of others, and to maintain supportive relationships within the team. Individuals must feel that they are contributing members of the team and are therefore valued citizens. There must be a mechanism to monitor performance of the task and adherence to established milestones.

Given the interdependent nature of groups, there must be coordination among the members of the team that ensures the involvement of others and encourages input from all team members. There should also be a shared responsibility of providing feedback to others. This feedback should be both positive and negative to provide a critical assessment of ideas. We see that high-performing groups are self-monitoring—they actively seek information about their performance and undertake their own actions to better achieve team goals.

Another important process is the handling of conflict. Members must appropriately react to conflict and be willing to address it when necessary.

They must understand that some degree of conflict is helpful, but they should also be aware of how to avoid potentially disruptive conflict.

In summary, Taggar's research found that there is a relationship between individual attributes, the behavior of individuals within groups, and the creativity of groups. What we see is that given the abilities and skills of individual members, the effective use of the specific processes will support group creativity. Individuals who function as viable members of the group can contribute creative ideas in conjunction with and in support of others. They must prepare for the task and feel like citizens who have responsibilities to the group in accomplishing the task. They must be willing to listen to and synthesize the ideas of others. They must have set goals that they are motivated to attain, and they must participate in the creative endeavors. When individuals function as members of a team, we find that Taggar's processes are helpful in supporting creativity. When groups consciously think about and apply these processes, they tend to be more creative and innovative.

ORGANIZATIONAL CULTURE AND INNOVATION

We have explored the influence of individual preferences on creativity, considered the roles that are important to addressing problems, and examined some processes that are helpful in developing the creativity of individuals and of groups. That said, the individual, the process, and the group atmosphere must all operate within the organizational context. So, finally, we will address the importance of leadership in establishing an organizational culture that supports the creativity of its members.

As organizations emerge and evolve, certain structures and procedures become accepted as standard practices in response to environmental challenges. The organizational paradigms or mental models become set in concrete, and these are even taught to new members as the "correct" way to think and act in challenging situations. The well-developed patterns of responses are difficult to break and are used to handle problems in the same old way. It is easy to see how individual creativity is naturally stifled in some organizations.

The challenge comes when the standard response is applied to a nonstandard problem in a complex and ambiguous environment and is, predictably, found to provide an ineffective or suboptimal solution. Solution sets that were optimal or good enough in previous settings become inadequate in the new context and thus require a new and different approach. Effective organizational learning occurs when the barriers to creativity are reduced, members of the organization are encouraged to be creative, and the organizational culture supports innovation.

As we have seen over the history of the U.S. military, necessity and crisis have been the drivers of innovation for our forces in the field. The German invasion of Poland in 1939 served as the impetus for the Army's Louisiana Maneuvers (LAM) training exercises, which were conducted from August to September 1941. Army leaders recognized the need to experiment, test, and learn mechanized tactics for the battlefields of the impending World War II. The LAM analogy was used as the Army implemented its Army Warfighting Experiments (AWE) in the mid-1990s to explore digitization of the force in the information age. Both examples demonstrate the willingness of the Army to modify existing organizations and processes with the incorporation of new technologies—a creative combination—to achieve greater capabilities. Whether it has occurred in maneuver training areas or on battlefields, the operational forces of our Army have exhibited a high degree of creativity and developed innovative solutions to survive in an unforgiving environment of high risk.

Army War College researcher Leonard Wong provides several examples in his monograph on the creativity and innovation exhibited by junior officers during contemporary operations in Iraq.[22] Consistently, in the conduct of the global war on terrorism, these young leaders shoulder great responsibilities that far exceed the level of their predecessors in recent conflicts. Wong's concern is that once these officers return to the functional Army, the innovativeness that served them so well in demanding and dangerous environments will be stifled.

The Army as an institution is seeking to develop a culture that can benefit from creativity at the institutional, group, and individual levels. In the article "Adapt or Die," the Army's institutional barriers to innovation are discussed, reflecting the concepts addressed earlier in this paper as mental blocks to creativity at the individual level of analysis.[23] The authors, from the Training and Doctrine Command (TRADOC) Futures Center, sound a clarion call to stress the imperative to develop and sustain a culture of innovation within the ranks by encouraging innovative behaviors throughout the organization. The goal is to attain a culture of innovation that promotes experimentation, feedback, learning, and renewal so that the Army becomes truly a learning organization. The challenges to our Army are numerous: high operational tempo; stretched resources in manpower, equipment, and dollars; and difficulties in assessing the long-term effectiveness of some military operations. These challenges require creative leadership to explore and develop strategies to support our national policy and security interests.

So what does this have to do with our students' creativity and leadership? Personal skills and preferences influence creative style. The information from the MBTI and KAI assessments should not be a surprise to students as they provide the data when completing the instruments, but it does give them a common framework and language to work with each other. The same applies to the Team Roles assessment that students receive with their Leader Feedback Program counseling. The assessments provide a self-awareness of their comfort zones and how they prefer to behave in groups. We encourage students to use that information to better manage themselves and to learn together with other members of the seminar.

During the course of the Army War College year and beyond, students will be members of groups that will be presented with situations ranging from trivial to just plain hard (VUCA will reign). Whether they are participating in bilateral negotiations, serving as staff officers on an operational planning team, or role-playing as members of an interagency working group, students are encouraged to work on developing relevant skills and overcoming personal barriers to creativity so that they will be more effective contributing members. That may mean assuming some of the functions required for effective teams. The self-awareness gained through the MBTI and KAI assessments, combined with the roles identified by Von Oech and Belbin, can support creative pursuits as an individual and as a team member.

The greater perspective is that as a senior leader in future assignments, an Army War College graduate will have a professional responsibility to develop innovative, ethical teams and organizations. These future senior leaders will understand that each individual member has a creative potential that can contribute to group success. Success will belong to those who are creative, agile, and adaptive to the strategic landscape.

The processes that Taggar identified should help to monitor and manage the interactions of team members, as well as those within organizations. Building an organization that is able to realize the creative potential of its individuals through their engagement with other members offers tremendous potential. This is the ultimate challenge faced by not only our students but also our Army. Our charter is to prepare Army War College graduates to be strategic leaders by providing an educational experience in how to think about national security issues. In the national security environment of the twenty-first century, developing national policies and implementing strategies require strategic and creative thinkers. Or, as Pulitzer Prize winner Thomas Friedman said recently, "The most important attribute you can have is creative imagination—the ability to be first on your block to figure out how all these enabling tools can be put together in new and exciting ways. . . . That has always been America's strength."[24]

NOTES

1. Stephen A. Shambach, ed., *Strategic Leadership Primer*, 2nd ed. (Carlisle, PA: U.S. Army War College, 2004): 12–14.

2. Abraham Maslow, *Toward a Psychology of Being*, 2nd ed. (New York: Van Nostrand, 1968).

3. Peter F. Drucker, "The Discipline of Innovation," *Harvard Business Review* 80 (August 2002): 95–103.

4. R. Duane Ireland and Michael Hitt, "Achieving and Maintaining Strategic Advantage in the 21st Century: The Role of Strategic Leadership," *Academy of Management Executive* 19 (2005): 63–77.

5. Mark A. Stoler, *George C. Marshall: Soldier-Statesman of the American Century* (Boston: Twayne, 1996).

6. William Duggan, *Napoleon's Glance: The Secret of Strategy* (New York: Nation Books, 2002).

7. Peter M. Senge, *The Fifth Discipline: The Art and Practice of the Learning Organization* (New York: Currency and Doubleday, 1990): 14.

8. Roger von Oech, *A Whack on the Side of the Head*, 3rd ed. (New York: Warner Books, 1998): 14–15.

9. Daniel Pink, *A Whole New Mind* (New York: Riverhead Books, 2005): 28–30.

10. John A. Nagl, *Learning to Eat Soup with a Knife* (Chicago: University of Chicago Press, 2005): 205–208.

11. H. G. Gough, "Studies of the Myers-Briggs Type Indicator in a personality assessment research institute," a paper presented at the fourth national conference on the Myers-Briggs Type Indicator, Stanford University, California, July 1981.

12. Diane F. Halpern, *Thought and Knowledge: An Introduction to Critical Thinking* (Mahway, NJ: Lawrence Erlbaum Associates, 2003): 396–429.

13. Teresa M. Amabile, *Creativity in Context: Update to the Social Psychology of Creativity* (Boulder, CO: Westview Press, 1996): 93–95.

14. Otto Kroeger, Janet M. Thuesen, and Hile Rutledge, *Type Talk at Work: How the Personality Types Determine Your Success on the Job* (New York: Dell Publishing, 2002): 27–28.

15. Ibid., 130.

16. Michael J. Kirton, *Adaption-Innovation in the Context of Diversity and Change* (New York: Routledge, 2003).

17. Roger von Oech, *A Kick in the Seat of the Pants* (New York: Harper and Row, 1986): 11–21.

18. Edward DeBono, *Six Thinking Hats* (New York: Bay Books, 1999).

19. Tom Kelley and John Littman, *The Ten Faces of Innovation* (New York: Doubleday, 2005).

20. Meredith R. Belbin, "Team Roles and a Self-Perception Inventory," *The Effective Manager: Perspectives and Illustrations*, Jon Billsberry, ed. (London: Open University Press, 1996).

21. Simon Taggar, "Individual Creativity and Group Ability to Utilize Individual Creativity Resources: A Multilevel Model," *Academy of Management Journal* 45 (2002): 315–330.

22. Leonard Wong, *Stifling Innovation: Developing Tomorrow's Leaders Today* (Carlisle, PA: U.S. Army War College, April 2002).

23. David A. Fastabend and Robert H. Simpson, "Adapt or Die: The Imperative for a Culture of Innovation in the United States Army," *Army* (February 2004): 20.

24. Thomas L. Friedman, *The World Is Flat: A Brief History of the Twenty-First Century* (New York: Farrar, Straus, and Giroux, 2005): 469.

PART III Strategic Leadership

CHAPTER 7

Visioning, Environmental Scanning, and Futuring for Strategic Leaders

COL James Oman, U.S. Army, and
COL Mark Eshelman, U.S. Army

Leaders operating at the strategic level must be adept in accomplishing a wide range of tasks that include providing vision, environmental scanning and futuring, shaping organizational culture, developing cultural competency, learning how to negotiate differences, and leading change.[1] Skillful practice of these tasks is necessary in order to successfully lead large, complex organizations.

Although there are many strategic leadership competencies, arguably one of the more difficult, yet extremely critical strategic leader skills is that of creating and implementing an organizational vision. The topic of visioning has been an enduring, prominent lesson embedded within the U.S. Army War College Strategic Leadership course. Visioning and its integral, interwoven components, environmental scanning and futuring, are examined in three lessons. Each focus represents a key component in the process and is necessary to posture an organization for mid- and long-term success.

This chapter describes the visioning process, along with the crucial role played by strategic leaders in posturing their organization for success; considers the environmental scanning process through the examination of the role of the strategic leader in understanding, interpreting, and responding to the external environment; examines the role of strategic leaders in considering, planning, and preparing for future outcomes; and concludes with an examination of the role of the strategic leader and the process for implementing a vision.

VISIONING

A review of current academic, governmental, corporate, and Department of Defense literature finds that organizational vision is a frequent topic for study, analysis, and discussion. Articles typically provide a definition of vision, focus on the importance of a vision to an organization, and examine some aspect of the need for a "shared vision."

Vision is defined in a multitude of ways. Peter Senge frames his discussion of vision within the context of governing ideas, which seek to answer the *what, why,* and *how* for an organization or enterprise. In this model, the *why* is the set of ideas that addresses the organizational mission and the *how* is the description of the core values. According to Senge, "Vision is the 'What?'—the picture of the future we seek to create."[2] General Gordon R. Sullivan, 32nd Chief of Staff of the U.S. Army, and Michael V. Harper take a broader, more complex view:

> Vision is a sense of the future. It is an imagined possibility, stretching beyond today's capability, providing an intellectual bridge from today to tomorrow, and forming a basis for looking ahead, not affirming the past or the status quo. The power of a vision is that it gives leaders a basis for positive action, growth, and transformation.[3]

John P. Kotter dedicates several chapters to the topic of vision, asserting that

> [v]ision refers to a picture of the future with some implicit or explicit commentary on why people should strive to create that future . . . a good vision serves three important purposes. First, by clarifying the general direction for change . . . it simplifies hundreds or thousands of more detailed decisions. . . . Second, it motivates people to take action in that direction. . . . Third, it helps to coordinate the actions of different people . . . in a remarkably fast and efficient way.[4]

The U.S. Army War College *Strategic Leadership Primer* qualifies vision as "the leader-focused, organizational process that gives the organization its sense of purpose, direction, energy, and identity."[5]

From these selected readings several common threads emerge. First, the leader must articulate and provide a view of the future that is easily understood by all. Further, the leader must succinctly propose a desired future state that most significantly inspires and motivates the members of the organization to embrace, as well as strive to attain, the vision. In a sense, the effective leader must be skilled in communicating and must constantly seek opportunities to make the vision relevant to the individual while remaining vigilantly focused on the common purpose. Second, a well-crafted vision significantly reduces the demands placed upon leaders by empowering subordinates to act for the common good of their organization, as well as harnessing the activities of many to work collectively toward a shared common purpose.

Indeed, strategic vision is one of the most important functions performed by strategic leaders. As the *U.S. Army War College Academic Year 2007 Curriculum Guidance* puts it, vision is an essential element of political, corporate, and military leadership. It directs and shapes the forces and trends that affect us individually and organizationally.... Leaders who have most successfully guided the destinies of people and organizations have understood the power of and communicated potent strategic visions.[6]

Characteristics of a Vision

A vision has multiple facets and components, typically including the following. It (1) portrays, conjures up, or creates a "mental picture" for the recipient; (2) describes an ideal end state; (3) is compelling; (4) leads to a "shared vision"; (5) is clear, focused, and understandable; and (6) is often targeted toward multiple recipients.[7]

Visual connotation. A key component routinely associated with the term *vision* is the mental visual idea or image created in the mind's eye. This visual image is often couched in phrases that describe where the strategic leader envisions the organization to be at some future point, whether defined in time; percentage of market share; or posture with regard to the environment, an enemy force, or (in the case of business) the competition or a competitor. The desired future state in a vision differs significantly from the short-term, immediate goal that characterizes a key element of the commander's intent statement familiar to members of the U.S. Army.[8] Mid- to long-term time horizons vary in length but are focused on a desired end state that may be as many as 5, 10, 20, or more years from the time when the vision is initially conceived, codified, and published.[9]

End state. A vision should have a measurable, quantifiable future end state.[10] The end state should be described in terminology that is rational, logical, and ambitious. Although the portrayed future end state should be ambitious, it also must be clearly credible and achievable. President John

F. Kennedy illustrated this concept when he issued the challenge and vision that led to the successful Apollo II mission, landing on the moon on July 20, 1969:

> "I believe that this nation should commit itself to achieving the goal, before this decade is out, of landing a man on the moon and returning him safely to the earth."[11]

Compelling. The vision should be compelling in that it generates enthusiasm, thereby convincing an organizational member to take action. It also needs to be compelling in the sense that it provides motivation, as well as inspiration, for members of the organization. The inspirational nature of a vision should create an energy and excitement across the entire organization. President Kennedy's statement superbly demonstrates this characteristic, particularly in consideration of the era in which this vision was articulated. His challenge—enhanced national focus on the space program—led Congress to increase funding for the National Aeronautics and Space Administration, and it laid the foundation upon which the United States would subsequently begin to regain its technological superiority in space over the Soviet Union.[12] A significant challenge for the strategic leader when crafting a strategic vision statement is that the vision must not only be communicated but also must reach every organizational stakeholder. Every member should be able to find value, attractiveness, and relevance in the vision.

Shared vision. Each organizational member must receive, understand, and embrace the vision. Organizational member buy-in to the vision, combined with empowerment of subordinates to exercise initiative within the greater organizational vision by the strategic leader, will lead to a "shared vision" between the leader and the team members. Shared vision, when combined with leadership that empowers individuals to use their initiative, leads to an increase in organizational effectiveness. Shared vision occurs when the strategic leader enables or sets the conditions for subordinates to demonstrate initiative by affording these members the freedom and opportunity to develop their own supporting vision. Subordinates who develop supporting visions are cast within the context of the larger organizational vision, leading to individual commitment. Individual commitment leads to greater productivity, better contributions from the members of the force, and a more effective organization. Senge captures the concept of individual commitment well:

> Organizations intent on building shared visions continually encourage members to develop their personal visions. If people don't have their own vision, all they can do is "sign up" for someone else's. The result is compliance, never commitment. On the other hand, people with a strong sense of personal direction can join together to create a powerful synergy toward what I/we truly want.[13]

Clear, focused, and understandable. The demands of operating within the strategic environment require today's strategic leader to be a skillful communicator and vocal advocate if he or she is to be successful in leading the organization forward. The strategic leader must be readily and competently able to deliver a vision that can easily be communicated to his or her constituents. The vision must be sharp, concise, and understandable so that members of the organization can act to achieve it. Communication of the vision must occur with regularity to reinforce the vision and encourage subordinates.

Multiple constituents. The strategic leader must always be cognizant of the multiple audiences that may receive and act upon the articulated vision. These audiences are in addition to the intended recipients, those primarily being the organizational stakeholders who will subsequently, with their personal commitment, become the future advocates of the vision. For example, President Ronald W. Reagan, "The Great Communicator," in his March 23, 1983, address to the nation on the topic of defense and national security, articulated the threat posed by the Soviet Union's strategic nuclear weapons. He argued for an alternative to the policy of mutually assured destruction. This address provides a superb example of a strategic leader communicating his vision of the future while being clearly mindful of the many audiences he is addressing:

> Let me share with you a vision of the future which offers hope. It is that we embark on a program to counter the awesome Soviet missile threat with measures that are defensive. Let us turn to the very strengths in technology that spawned our great industrial base and that have given us the quality of life we enjoy today.
>
> I know this is a formidable, technical task, one that may not be accomplished before the end of the century. Yet, current technology has attained a level of sophistication where it's reasonable for us to begin this effort. It will take years, probably decades of efforts on many fronts. There will be failures and setbacks, just as there will be successes and breakthroughs. And as we proceed, we must remain constant in preserving the nuclear deterrent and maintaining a solid capability for flexible response. But isn't it worth every investment necessary to free the world from the threat of nuclear war? We know it is. . . .
>
> America does possess—now—the technologies to attain very significant improvements in the effectiveness of our conventional, nonnuclear forces. Proceeding boldly with these new technologies, we can significantly reduce any incentive that the Soviet Union may have to threaten attack against the United States or its allies. . . .
>
> I clearly recognize that defensive systems have limitations and raise certain problems and ambiguities. If paired with offensive systems,

they can be viewed as fostering an aggressive policy, and no one wants that. But with these considerations firmly in mind, I call upon the scientific community in our country, those who gave us nuclear weapons, to turn their great talents now to the cause of mankind and world peace, to give us the means of rendering these nuclear weapons impotent and obsolete. . . .

My fellow Americans, tonight we're launching an effort which holds the promise of changing the course of human history. . . .[14]

Value of a Vision

Vision can provide the foundation for and contribute to the shaping of an organization's culture; in fact, it is invaluable in doing so. It provides the lens through which the members of the organization view the operating environment, and it provides the impetus for change within an organization.[15] Vision, when viewed through an organizational culture lens, provides a purpose for the individual, his or her activities, and the organization by establishing a broad direction to reach a future end state. The vision statement often states and/or reinforces the values of the organization. Reinforcement of values provides a touchstone or a moral compass for the members of the organization and consequently becomes more significant during turbulent times.[16]

From an internal organizational perspective, a vision statement empowers and enables subordinates and the organization to develop supporting plans, policies, and procedures. As would be expected, these supporting efforts would have a greater level of specificity and would include such things as goals, objectives, activities, pathways with anticipated trajectories, and metrics. From an external perspective, the vision statement helps to focus the members of the organization on the environment in which they operate. Specifically, this focus is important to the organization because it empowers and sensitizes members to seek opportunities within the context of the vision; yet, conversely, this awareness also should contribute to threat avoidance and/or mitigation.[17]

When viewed as a change in organizational direction, Kotter believes a vision is essential and accomplishes three things: "It simplifies numerous detailed decisions . . . it motivates people to take action in the right direction . . . and it helps to coordinate the actions of different people, even thousands and thousands of individuals, in a remarkably fast and efficient way."[18]

An appreciation of the multiple elements of a vision, their relative importance and merits, and the value added by a strategic vision is a necessary first step for the strategic leader. This familiarity and understanding are essential elements in providing the strategic leader with both the capability and the incentive to begin the vision-formulation process. Illustrative examples are tremendously helpful in giving the entire vision concept "meaning" and provide the backdrop in deepening understanding and comprehension of this major strategic leader task. Equally important, though, is an understanding that the concept of providing a vision is merely the stage setter for the acts that follow, described in the upcoming sections.

CREATING THE VISION

Visioning is often viewed as predominantly a leader task. Stephen Shambach points out, however, that this occurs "because of [the leaders'] critical role in developing and articulating it and their position as the representative of the organization. . . ."[19] He continues, "Vision does not reside only in leaders; rather, vision is developed as a collaborative effort, with leaders performing the critical role of integrating and guiding the process."[20]

Strategic leaders rarely develop effective visions within a vacuum. Vision development usually requires significant assistance from others or from subordinate staffs. Strategic leaders of high-performing organizations successfully tap into the reservoir of experience found among intermediate leaders. Strategic leaders judiciously use their subordinate leaders' knowledge and recommendations throughout the entire vision-formulation process. Large and complex organizations routinely have permanent committees responsible for strategic planning, which includes such tasks as maintaining the vision, monitoring the environment, seeking future opportunities, and avoiding threats.

Authors Todd D. Jick and Maury A. Peiperl expand on these processes by identifying three ways in which visions are created. The first process, the CEO/Leader Visioning Model, assumes that inspiring a shared vision is the key to leadership, and as Jick and Peiperl emphasize, this model is highly grounded in the domain of charismatic or inspirational leaders.[21]

The second model, the Leader-Senior Team Visioning Model, is much more collaborative than the CEO/Leader Visioning Model; it is more iterative and involves more give and take. The Leader-Senior Team Visioning Model mirrors the examples of the U.S. Army's and the U.S. Navy's vision statements, which are provided and expanded upon in the *Strategic Leadership Primer*.[22]

Jick and Peiperl's third model, the Bottom-Up Visioning Model, involves more bottom-up or middle-up involvement. This version alludes to greater involvement as a positive characteristic, yet it wisely offers the following cautionary note: "With this bottom-up approach, visions are only effective insofar as they are meaningful and motivating to those that have to implement them. Thus, it is better to solicit or be responsive to those in the middle particularly. Otherwise there will be resistance or apathy, and the vision will be an unrealized dream or an empty slogan."[23]

Vision Formulation

Vision formulation is an iterative, dynamic, resource-consuming process that involves multiple steps, including the consideration of a comprehensive environmental assessment, plausible future scenarios, and organizational goals.

Environmental Scanning

Environmental scanning is an integral part of the vision-development process. It begins by collecting information and conducting a comprehensive assessment. Including as many members of the organization as feasible should be the goal, which in turn leads to a more diverse product that will provide a richer, more robust assessment. The assessment should include an appraisal of the organization's current position with regard to the history of the organization, the operating environment, the organization's values and culture, and current critical trends and interactions that could be expected to have a significant impact upon the organization.

Environmental scanning is an absolute must in any assessment. An examination of the external operating environment should be systematic, thorough, and as expansive as time and resources permit. An environmental scan will be a major contributing factor in keeping an organization abreast of events that, if they are not considered and potentially planned for, may result in serious, disruptive, and consequential outcomes with long-lasting implications that ultimately may lead to a failure to attain the stated vision. The following statement, made by former Secretary of Defense Donald H. Rumsfeld on May 16, 2001, during an interview with several *New York Times* reporters, illustrates this point:

> Your opening question was if things are not bad, why do you need to change anything? And of course that's exactly when institutions suffer. If they think things are good and they relax and don't recognize the changes taking place in the world, they tend to fail. And the landscape is littered with institutions that have [cratered] shortly after. . . . If they look back five or ten years, they look back and say we were on top of the world, and all of a sudden they don't exist. I mean think of the major, major, major blue chip corporations that are gone today.[24]

Richard L. Daft and Karl E. Weick provide a strong foundational reading that provides a construct for future leaders as they examine the topic of the external environment.[25] Applying their approach to a military example may help clarify what is admittedly abstract at first glance. Their model describes a three-phase process: *scanning or data collection, interpretation, and learning.* The **scanning or data collection** phase is the monitoring or scanning of the external environment, which is simply information gathering. Organizations gather external environmental information through informal and formal means. Information is gathered for a variety of reasons. Typically, it is assembled with the intended purpose of recognizing opportunities, as well as potential threats, and seeking to garner a strategic advantage; ultimately, it is assembled for the role it plays in informing the leader before and during the development of the strategic plans. Continual information acquisition also enables leaders to make the informed mid-course corrections that may be needed in response to environmental changes or new information.

The second phase of the model is the *interpretation* phase. This is a key strategic leader task that requires the leader and those who support the leader to examine, interpret, and determine the meaning behind the gathered information. Leader interpretation of data leads to the third and final phase of the model, which Daft and Weick call the learning phase.

They describe the *learning* phase as the organizational response or reaction that occurs as a result of the data that have been gathered and interpreted. As they point out, "Feedback from organizational actions may provide new collective insights."[26] Accordingly, these insights can be fed back into the other two phases, and this interconnectivity or feedback loop between the phases contributes to a dynamic system.

Daft and Weick further expand upon their concept of organizational interpretation and use the Model of Organizational Interpretation Modes (Figure 7-1)[27] to show the ways in which organizations interpret or give meaning to information that has been gathered. The axis labeled *Environmental Analyzability* is intended to illustrate how organizations view their ability to analyze the environment. The other axis, labeled *Organizational Intrusiveness*, illustrates the scope of organizational intrusion into the environment as it seeks to make sense of its surroundings.

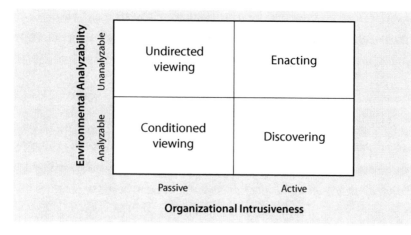

FIGURE 7-1. Model of organizational interpretation modes.

The Model of Organizational Interpretation Modes serves as a spring-board for dialogue about each quadrant and its implications for organizations and the people who lead them. The quadrants in the model are defined as follows. **Undirected viewing** means the environment is unanalyzable and passive with respect to environmental intrusiveness. Accordingly, information gathering often is haphazard, and managers act with limited information.[28]

Conditioned viewing occurs when the organization believes that the environment is analyzable but is passive about information gathering and, consequently, there is no intrusion into the environment. These organizations are characterized as ones that "rely upon established data collection procedures, and the interpretations are developed within traditional boundaries."[29]

The **enacting** quadrant occurs when the organization believes that the environment is unanalyzable and actively intrudes into the environment while in the data-gathering mode. The organization deliberately seeks to influence outcomes and events.[30] The final quadrant, the *discovering* mode, reflects organizations that believe that the environment is analyzable; it is characterized by the organization's aggressively intruding into the environment as it seeks to obtain information.[31] Organizations that fall within this quadrant use formal data-gathering means to seek opportunities and avoid problems.[32]

Interpretations of each of the quadrants could include "over the horizon" technologies, potentially representative of the undirected viewing mode; nongovernmental organizations and private voluntary organizations, representative of the conditioned viewing mode; the global war on terror, an example of the enacting mode; and finally, clearly established operations such as those found within NATO, an example of an analyzable environment that offers known correct answers.[33] Craig Bullis and Stephen Gerras postulate that by using "this model, we might be able to understand some of the military's 'identity crisis' after the Cold War. We were required to move from a 'discovery' mode with a well defined enemy to missions that were 'less analyzable.'"[34]

Unequivocally, the strategic leader plays a unique role in the environmental scanning process. It is an inherent responsibility of strategic leadership. Strategic leader understanding, correct interpretation of environmental data, and consideration of the external environment are of vital importance to the future effectiveness of the organization. Arming the strategic leader with this understanding will posture him or her to conduct an assessment of the future with its many possibilities.

Examining and Considering Future Scenarios

The role of strategic leaders in anticipating the future is a key competency skill.[35] Like the previously examined topic of environmental scanning, it is an integral component of the vision-development process. There are many different methods for examining and considering the future and change and its impact on organizations. Some of the more common methodologies are trend extrapolation, dynamic systems analysis and computer modeling, simulations and games, technological forecasting, technological impact assessment, and scenarios.[36]

Scenario-Based Planning

The Army War College currently uses the scenario-based planning model to facilitate students as they think about the future, its many potential impacts upon their organizations, and the decisions they will be asked to make as strategic leaders. The scenario-based planning methodology has existed since the early 1970s as a widely accepted practice, and it is used by numerous complex public and private organizations.[37] Routinely, some students have had experience with this type of methodology. Most, however, have not had the depth of exposure or experience in the systematical approach that we provide for their future use.

The article entitled "Plotting Your Scenarios," by Jay Ogilvy and Peter Schwartz, describes a deliberate methodology that the Army War College uses to examine the future through the development of plausible alternatives.[38] The value afforded the leader by this type of methodology is that

> Thoughtfully constructed, believable plots help managers to become deeply involved in the scenarios and perhaps gain new understanding of how their organization can manage change as a result of this experience. The more involved managers get with scenarios, the

more likely they will recognize their important but less obvious implications.[39]

Following a deliberate, team-focused, and scenario-based methodology such as that espoused by Oglivy and Schwartz offers clarity, reduces ambiguity, and provides leaders a useful framework in which they can consider abstract thoughts as they posture their organization for success. This approach consists of the following steps:[40]

Identify the key decision facing the organization. Identify the key decision, develop useful questions that address this decision, and identify the time frame for the scenario.

Identify driving forces and key trends. Identify key forces and trends that will drive the key decisions and determine their outcomes. The authors suggest brainstorming as a good technique to identify, select, and define forces and trends.

Distinguish predetermined elements from uncertainties and rank them. Which key forces seem inevitable or predetermined? Which forces are most likely to define or significantly change the nature or direction of the scenarios? Rank-order identified forces by taking into account both the importance and uncertainty of a future scenario. These forces will be subsequently inserted into a scenario matrix.

Select and construct a scenario matrix. Use a deductive approach—i.e., an approach that focuses on specificity. This will lead to an effective matrix. Construct four logical, realistic scenarios and a fifth "wild card" scenario— a dramatic event that will radically change potential outcomes.

Flesh out the scenarios. With the scenario matrix built, the challenge now is in the development and expansion of the scenarios for each quadrant. Using a systems approach and creating a narrative will qualitatively improve and expand the scenarios.

Interpret or make sense of the scenarios. Answering the strategic So what? question provides the basis for, and enables the leader to make, the strategic plans and appropriate decisions to posture the organization for success.

Visualize a future organizational state. A critical examination of each of the likely future scenarios and their end state should inform the strategic leader when developing a broad-based vision statement. Further refinement of the initial vision statement occurs over time, which allows the strategic leader greater flexibility to develop strategies and make resource allocation decisions.

Before implementing a vision, it is imperative that the strategic leader pause and review the newly crafted vision. The leader must critically review the document, looking for inconsistencies, inaccuracies, and logic gaps. The leader must be mindful that the final review of the proposed language must also ensure that the vision is unambiguous, meaningful, and consistent with the organizational values. The vision must also add value to the organization by providing goals and a future end state. Once the leader is comfortable with the vision statement and is confident that it meets all of these criteria, the next step is to take the necessary actions to implement the vision.[41]

IMPLEMENTING THE VISION

Vision implementation requires leader involvement and a great expenditure of personal energy to see the vision embraced and propagated throughout the organization. Marshall Sashkin and Molly G. Sashkin, in their book, *Leadership That Matters*, describe four distinct actions or steps in a process that focuses on the thinking skills required by the leader.[42] The steps include expressing the vision, explaining the vision, extending the vision, and expanding the vision.

Expressing the Vision

This first step describes a leader who must be able to communicate the vision and determine, consider, and anticipate the full range of required activities associated with seeing the vision through to fruition. Most significantly, the leader must be able to oversee, execute, and express these important activities in an actionable manner.[43]

For example, General Dwight David Eisenhower's masterfully crafted "D-Day Message" gives a clear expression of his vision: victory in Europe through the destruction of Nazi Germany's war machine.[44] He wrote:

> **Soldiers, Sailors and Airmen of the Allied Expeditionary Force!**
>
> You are about to embark upon the Great Crusade, toward which we have striven these many months. The eyes of the world are upon you. The hopes and prayers of liberty-loving people everywhere march with you. In company with our brave Allies and brothers-in-arms on other Fronts, you will bring about the destruction of the German war machine, the elimination of Nazi tyranny over the oppressed peoples of Europe, and security for ourselves in a free world.

Your task will not be an easy one. Your enemy is well trained, well equipped and battle hardened. He will fight savagely.

But this is the year 1944! Much has happened since the Nazi triumphs of 1940–1941. The United Nations have inflicted upon the Germans great defeats, in open battle, man-to-man. Our air offensive has seriously reduced their strength in the air and their capacity to wage war on the ground. Our Home Fronts have given us an overwhelming superiority in weapons and munitions of war, and placed at our disposal great reserves of trained fighting men. The tide has turned! The free men of the world are marching together to Victory!

I have full confidence in your courage and devotion to duty and skill in battle. We will accept nothing less than full Victory!

Good luck! And let us beseech the blessing of Almighty God upon this great and noble undertaking.

SIGNED: Dwight D. Eisenhower[45]

Explaining the Vision

The second step requires the leader to simplify, clarify, and spell out the intermediate steps that will lead to the attainment of the vision. As the authors caution, the inability of a senior leader to adequately explain the vision to others will lead to constant uncertainty about handling day-to-day program details and any problems and issues that arise.[46]

Explaining the vision implies much more than simply a restatement of the vision; it is more akin to a skillful narration that involves articulating how multiple actions are woven and linked together to form a comprehensive mosaic that will lead to vision attainment. Eisenhower's interpretation of strategic policies and his subsequent directives to his subordinates demonstrates the kind of action senior leaders must take to achieve their organization's vision.

Extending the Vision

The third step involves the leader extending the vision throughout the organization. This occurs when the leader skillfully applies the vision to activities, implementing the vision. This step requires the leader to articulate, oversee, and flexibly shape and alter activities in a manner that leads to the desired vision.[47] Eisenhower, for instance, achieved victory in Europe by constantly articulating the vision, leveraging support, and setting the conditinos for tactical success.

Expanding the Vision

The fourth and final step is the most complex, most difficult, and very likely most time-consuming step in the process—expanding the vision through alternative activities.[48] Eisenhower's frequent front-line visits with subordinate commanders improved his situational awareness, and it illustrates how he extended his vision by reinforcing the road ahead.

Successfully leading organizations at the strategic level requires leaders who are effective at operating in a dynamic environment characterized by uncertainty and complexity. All too commonly, the expectations, demands, and requirements that confront the strategic leader on a daily basis, when combined with the volume and availability of real-time information, can easily overwhelm the leader, the organization, and their shared goals.

Unfortunately, focusing on resolving short-term issues can distract or even prevent the strategic leader from accomplishing his or her primary organizational duties and responsibilities. The strategic leader must be disciplined and focus energy on the accomplishment of mid- and long-term tasks, which ultimately will lead to the achievement of long-term organizational objectives.

The demands facing strategic leaders today are of such importance that leaders simply must conduct a thoughtful and rigorous examination of the environment, always mindful of opportunities and threats, develop a vision that considers realistic possibilities, and chart a pathway for their organizations to reach ideal, relevant goals.

NOTES

1. Stephen Shambach, ed., *Strategic Leadership Primer*, 2nd ed. (Carlisle, PA: U.S. Army War College, 2004): 47.

2. Peter M. Senge, *The Fifth Discipline: The Art and Practice of the Learning Organization* (New York: Currency and Doubleday, 1990): 223.

3. Gordon R. Sullivan and Michael V. Harper, *Hope Is Not a Method* (New York: Broadway Books, 1996): 79.

4. John P. Kotter, *Leading Change* (Boston: Harvard Business School Press, 1996): 68–69.

5. Shambach, 29.

6. Shambach, enclosure 5.

7. For additional background on an alternative view of vision characteristics, see Kotter, *Leading Change*, 72–76.

8. For additional information on the role of the commander in the development of the commander's intent, see "Field Manual 6-0—Mission Command: Command and Control of Army Forces (Washington, D.C.: Department of the Army, 2003), Chapter 4.

9. U.S. Army War College, *Strategic Leadership Primer* (Carlisle, PA: Department of Command, Leadership, and Management, 1998): 21.

10. Although the term *end state* is used to describe what needs to be accomplished when crafting a vision, many of the faculty instructors in the Department of Command, Leadership, and Management routinely initiate a dialogue with their students about the limitations of the term at the strategic level. We suggest that many of the long-term issues that strategic leaders deal with are so long-term they are effectively never-ending. An end state may describe a future objective for a point in time, but time will continue once that objective is achieved, and some future strategic leader will probably have to continue to manage the issue and evolve it further.

11. John F. Kennedy, "Special Message to the Congress on Urgent National Needs," 25 May 1961, available online at http://www.jfklibrary.org /Historical+Resources/ Archives/Reference+Desk/Speeches/JFK/Urgent+National+Needs+Page+4.htm (accessed 29 December 2006).

12. James E. Webb, "Statement by NASA Administrator, Budget Briefing," news release 61-112 and 61-115, 25 May 1961, available online at http://www.hq.nasa.gov/ office/pao/History/SP-4205/ch1-9.html (accessed 25 February 2007).

13. Senge, 211.

14. President Ronald W. Reagan, "Strategic Defense Initiative Speech," 23 March 1983, available online at http://www.atomicarchive.com/Docs/Missile/Starwars. shtml (accessed 29 December 2006).

15. U.S. Army War College, 24–25.

16. Shambach, 23.

17. U.S. Army War College, 20.

18. Kotter, 68–69.

19. Shambach, 24.

20. Shambach, 24.

21. Todd D. Jick and Maury A. Peiperl, *Managing Change: Cases and Concepts* (New York: McGraw-Hill/Irwin, 2003).

22. Ibid.

23.

24. Ibid., 98–100.

25. An interview of Secretary of Defense Donald H. Rumsfeld by Jim Dao, Thom Shanker, and Eric Schmitt of *The New York Times*, 16 May 2001, available online at http://www.defenselink.mil/transcripts/2001/t05242001_t0516sdc.html (accessed 4 January 2007).

26. Richard L. Daft and Karl E. Weick, "Toward a Model of Organizations as Interpretation Systems," *Academy of Management Review* 9.2 (1984): 284–295.

27. Ibid., 286.

28. Ibid., 287–290.

29. Ibid., 289–290.

30. Ibid., 289.

31. Ibid., 288–289.

32. Ibid., 289.

33. Craig Bullis and Stephen Gerras, U.S. Army War College strategic leadership course text, *Lesson 5–L/S Environmental Scanning, 2006 Instructor Notebook*, Tab E, 7.

34. Ibid., Tab E, 5.

35. Ibid.

36. U.S. Army War College, 56.

37. Linda Groff and Paul Smoker, "Methodologies for Studying Change and the Future," available online at http://www.csudh.edu/global_options/IntroFS. HTML#FSMethodols (accessed 6 January 2007).

38. Joel Garreau, *Radical Evolution* (New York: Doubleday, 2005): 78. See also "Long-Range Planning Analysis for USARPAC Requirements," memorandum for Deputy Chief of Staff of Operations and Plans (17 May 1996).

39. Jay Ogilvy and Peter Schwartz, *Plotting Your Scenarios* (San Francisco: Global Business Network, 2004).

40. Ibid., 2.

41. Ibid., 3–16.

42. U.S. Army War College, 24.

43. Marshall Sashkin and Molly G. Sashkin, *Leadership That Matters: The Critical Factors for Making a Difference in People's Lives and Organizations' Success* (San Francisco: Berrett-Koehler, 2003).

44. Ibid., 100.

45. General Dwight D. Eisenhower, "D-Day Message—Order of the Day: 6 June 1944," available online at http://www.kansasheritage.org/abilene/ikespeech.html (accessed October 28, 2008).

46. Ibid.

47. Sashkin and Sashkin, 100.

48. Ibid., 100–101.

49. Ibid., 102.

Strategic Leadership and Organizational Culture

8

*Stephen Gerras, PhD, and
COL Charles Allen, U.S. Army*

One of the principal purposes of the U.S. Army War College is to instill an appreciation for the methods of formulating national security strategy for the Department of Defense (DoD). Organizational culture has a significant impact on DoD's ability to change its strategy to align with the environment. Why did the Army resist letting go of horses and mules when mechanization of warfare with tanks and automobiles was clearly the future after World War I? Why did the Navy hold on to battleships well beyond their useful purpose after the Cold War ended? Why is the Air Force resisting the use of remotely piloted vehicles when they are demonstrating great capabilities during current operations across the globe? Why has there been so much discussion about how the Army's culture must transform in order to align itself with the contemporary operating environment?[1] The answer to these questions centers around *organizational culture.*

Asserting that the military needs to shift its culture to a more innovative, agile, and initiative-centric force is akin to positing that Americans need to lose weight. Everyone agrees with the assertion, but without significant, well-planned, and painful steps, neither of these goals will become a reality. Many organizations—public and private—face the same dilemma. The rank and file understand that an organization's culture is antiquated and that it needs to change, but many leaders struggle with the change process. This chapter describes how the Army War College faculty teach future leaders to assess culture and change it.

ORGANIZATIONAL CULTURE

There have been many definitions of *organizational culture*. For the purpose here, *culture* is a set of shared, subconscious assumptions that define how an organization relates to both its internal and external environment.[2] Why do many Iraqis think U.S. soldiers seem elitist toward all foreigners, not just Iraqis?[3] Why have press reporters asserted that Army generals tend to smartly salute and blindly follow the directions of civilian superiors, no matter how wrongheaded those superiors are?[4] Why does an officer's career end immediately after it has been discovered that the officer is guilty of ethical lapses (lying, adultery, etc.)? The answers to these questions can be discovered by thoroughly assessing the pattern of shared, subconscious assumptions that form the organization's collective "state of mind."[5]

Noted social psychologist Edgar Schein has developed one of the more influential theories of organizational culture and one that is much used at the Army War College.[6] Schein posits that assumptions form the core of an organization's culture. Assumptions represent what organizational members believe to be reality and thereby influence what they perceive and how they think and feel. Assumptions exist in the subconscious; they are taken for granted.[7]

The Army is a good example. Although Field Manual 1, *The Army*, outlines the institutional purpose, functions, and vision by describing "what the Army is, what the Army does, how the Army does it, and where the Army is going,"[8] the Army's assumptions are not listed. Rather, to understand the Army's assumptions or those of any organization and then attempt to change these cultural assumptions to align them with the environment, one needs to appreciate Schein's three levels of culture: (1) artifacts, (2) norms and values, and (3) underlying assumptions.

Artifacts

It would be fruitless to walk into an infantry division's readiness meeting at its home station or a brigade tactical operations center in Iraq and think you can quickly divine the Army's cultural assumptions. What Schein posits, however, is that you can observe the *artifacts* of the organization's culture. Artifacts represent the first level of culture. They are the visible, but often undecipherable, physical, behavioral, and verbal manifestations of the culture.[9]

Artifacts can be observed by anyone; they represent the most accessible elements of culture. Dress and appearance (physical manifestations), ceremonies, rewards and punishments (behavioral manifestations), and stories and jargon (verbal manifestations) are examples of artifacts. When you sit in on an Army briefing, you can often infer from the way the soldiers talk to each other, the form of the PowerPoint charts (with unit motto and insignia), and the condition of the conference room (adorned with lineage and awards) what the organization values and what its norms are.

Norms and Values

Norms and values are the second level of culture. Unlike artifacts, you cannot typically observe them. *Values* are more conscious than basic assumptions but are not usually at the forefront of members' minds.[10] *Norms*, which are closely associated with values, are the unwritten rules that allow members of a culture to know what is expected of them in a wide variety of situations.[11] According to Schein, organizational members hold values and conform to norms because their underlying assumptions nurture and support the norms. The norms and values, in turn, encourage activities that produce surface-level artifacts.[12]

When a senior officer walks into a room of soldiers, the soldiers stand. This is an observable artifact of the culture, in this case a manifestation of the Army norm to respect rank and authority. It can be inferred from this norm that the Army has a shared cultural assumption about the importance of position power in determining day-to-day interactions. The values of the Army have been codified in the contrived acronym *LDRSHIP*. All soldiers can recite those values without hesitation—Loyalty, Duty, Respect, Selfless Service, Honor, Integrity, and Personal Courage—and carry the Army Values card as an artifact in their wallets and on their identification tag ("dog tag") chains.

How does culture work? Schein posits that when new members are brought into a culture, they are either selected (or in the Army's case, recruited) on the basis of the match between their values and those of the culture, or they are socialized to accept cultural values. Anyone who has ever been through Basic Training, ROTC Advanced Camp, or West Point's New Cadet Training (formerly known as Beast Barracks) can attest to the important socialization component of these programs. Members who don't fit into the culture because the culture is different from what they anticipated, or have a hard time adjusting to changes in the organization's culture, are typically dissatisfied with the organization and leave. They also may be forced out by existing members. When left unchecked by responsible members of the organization, socialization can quickly deteriorate to hazing and become dysfunctional. Once a group has a culture, it will pass elements of this culture on to new generations of group members.[13] And so the cycle of cultural indoctrination continues.

Assumptions

If artifacts are observable manifestations of norms and values, which are reflections of underlying shared assumptions, how do we identify, understand, and change these assumptions? Schein would argue that unless you can dig down to the level of the basic assumptions, you really can't decipher the artifacts, values, and norms.[14] Picture yourself walking into a human resource management office as the first stop upon arriving in a new unit or organization. You see on the wall a sign that reads, "People are our focus." If there were a direct link between artifacts, values, and assumptions, you could infer that this new organization really cares about people.

But as we're sure everyone has experienced, there is often a disconnect between espoused values and practiced values, as reflected in the behavior of the organizational members. After waiting two hours and eventually seeing a rude administrator, you'll quickly recognize the disparity between what is said and what is done. This example is meant to demonstrate the intriguing nature of culture as a concept because it points us to phenomena that are below invisible and, to a considerable degree, unconscious.

Schein further posits, "Culture is to a group what personality or character is to an individual."[15] In fact, distinctive cultures extend to the armed
services, as Carl Builder explains in *The Masks of War*.[16] Builder contends
that each service has its own unique culture as manifested by distinct
identities: the Army has a culture of service to the nation; the Navy has
a culture of tradition; and the Air Force, a culture of technology. These
cultures shape how the service views itself and its environment, and how it
develops strategies to fulfill its perceived role in the defense of the nation.

Culture and cultural assumptions are a multidimensional and multifaceted phenomenon, not easily reduced to a few dimensions. Schein first
examines an organization's internal integration and external adaptation
and then begins to analyze the deeper dimensions around which shared
basic *underlying assumptions* form. These dimensions include the nature
of reality and truth, time and space, human activity and relationships, and
human nature itself.

For example, if we try to decipher an organization's assumptions about
human nature, we would try to answer the question, "Does this organization see people as good or bad?" If, for instance, the organization saw
people as bad or lazy, it might have TV cameras watching over the assembly
line, require permission slips to miss any type of work, or hold military
formations more often than usual to ensure that nobody had slipped off
to loaf and avoid work. As an outsider approaching this organization,
you would see the TV monitors, permission slips, formations, and other
"artifacts," and you would probably start to develop an interpretation of
the culture of this organization. You might use Schein's dimensions to
develop a perception of the various deeper assumptions that underlie this
organization's culture.

The Power of Culture

The power of culture comes about through the fact that the assumptions are shared and therefore mutually reinforced. In other words, the essence of a culture lies in the pattern of basic underlying assumptions, and once one understands those, one can easily understand the other more surface-level artifacts and deal appropriately with them.[17]

Anyone who has spent time with the U.S. Army probably recognizes the importance of subcultures. While the Army has a distinct culture, subordinate units like a Ranger company and an Army hospital clearly have very different subcultures. Although the underlying assumptions of Army culture serve as the foundation of these subcultures, as we attempt to assess Army culture or the culture of any complex organization, we must untangle how all the subcultures relate to each other and discover how they fit together to form the larger Army culture.

Why do subcultures form? People tend to gravitate toward people like themselves; they also tend to become more cohesive with people they interact with often. Psychologist Mary Jo Hatch asserts that task interdependence, reporting relationships, proximity, design of offices and workstations, and sharing of equipment or facilities all bring members of the organization into contact with each other.[18] This dependence and interaction tend to serve as a catalyst to subgroup formation. The Army's branch schooling system, unit structure, and mission requirements are just a few factors that facilitate the creation of subcultures in the Army.

Are subcultures bad? It depends. If the subculture enhances the dominant values of the overall culture, it is probably a good thing. If, however, the subculture denies the values of the overall culture, it is something that the organization's leadership needs to address. Some might argue that former Army Chief of Staff General Eric Shinseki was attempting to address diverse subcultures by ordering the wearing of the beret for all Army soldiers as a symbol of a transformed force unified in purpose for a changed environment. Even the choice of the date to formally institute the change, June 14, 2001, was symbolic—the Army's first birthday in the new century.

Was the black beret initiative an attempt to change Army culture? Many of us remember the resistance from many camps to adopting the beret. The black beret was a mark of distinction for the Rangers, the purple beret was a symbol of the elite paratrooper division, and the green beret was uniquely associated with the Special Forces. These three groups have very strong and well-defined subcultures that actively resisted the "big Army's" encroachment on their cultural artifacts.

Consider this example: If the Chief of Staff of the Army wants to develop and reinforce an underlying cultural assumption about the importance of values, what is the best way to do it? One way might be to ask all soldiers to wear an Army Values card on their dog tag chain as a mechanism to keep the values at the forefront of each soldier's conscience. Another way might be to court-martial a two-star general who had an affair with his aide's spouse as a symbol of how seriously the Army takes violations of its values.

These two examples serve as a transition to understanding the right way and the wrong way for senior leaders to change culture. The easiest approach, but more questionable in its effectiveness, is plastering posters that list vision statements, objectives, and values throughout the organization's buildings. Although highly visible to its members, these artifacts are quickly discounted when everyday behavior does not match the espoused values. It is difficult to enforce values, especially among senior members, unless there are consequences for violators. However, taking such action is best for the health of the organization. As senior leaders, we must remember that people may hear what we say, but they see and will do what we do.

Kim Cameron and Robert Quinn argue that for cultural change to occur in large, mature organizations, it must be managed consciously.[19] Schein maintains that basic, underlying assumptions tend to be considered undeniable and therefore extremely difficult to change. To learn something new in this realm requires us to resurrect, reexamine, and possibly change some of the more stable portions of our cognitive structure. Such learning is intrinsically difficult because the reexamination of basic assumptions temporarily destabilizes our cognitive and interpersonal world, evoking considerable personal anxiety.[20]

Clearly, changing a culture is very hard. Dominant members or coalitions in the organization will attempt to preserve and enhance existing culture. Schein argues that the only force that might unfreeze such a situation is an external crisis of survival.[21] For those who are overweight, a heart attack might be the critical event that causes a change in diet and exercise habits, behaviors that lead to weight loss.

For instance, since the early 1970s and the creation of an all-volunteer force, the Army has been challenged by several significant external crises. An assessment by Army leadership determined that the Army's culture after the U.S. withdrawal from Vietnam was one characterized by ill discipline and low morale, which were manifest in several problems of the era. An institution whose identity was tied to service to the nation, the Army had lost the respect of the American public. Based on that assessment, Army leadership developed a strategy to change the force, and one instrument in the 1980s was a series of coherent annual themes (the "Years" of Values, Leadership, Family, and the Noncommissioned Officer) that clearly identified what the Army wanted to change and its expectations of its members.

After a period of 15 years (1975–1990), the Army looked to the operational successes of the first Gulf War (Operation Desert Storm) as confirmation that it had effectively exorcised the ghosts of the Vietnam War and the initial problems with the volunteer army (VOLAR). We then assessed our culture to be one of confident military professionals willing and able to answer the nation's call. But again, more than 15 years later, we think that an honest, self-reflective look at the Army's performance in Operation Iraqi Freedom might reveal that the Army's culture needs to change to face the challenges of the twenty-first century.

In terms of how a culture is formed and can be changed, Schein focuses on concepts labeled *primary embedding mechanisms* and *secondary reinforcing mechanisms*. We see these as the key to successful cultural change in the Army and in any complex organization.

CULTURE CHANGE

How do senior leaders change the culture of their organization? Schein postulates that "even if the assumptions are brought to consciousness, the members of the organization are likely to want to hold on to them because they justify the past and are the source of their pride and self-esteem."[22] Whether it is creating a culture in a new organization or changing a culture in a more mature entity, the Army War College's faculty suggests that

Schein's model for embedding and transmitting a culture serves as the best reference.[23] He argues that leaders change cultures through the use of primary embedding mechanisms and secondary reinforcing mechanisms. Changing a culture requires an alignment of the embedding and reinforcing mechanisms by embedding mechanisms that have primacy.

Embedding Mechanisms

So what are the embedding mechanisms, and how do they work? The first mechanism is *what leaders pay attention to, measure, and control on a regular basis*. The old adage is that units do best what the commander checks. While this is easily seen and understood at the battalion level and below, it can also be effective at higher levels in the institution. If every morning the Chief of Staff of the Army holds a 20-minute meeting to review any safety accidents over the last 24 hours, over time this focus on safety will cascade down through the organization, especially if the Chief makes follow-up phone calls after the meeting to commanders of units that have had accidents. This attention will eventually shift the culture to one that focuses on safety when subordinates are held accountable for what the Chief thinks is important.

Another embedding mechanism is *how leaders react to critical incidents and organizational crises*. Suppose the Army decided there was an unacceptable underlying cultural assumption of marginally accepted sexual harassment. How the Army's senior leaders react to reports of senior officers or noncommissioned officers charged with sexual harassment would have a significant effect on this underlying assumption. If, for instance, a senior general admitted to sexually harassing a subordinate and was allowed to retire with just a verbal reprimand, how successful would such a reaction to this critical incident be in changing the underlying assumption? Compare that approach with a reaction in which the general was tried by court-martial, reduced in rank, and forced into retirement.

How leaders allocate resources is another mechanism. If you think back to the drawdown in the early 1990s after the fall of the Soviet Union, many of the personnel cuts seemed to come from the institutional, not the operational, Army. One must remember that the Army reduced its force structure from 18 to 10 active component divisions. However, to preserve war-fighting capability and avoid the "hollow Army" of post-World War II, the budget, personnel manning directives, and equipment programs focused on protecting field units at the expense of organizations whose missions were to educate, train, equip, and sustain the Army. In terms of cultural assumptions, this prioritization of resources could easily lead to the inference, and hence reinforcement, of the underlying assumption that the Army values operational units over school and doctrine writers. Any commander who served as a Forces Command (FORSCOM) unit commander on a Training and Doctrine Command (TRADOC) installation in the 1990s can attest to the "haves versus have-nots" climate that existed between these two major commands. This allocation of scarce resources had a clear effect on the Army's culture.

The next mechanism focuses on *the leader's use of deliberate role modeling, teaching, and coaching*. If each time the Chief of Staff of the Army talks to groups of general officers he discusses and teaches the benefits of lean and six sigma techniques and identifies enterprise management as an essential competency of Army leaders, over time this focus will send a signal about the importance of these concepts. Clearly, this example could also be interpreted as the use of the mechanism of what leaders pay attention to, suggesting that these embedding mechanisms are not mutually exclusive. What is important, however, is that the leader ensures an alignment of whatever mechanisms are used to make certain that a consistent message is sent to the organization.

Many would argue that the next mechanism, ***how leaders allocate rewards and status***, is probably the most effective mechanism in terms of changing Army culture. This assertion is based on the impact of the Officer Evaluation Reports (OERs). As examples, a senior leader could talk about the importance of physical fitness and, in fact, review unit physical fitness data each week. However, as we've seen in the Army, mandating comments on the OER is probably the most effective way to change the culture to one that values physical fitness. With the Army's focus on Physical Training (PT) in the 1980s, officer and enlisted evaluations required information on whether the soldier had passed the Army Physical Fitness Test (APFT) and met the standards for height and weight. An annotated "No" or "Fail" for either of these items might hinder promotion or selection for key schooling. This was a substantial cultural change from the 1970s, when PT was not emphasized.

Similarly, many of us remember that in the mid-1980s, the Chief of Staff of the Army directed that officers who were caught driving under the influence (DUI) would get a General Officer Memorandum of Reprimand (GO-MOR) in their official military personnel file, which would significantly reduce their chances of subsequent promotion. The power of a mechanism that affects evaluations and promotions cannot be overstated.

Closely related to this mechanism, the last embedding mechanism focuses on ***how leaders recruit, select, promote, and retire or "fire" personnel***. As an example, in the late 1980s the Army Chief of Staff's guidance to promotion boards directed that board members emphasize that a tour in a combat unit was a must if an officer or noncommissioned officer wanted to be promoted to senior ranks. Over time, this guidance has had a significant effect on the career-progression desires of the officer and noncommissioned officer corps.

The Army struggled to find volunteers for assignments in the 3 R's— Reserve Component support to the Army National Guard, Recruiting Duty, and Reserve Officer Training Course (ROTC) instructors—because the institution rewarded time on active duty in war-fighting units. The contemporary challenge for the recruitment of enlisted personnel for a nation at war also exists with respect to the recruitment and selection of junior officer leaders. Today, it would seem a viable argument to say that the Army's difficulties in filling ROTC cadet positions at the nation's colleges and universities, along with a potential lowering of standards for enlisted recruits, will have a long-term effect on the Army's culture.

Reinforcing Mechanisms

In addition to the embedding mechanisms, Schein highlights the importance of what he labels as secondary or reinforcing mechanisms.[24] Certainly, the use of these mechanisms alone will not change a culture (you need to use the embedding mechanisms, too); however, if the reinforcing mechanisms are not aligned with the embedding mechanisms, cultural change is almost impossible.

The first of these reinforcing mechanisms is ***organizational design and structure***. Picture a senior leader who wants to change the culture of his or her organization to one that is agile and flexible (commonly desired attributes for turbulent environments). If at the same time the leader creates or maintains an extremely hierarchical, rank-driven structure, it will be very difficult for subordinates in the organization to demonstrate the kind of agility espoused. It could be argued that our main enemy in the global war on terror, Al Qaeda, has a decentralized structure and design that makes change and flexibility much easier to effect than the American military, which has centuries of tradition as a bureaucratic, hierarchical organization.

The next reinforcing mechanism focuses on **organizational systems and procedures.** We sometimes discuss how ironic it is that for Army War College faculty to go on temporary duty to a conference on agile leadership, we need to get six permissions and spend two hours in the automated Defense Transportation System to get the conference attendance approved. This irony is not unique to the Army and has been accurately captured by the "Dilbert" comic strip, which parodies corporate business practices. As another example, the Army's use of After Action Reviews (AARs) and the Center for Army Lessons Learned (CALL) are clearly systems and procedures established to emphasize the Army's focus on learning from the past. The intent is to support organizational learning and share knowledge across the force to enable the force to be more effective in its missions.

The design of physical space, facades, and buildings is the next mechanism. Anyone who has ever walked into the headquarters of a senior general officer is clearly impressed by the layers of secretaries, executive assistants, and deputies who serve as gatekeepers to the general, whose office is typically quite impressively decorated in mahogany, with the walls covered in acknowledgements of military accomplishments. This design tends to reinforce the Army's assumption about the importance of command and the emphasis on positional power. As an example of cultural change, you could not simply move the general's office out to a cubicle and think the unit would become a decentralized, agile entity. Nevertheless, given the sensible use of several of the embedding mechanisms, some repositioning of these cultural artifacts might reinforce the embedding mechanisms necessary for an agile culture to emerge.

The next mechanism relates to ***the use of formal statements of organizational philosophy, creeds, and charters.*** Earlier we mentioned the Army's use of the Army Values card on the dog tag chain. This is a perfect example of attempting a cultural change by using only the reinforcing mechanism, with no accompanying embedding mechanism. Clearly, wearing the values card won't change someone's values. However, wearing the values card as a reinforcing tool for embedding mechanisms such as firing a senior officer who violates the Army's values or not allowing recruits who require moral waivers to enter the service (i.e., how leaders recruit and select) would clearly be important. Perhaps a more effective strategy is the development of the Soldier's Creed, which has embedded *The Warrior's Ethos* within the Army:

- ▶ I will always place the mission first.

- ▶ I will never accept defeat.

- ▶ I will never quit.

- ▶ I will never leave a fallen comrade.

These statements are inculcated during the entry programs for new members and reinforced through multiple media (print, video, and web) to all soldiers.

The last two reinforcing mechanisms, ***rites and rituals of the organization*** and ***stories about important events and people***, focus on the importance of symbols in organizational culture. Senior leaders often use anecdotes to communicate important concepts to members of their organization. These stories, along with the emphasis we place on events such as changes of command, retirement ceremonies, hails and farewells for incoming and departing personnel, and a sergeant's promotion to the ranks of the noncommissioned officer corps, all serve as intentional reinforcing mechanisms for the Army's cultural assumptions and values.

Any time a leader starts to detect resistance to changes that he or she has enacted, the leader should sit down and attempt to assess the impact of the organization's culture, because culture is probably the root issue in the resistance to change. Leading and managing change is a strategic leader responsibility. The strategic leader should be proactive, because in the Army it is said that "culture eats strategy for lunch." If a leader attempts to direct change without understanding the organizational culture and its friction points, that change could be doomed to failure.

The leader needs to have a process to methodically assess the underlying assumptions that form the foundation of the culture. This is not an exercise that can be conducted alone; the leader needs to interact with all of the levels of the organization to really be exposed to the artifacts and norms of the organization that may allow him or her to infer some of the underlying assumptions that may be at the root of the resistance to change. In addition, as addressed in other chapters of this book, the strategic leader needs to scan the external environment proactively to anticipate changes and then attempt to align the organization's vision and culture with these anticipated changes.

NOTES

1. Andrew Garfield, "Succeeding in Phase IV: British Perspectives on the U.S. Effort to Stabilize and Reconstruct Iraq," 8 September 2006, available online at http://www.fpri.org/enotes/20060908.military.garfield.britishperspectiveiraq.html (accessed 16 July 2007).

2. Edgar H. Schein, "How Founders and Leaders Embed and Transmit Culture: Socialization from a Leadership Perspective," *Organizational Culture and Leadership*, 2nd ed. (San Francisco: Jossey-Bass, 1992): 17.

3. Garfield, 4.

4. John Barry and Evan Thomas, "Iraq: Blame the Top Brass," *Newsweek* (22 January 2007), available online at http://ebird.afis.mil/ebfiles/e20070115480997.html (accessed 23 January 2007).

5. David A. Fastabend and Robert H. Simpson, "Adapt or Die: The Imperative for a Culture of Innovation in the United States Army," *Army Magazine* (February 2004): 16.

6. Schein, *Organizational Culture and Leadership*, 2nd ed.

7. Mary Jo Hatch, "Organizational Culture," *Organization Theory* (New York: Oxford University Press, 1997): 210.

8. Department of the Army, "FM-1—The Army" (Washington, D.C.: Department of the Army, 14 June 2005): iii.

9. Schein, 217.

10. Ibid., 214.

11. Ibid., 214.

12. Ibid., 216.

13. Schein, 18.

14. Ibid., 59.

15. Ibid., 8.

16. Carl H. Builder, *The Masks of War: American Military Styles in Strategy and Analysis* (Baltimore: Johns Hopkins University Press, 1989): 18–20.

17. Ibid., 36.

18. Hatch, 229.

19. Kim S. Cameron and Robert E. Quinn, *Diagnosing and Changing Organizational Culture* (San Francisco: Jossey-Bass, 2006): 57.

20. Schein, 31.

21. Ibid., 293.

22. Ibid., 312.

23. Schein, Chapter 13.

24. Ibid., 246.

CHAPTER 9

Cultural Diversity and Leadership

COL Julie T. Manta, U.S. Army

A great many people think they are thinking when they are merely rearranging their prejudices.

—WILLIAM JAMES

The U.S. military is no different from most large organizations, both public and private, whose leaders are studying the impact of globalization and the interdependence of nations and diverse peoples. Thomas Friedman labels this phenomenon "Globalization 3.0" and characterizes it as "the newfound power for individuals to collaborate and compete globally to flatten and shrink the world." He emphasizes that the people driving Globalization 3.0 will become more diverse and that "non-Western, non-white . . . individuals from every corner of the flat world are being empowered" through the development of technology and their ability to connect. Friedman's observations encourage leaders to think about the forces of globalization and the implications of leading in a multicultural and diverse environment.[1]

The effects of globalization within and across nations have sparked interest in the disciplines of multiculturalism, intercultural communications, and cross-cultural psychology. As outgrowths of anthropology, sociology, and psychology, these cultural fields of study historically have not generated much attention within broader military circles. As an exception, the U.S. Army War College's *Strategic Leadership Primer* emphasizes the importance of what we call "cross-cultural savvy" as one of six *metacompetencies* necessary for the professional development of strategic leaders. The *Primer* defines *cross-cultural savvy* as "the ability to understand cultures beyond one's organizational, economic, religious, societal, geographical, and political boundaries."[2]

One of the military's twenty-first–century challenges is to develop leaders who possess cross-cultural savvy and can successfully manage cultural diversity. To raise awareness and encourage study of successful leadership in multicultural and diverse environments, this chapter first addresses the relevance of understanding cultural diversity. Second, a three-stage model (cultural awareness, cultural knowledge, cultural skills) is provided to evaluate cultural diversity and develop culturally competent strategic leaders; it serves as a basis for exploring various efforts by the Army in developing culturally competent leaders.[3] Last, this chapter concludes by offering implications for senior leaders to consider when leading in a multicultural environment.

CULTURAL DIVERSITY

The military has long been at the forefront of efforts to integrate and manage issues of cultural diversity. Long before the United States codified racial equality into law, President Franklin D. Roosevelt signed Executive Order 8802,[4] and later President Harry S. Truman signed Executive Order

9981,[5] which mandated equality of treatment and opportunity in the armed services for people of all races, religions, or national origins.

In 1995, senior Department of Defense (DoD) civilian and military leaders addressed the ability to manage diversity in the DoD Human Capital goals, stating that "our nation was founded on the principle that the individual has infinite dignity and worth," and included two objectives supporting diversity management. These goals were "to make military and civilian service in the Department of Defense a model of equal opportunity for all" and "to create an environment that values diversity and fosters mutual respect and cooperation among all persons." Likewise, many current DoD documents, such as the 2006 *Quadrennial Defense Review* and the 2006 *Strategic Plan for Transforming DoD Training*, also include recognition, if not an exhortation, that DoD should develop more culturally aware leaders.[6]

More recently, the Department of the Army (DA) began focusing its leader development efforts on how to improve cultural awareness education and develop adaptive leaders, as exemplified by the Army's pentathlete model.[7] The pentathlete depicts a "multi-skilled, innovative, agile and versatile" leader who can comfortably lead during changing and uncertain times. The model encourages leaders to be educated, lifelong learners who display empathy and can effectively communicate with others. To do so, one must become a builder of leaders and teams and be able to understand and work effectively across contexts. To a pentathlete, leadership is an interactive process between leaders and followers—a process that Peter Northouse states occurs when "an individual influences a group of individuals to achieve a common goal" and initiates and maintains the relationship and develops critical communication linkages.[8]

Similarly, in the business sector, developing culturally aware leaders who can manage diversity has become an important component of many leader development programs. Although many large organizations recognize the importance of developing culturally savvy leaders, there has not been agreement about how to do it. As a result, leader development experts continue to study how best to develop leaders who can successfully, and comfortably, lead others in a multicultural environment and capitalize on the talents of an increasingly diverse workforce.

Mary Connerley and Paul Pedersen's Three Stage Developmental Sequence demonstrates the developmental stages of becoming multiculturally aware and cross-culturally savvy.[9] The following paragraphs refer to the three stages as developing cultural awareness, acquiring cultural knowledge, and developing cultural skills.

Most traditional diversity management and multicultural awareness education has focused on Connerley and Pedersen's stage two: acquiring knowledge about a particular culture (i.e., learning about the culture's demographics, customs, formalities, and language). While researchers contend that learning a foreign language is an "effective way to increase one's information"[10] about another culture, it is generally understood that learning another language in and of itself will not automatically improve cultural awareness or competence. In short, culturally savvy leaders begin with Connerley and Pedersen's stage one: developing cultural awareness.

DEVELOPING CULTURAL AWARENESS

> *Many leaders are unaware of the cultural lenses they use to view the world, or how their own cultural background affects the way in which they view others.*[11]
>
> —MARY L. CONNERLEY AND PAUL B. PEDERSEN,
> *LEADERSHIP IN A DIVERSE AND MULTICULTURAL ENVIRONMENT*

Military leaders' interest in learning about other cultures and improving cultural awareness has increased significantly. However, that interest and desire may obscure a willingness to explore and learn about oneself. Developing cultural awareness requires initial assessment of one's own cultural assumptions or the ability to judge a cultural situation accurately from one's own and the other's cultural viewpoint. Self-awareness, or the ability to know how and why you're thinking what you're thinking, is an important part of this process. Likewise, encouraging leaders to think about *how* they think contributes to developing self-awareness.

This process is similar to many leader development programs—including the one at the Army War College (comprising systems thinking, critical and creative thinking, ethical reasoning, decision-making, organizational culture and climate, etc.)—which focus on cognitive and interpersonal competencies useful to leaders in a culturally diverse environment. Connerley and Pedersen stress the importance of being aware of one's implicit learned assumptions in order to know about the culture of others. One must be willing to change one's "attitudes, opinions and personal perspectives about [oneself] and the other culture" so that multicultural awareness can develop.[12]

Developing cultural awareness includes understanding that all leadership actions and interactions between members in an organization occur within a particular cultural context. Numerous researchers support the approach of recognizing one's own culturally learned assumptions as a starting point for understanding cultural diversity. Glen Fisher emphasizes that

> [t]he human mind is a cognitive system: a framework of mental constructs of the external world and of beliefs, images, assumptions, habits of reason . . . by which the continuing barrage of stimuli a

person receives can be sorted out and given meaning. . . . Mindsets are a means of simplifying the environment and bringing to each new experience or event a pre-established frame of reference for understanding it.[13]

Psychologists contend that when confronted with new and different cultures, people tend to perceive selectively and in ways that minimize disruption to their own cognitive system and therefore "interpret what they perceive in a manner consistent with [their] own particular mindset." In other words, one's perceptions are much more *fixed* than one realizes, and the most common response is to "project [one's] mindset onto other people." Fisher also cautions that using one's own mindset to interpret the words and actions of others is especially problematic when attributing motives to others in foreign affairs.[14] Therefore, to develop multicultural awareness and understand cultural diversity, leaders must learn that they possess a particular mindset that predisposes them to certain responses to others who are different.

How leaders perceive and experience others is part of the process of developing cultural awareness. Typically, leaders see others based on their physical or most obvious attributes, such as race and gender. Marilyn Loden and Judy Rosener identify primary and secondary dimensions of diversity as a way of describing how people see difference.[15] The primary dimensions are age, gender, ethnicity, physical abilities/qualities, race, and affection/sexual orientation.

The secondary dimensions, which are less apparent, may change in each individual over time because of life circumstances, decisions, or experiences or through the person's own will. The secondary dimensions are education, geographic location, income, marital status, military experience, parental status, work background, and religious beliefs.[16]

Awareness of these many dimensions highlights diversity as more than race- and gender-based and begins to emphasize that the *interconnectedness* of the dimensions is what shapes people.[17] Viewing diversity as a kaleidoscope in which the primary and secondary dimensions move independently can be helpful when attempting to understand what aspects of an individual's identity are most important to him or her and what aspects shape the individual's view of others.

DoD military and civilian leaders benefit from learning how they and their peers identify themselves because an individual's self-identity is very often different from how someone else would characterize the individual.

In a recent Defense Equal Opportunity and Management Institute (DEOMI) Leader Team Awareness course for senior military leaders, instructors asked each participant which dimension(s) was most important to him or her. The DEOMI instructor first wrote the primary and secondary dimensions of diversity on placards, hung randomly around the classroom. Once the students had assembled, the instructor had them write the numbers 1, 2, and 3 on a piece of paper. Using the Loden and Rosener dimensions of diversity, the students identified and recorded the dimension each believed best described or defined himself or herself, beginning with the third choice, then the second choice, and finally the first choice. The students' first choice was the most important dimension in how they see themselves, compared with their second and third choices.

Once the students had identified their choices, the instructor directed them to stand next to the placard showing the dimension that was their third choice. The instructor encouraged everyone to scan the room and ask other students what they saw as the advantages of being a member of the group identified as their third choice. Students shared their observations with the class. Next the students moved to their second choice, and this time the instructor asked the students to describe the disadvantages of being in their second-choice group. It was important for students to share their observations about the disadvantages because it provided insight to others about what students saw as the negative descriptions of certain dimensions. Last, the students moved to the location naming their first choice and were asked to explain what they would not want people to say about the group to which they had assigned their first choice.

What is interesting about the exercise results is the different ways individuals defined themselves. Many saw their professional role or military experience as central to their identity. Similarly, just as many defined themselves by their ethnic group, their parental or marital status, or their religious beliefs. In addition, when the instructor asked group members to share what they saw as the advantages, what they saw as the disadvantages, and what they would not like to have said about a group with which they had self-identified, the students gained an appreciation for other perspectives. Likewise, this exercise provided an opportunity for the participants to express how their life experiences had shaped their views.

The DEOMI exercise demonstrates an important lesson for developing leaders' cultural awareness and enables student leaders to explain how they view themselves rather than allowing others to define them. It also requires student leaders to listen to others' descriptions of themselves, as well as hear what they perceive are the advantages and disadvantages of being a member of a particular group or multiple groups. Perhaps, more important, student leaders typically define themselves with multiple dimensions based on their life experiences rather than based on an observed dimension.

Loden and Rosener are not alone in raising awareness that diversity is more than race- and gender-based and that people prefer to define or see themselves as more than their race or gender. One group of management consultants focuses on ten dimensions of diversity they believe are most critical to the workplace. Their dimensions closely mirror Loden and Rosener's: class, ethnicity, age, race, hierarchy/status, gender, religion, physical ability/disability, family situation, and sexual orientation. Their research is instructive because it offers practical examples and case studies with questions and answers for leaders confronted with issues associated with group diversity.[18]

Mark A. Williams, the founder and CEO of the Diversity Channel, progresses beyond categories by identifying ten lenses that "provide a framework to understand what is at the heart of an individual's cultural belief system." His efforts indicate that we see the world "through our own set of perceptual filters or lenses that are made up of what we have been taught and what we have seen, heard and experienced." He further provides examples of the layers influencing those lenses:

> race, color, gender, ethnicity, sexual orientation, age, nationality, marital/parental status, family background, socioeconomic level, physical/mental ability, region of country, education level, religion or spiritual path, political affiliation, profession and leisure activities.[19]

Williams labels the ten lenses: (1) Assimilationist, (2) Colorblind, (3) Culturalcentrist, (4) Elitist, (5) Integrationist, (6) Meritocratist, (7) Multiculturist, (8) Seclusionist, (9) Transcendent, and (10) Victim/Caretaker.[20] Williams' analyses are most instructive because of the characteristics he ascribes to each lens in terms of archetype, profile, strengths, and shadows (or blind spots) as a way of identifying perspective and identity.

Williams recognizes that significant historical events, which he calls *legacies*, contribute to the development of an individual's lens. An example of a legacy is "the processing of immigrants at Ellis Island, New York and other ports of entry."[21] He provides a formula for the development of a lens: legacy + layers = lens. Experiences shaped by one's family, community, and ancestors shape an individual's legacy. This concept of learning about legacies and significant historical events is particularly relevant for military, government, and business leaders, who often interact with people outside their own culture, and it offers a useful template for understanding others' experiences.

Fisher adds that international leaders and managers who routinely interact with others must be able to anticipate how they "are programmed to perceive the issue at hand [as well as] to understand the substance of the issue." He points out that few international leaders make decisions based purely on logic, and "certainly their publics and clients do not." As a result, leaders may need to understand the historical facts, as well as the operant or remembered past.[22]

Regardless of the model used, leaders' efforts to understand the cultural assumptions they make about others increase their self-awareness and appreciation for other people and cultures. Most scholars agree that challenging leaders' prevailing attitudes and norms and eliciting their own unspoken opinions promotes self-awareness. Stage one of Connerly and Pedersen's model—developing self-awareness—is typically overlooked in most cultural diversity education programs, whereas stage two—acquiring cultural knowledge—has been overemphasized.

ACQUIRING CULTURAL KNOWLEDGE

I had never visited Indochina, nor did I understand or appreciate its
history, language, culture or values. When it came to Vietnam, we
found ourselves setting policy for a region that was terra incognita.

—ROBERT S. MCNAMARA, SECRETARY OF DEFENSE (1961–1968)

The second stage, acquiring cultural knowledge, is a process familiar to many. Common examples are learning a foreign language, participating in ethnic celebrations, and attending diversity awareness and equal opportunity seminars. Acquiring cultural knowledge at its most basic level occurs whenever an individual enters a new or unfamiliar environment or organization, such as attending new employee orientation for a new job or going through basic training in the military.

As a leader, perhaps the greatest challenge is staying abreast of cultural changes that affect the dimensions of diversity within one's sphere of influence. At the strategic level, cultural knowledge can include the process of environmental scanning or the identification of trends in the external environment. The leader's role in managing this information is one way of gaining knowledge about the world and the forces of globalization, which the leader can then apply in his or her organization.

A common way of gaining knowledge about world trends is to review the findings of government or research organizations like the Center for Strategic and International Studies (CSIS). Erik R. Peterson, director of the Global Strategy Institute, CSIS, offers Army War College students an informative and thought-provoking presentation called "The Seven Revolutions." It analyzes the seven major forces that will shape our world in the future: population, resource management, technology innovation and diffusion, development and diffusion of information and knowledge, economic integration, conflict, and the challenge of governance. A leader's challenge, then, is to determine how to best position the organization to respond to the major forces of the future.[23]

At the societal and organizational level, cultural knowledge involves learning about a culture as a whole. Learning facts and information about cultures can be a fairly straightforward process and may include studying the demographic makeup of the culture's population. For example, Loden and Rosener's dimensions of diversity provide a framework in which one can assign demographic data by category (gender, age, race, ethnicity, religion, education level) depending on the population of interest. Management consultants offer models similar to Loden and Rosener's as a way to determine the diversity among people they serve. They suggest that it is necessary for leaders to ascertain the "current demographic complexion of their workforce before developing plans for recruiting, training and retention."[24]

Similarly, many organizations use demographic data to assess the diversity within the organization compared to that of the population as a whole. Mady Wechsler Segal and Chris Bourg argue that as the Army becomes more representative of the U.S. population, it will improve its public standing. They also highlight the Army's progress over time in the representation of African Americans and women, one of the most common ways organizations demonstrate they are making progress in cultural diversity. While Segal and Bourg focus on the Army, the definitions and concepts addressed could easily pertain to the military overall or to a global corporation.[25]

More recently, Remi Hajjar and Morten Ender have provided an extensive review of the U.S. Army's culture as part of the larger American culture and America's core values. Their analysis includes detailed demographic statistics about seven categories: race and ethnicity, religion, social class, sex and gender, age, physical ability and disability, and sexual orientation. In addition, the authors provide interesting and useful insights to Army unit leaders into improving performance by influencing a unit's culture.

Being aware of organizational demographics and member diversity dimensions can give leaders valuable insight about cultural diversity; however, when examining a particular dimension of diversity, it is important to understand how the organization defines or describes the dimension. A key point highlighted by Hajjar and Ender is the way the U.S. census now classifies race: by asking individuals what race they consider themselves to be. Permitting people to define their own race or other dimensions of identity can be more informative for organizational leaders. How individuals perceive themselves is often more important than how a leader or organization assumes people see themselves.[26]

To acquire information and improve knowledge about a particular organization or culture, leaders may also find it useful to assess the cultural environment of the population or workforce to determine people's views about diversity and to identify challenges and barriers to managing diversity.[27] Climate surveys and other organizational assessment instruments that solicit opinions and viewpoints provide a way for leaders to know more about their organizations' cultural beliefs and values than what they can see or what demographic categories describe.[28] For example, in 2004, the Army War College's Division Commander Study evaluated behaviors demonstrated by senior officers in creating a climate that supports excellence and motivates competent people to continue military service. The study concluded that leaders should pay equal attention to the development of interpersonal skills in building effective leadership teams and to the development of technical and tactical skills for subordinates.

Given that globalization is fostering interest in leaders' being able to successfully interact and communicate with those in other cultures, knowledge about how cultures communicate and view leadership is especially relevant. In *When Cultures Collide,* Richard D. Lewis examines how people's culture conditions their thinking and affects their interactions with others. Lewis's work helps leaders identify similarities and differences between populations, which is an important part of this stage of developing multicultural competence.[29]

An extensive work on intercultural characteristics, the Lewis study classifies more than 70 countries and regions of the world and offers an intercultural framework about how different cultures interact and interrelate globally. Two of his key concepts can be instructive here. First, categorizing cultures can foster cultural understanding and enhance intercultural communication. Second, leadership concepts, styles, and organizational structures reflect historical and cultural changes.

Parts I and II of Lewis's book focus on defining cultural diversity and describing cultural categories—how cultures use time, view status and leadership, and interrelate in terms of mannerisms and team-building. However, what many find fascinating, and perhaps most useful, is Part III, "Getting to Know Each Other." In this section, Lewis provides an analysis and assessment of the characteristics of specific countries and regions of the world.

Lewis's research demonstrates that learning how cultures are similar and dissimilar can improve one's ability to interact with other cultures. He examines this ability to interrelate by classifying several hundred cultures into three groups: (1) linear-active cultures, described as task-oriented and highly organized planners; (2) multi-active cultures, described as people-oriented and talkative interrelators; and (3) reactive cultures, characterized by introverted and respect-oriented listeners.[30]

Each of Lewis's categories has more than 30 descriptors or common traits to further elucidate his categories. For instance, a Linear-Active group may include the descriptors of being introverted, patient, quiet, and "minds own business." On the other hand, a Multi-Active group would be described as extroverted, impatient, talkative, and inquisitive.[31] Such categorization allows Lewis to address how different cultures view leadership and status within organizations, explains the difference between Eastern and Western perspectives, and questions whether there can be one successful global leadership style. He explains the cultural underpinnings of organizations and leadership and distinguishes between individual and collective leadership styles by providing examples of how different regions view the concepts of status, leadership, and organization. He offers in-depth explanations about how various cultures (France, Germany, Britain, United States, and Japan) understand leadership and organizations. He includes other cultures to a lesser degree.[32]

What may be perhaps most instructive for Western leaders is Lewis's assessment of cultural skills. He contends that while the Big Five countries—the United States, Japan, Germany, Britain, and France—have the largest economies and the most resources, these countries and their business interests are the least sensitive in managing intercultural issues. To successfully compete in future world markets and maintain their preeminence, he postulates, Western leaders should rely on their "dynamic leadership, perspicacity, psychological skills, and willingness to innovate as well as cleverly [making use of their] democratic institutions...such as clubs, societies, committees, charities, associations . . . and alumni fraternities."

Again, this assessment of leaders' knowledge about intercultural issues is not just for business leaders. Colonel Maxie McFarland, U.S. Army (Ret.), supports the emphasis DoD is placing on improving cultural awareness among military personnel, specifically soldiers. McFarland agrees that cultural education should be a part of all Army leader development programs because cultural education means developing both culturally literate and culturally competent soldiers.[33]

McFarland's explanation of cultural literacy is similar to Connerley and Pedersen's Awareness and Knowledge stages. He describes cultural literacy as understanding one's own cultural heritage and self-identity in terms of values, norms, assumptions, and history, as well as understanding the basic diversity management concepts of prejudice and bias. He proposes that knowing about the beliefs, values, history, and behaviors of another culture, learning a second language or multiple languages, and becoming aware of the similarities and differences of various cultural groups are part of cultural literacy. In addition, McFarland suggests that military leaders' study of cultural norms should start with learning about "communication styles [especially nonverbal ones such as facial expressions and gestures] . . . attitudes toward conflict . . . approaches to completing tasks . . . decision-making styles . . . attitudes toward personal disclosure . . . [and] approaches to knowing," whether through cognitive means (learning based on thinking) or affective means (learning based on emotions or feelings).[34]

It is apparent that information about different cultures comes in various forms and through many venues. Certainly learning a new language and studying another culture, including its literature, history, and values, enables leaders to acquire knowledge to increase their understanding of other cultures' viewpoints. Likewise, leaders should know that increasing comprehension is "essential to meaningful understanding of how to present a problem in its cultural context."[35]

Being able to empathize and understand others from their point of view is necessary for developing cultural competence. Peter Senge, a guest of the Army War College, addresses how each individual has a unique perspective on a larger reality. He asserts, however, that the key to building consensus among those who do not share common ground is to "look out" through another's lens so one can see another idea or reality. In summary, Connerly and Pedersen's second stage provides baseline knowledge and facts that allow one to move beyond awareness and progress to the third stage of developing successful cultural skills.[36]

Multicultural training for most organizations, including the military, focuses on behavior modification designed to raise awareness and improve sensitivity, but it stops short of developing cultural skills.[37] Developing skills within a cultural context requires more than simply modifying one's behavior, leading us to stage three.

DEVELOPING CULTURAL SKILLS

The value of military intelligence is exceeded by that of social and cultural intelligence. We need the ability to look, understand, and operate deeply into the fault lines of societies where, increasingly, we find the frontiers of national security.

—Arthur K. Cebrowski, Admiral (Ret.), USN,
former Director of the Office of Force Transformation,
Office of the Secretary of Defense

The third stage of Connerley and Pedersen's model, developing cultural skills, progresses from cultural awareness and knowledge and focuses on *executing what needs to be done rather than just knowing what needs to be done.* This suggests that a multiculturally aware leader uses culturally appropriate skills to effect change, or uses "strategies to match the right method to the right situation in the right way at the right time."[38] The third stage of the model supports Christopher Earley and Randall Peterson's description of cultural intelligence as the

> capability for adaptation across cultures [reflecting] a person's ability to gather, interpret, and act upon . . . radically different cues to function effectively across cultural settings or in a multicultural situation . . . [and] requires that novel ways of dealing with others be discovered . . . [and that] existing strategies must be adjusted, adapted, or reinvented depending on the situation or culture.[39]

In addition, Earley and Peterson suggest that an individual's cultural intelligence consists of three components: metacognition and cognition, motivation, and behavior. They theorize that an assessment of an individual's cultural intelligence and ability to adjust and adapt to other cultures can identify shortcomings, which the individual can then use to improve upon intercultural training and education.

As a result, Earley and Peterson tend to be critical of educational and developmental methodologies that focus primarily on cognitive awareness skills, such as learning country-specific knowledge and idiosyncratic lists of cultural values, because these efforts can lead to stereotyping national cultures and cause misunderstanding about the actual behavior of members of the culture. It is worth noting that other scholars also question the utility of teaching cultural awareness and knowledge by simply teaching a language or providing lists of social dos and don'ts. Developing cultural skills requires a more individualistic approach to education.

Earley and Peterson's description of cultural intelligence and their focus on developing cultural skills based on the ability to adjust to others is comparable to the metacognitive skill identified in the U.S. Army War College *Strategic Leadership Primer* as the metacompetency of *mental agility*. Mental agility refers to

> the ability to recognize changes in the environment; to determine what is new, what must be learned to be effective, and includes the learning process that follows that determination, all performed to standard and with feedback. [It is also the] ability to scan and adjust learning based on the environment and includes aspects of cognitive complexity and improvisation.[40]

DoD's 2006 Quadrennial Defense Review reflects this projected need for leaders with the capabilities to support the objectives of the National Defense Strategy. One of the capabilities DoD explicitly identifies is the following: "Human intelligence, language skills and cultural awareness to understand better the intentions and motivations of potential adversaries and to speed recovery efforts."[41]

The Army's recently published Field Manual 6-22, *Army Leadership,* advises senior leaders to invest time in learning about the economic, political, and social aspects of their international and geopolitical partners' cultures. Possessing cultural sensitivity and geopolitical awareness skills is now recognized as essential for building relationships and accomplishing tasks outside one's organizational hierarchy. This approach is unique for the Army because of the insistence on considering others' interests when developing plans and courses of action.[42]

McFarland's description of cultural competency attempts to move military cultural education closer to the attainment of cultural skills as defined by Connerley and Pedersen. He prescribes a decidedly practical approach, saying the Army should focus soldiers' development of cultural competence on one country or one region of the world. He contends that cultural competency is a necessity for "managing group, organizational, or community cross- or mixed- cultural activities and demands a more in-depth and application-oriented understanding of culture than cultural literacy requires." This is because he believes leaders exhibit cultural competency when they can interact successfully between the cultural divides within organizations and can build cooperative bridges between different cultural groups.[43]

Cultural competency must involve diverse people in all organizational activities in an effort to create "an environment that allows each culture to contribute its values, perspectives, and behaviors in constructive ways to enrich the outcome."[44] Similar to Connerley and Pedersen's suggestion that cultural skills allow one to do what needs to be done, cultural intelligence for Earley and Peterson includes being able to adapt and develop new ways to work across cultures. McFarland explains that cultural competence

> might entail changing how things are done to acknowledge differ-
> ences in individuals, groups, and communities. One must develop
> skills for cross-cultural communication and understand that com-
> munication and trust are often more important than activity. Institu-
> tionalizing cultural interventions for conflicts and confusion caused
> by the dynamics of difference might also be necessary.[45]

Central to acquiring cultural skills is progressing beyond the level of cultural literacy and knowledge of behaviors to developing cultural intelligence or an ability to adapt based on changing situations in any cultural environment. The real key is for each leader to develop the cognitive competencies and thinking skills to not just see the world from another's perspective but also act appropriately in the interest of the other culture as well as one's own. Ultimately, cultural leadership is demonstrated by an ability to (1) see the dignity and value of each individual, (2) make judgments about cultural diversity in order to foster the goals of the organization, and (3) partner successfully with others rather than imposing.

> *In short, Army leaders in this century need to be pentathletes, multi-skilled leaders who can thrive in uncertain and complex operating environments . . . innovative and adaptive leaders who are expert in the art and science of the profession of arms. The Army needs leaders who are decisive, innovative, adaptive, culturally astute, effective communicators and dedicated to lifelong learning.*
>
> —DR. FRANCIS J. HARVEY, SECRETARY OF THE ARMY
> SPEECH FOR U.S. ARMY COMMAND AND GENERAL STAFF COLLEGE
> GRADUATION (2005), FM 6-22 (OCTOBER 2006)

Globalization is fostering multicultural interactions and communications more than ever before. In an increasingly flat world, leaders are successful when they can interact in multicultural, intercultural, or cross-cultural environments. Managing cultural diversity is a prerequisite for success within one's own organization but also in multicultural environments. Ever-demanding future challenges will require leaders in the United States and the rest of the world to continually assess their view of others and the way they lead. Successful interaction between leaders from other cultures and an understanding of cultural context are essential. Successful leaders will recognize that multicultural awareness and diversity management require more than behavioral actions like supporting monthly ethnic celebrations and exhibiting proper pleasantries in multicultural settings.

A wealth of research offers guidance for leaders to successfully interact and communicate with other cultures. Leader development experts studying diversity management and cultural awareness generally support Connerley and Pederson's three-stage process as a framework for developing cultural skills and cultural intelligence. Such models can assist leaders in understanding how to develop multicultural awareness, knowledge, and skills by affirming that (1) cultural awareness, cultural knowledge, and cultural skills development are different and require varying degrees of effort; (2) demographics are more than race and gender; (3) individuals are better at defining themselves than others are at defining them; (4) assessing an individual's values, beliefs, and perspectives provides valuable insight; (5) using cultural labels in interactions with others should be avoided; (6) learning one's own cultural assumptions and mindsets develops cultural awareness; (7) cultural knowledge is more than learning a new language; (8) cultural diversity exists everywhere, so look for it; (9) cultural skills and intelligence require adaptability; and (10) globalization and diversity management are here to stay.

Leaders need to gain self-awareness and knowledge about culture—both national and organizational—and to learn how the impact of diverse cultures and the dimensions of diversity affect the development of highly productive, cohesive, and mission-focused teams. The successful leaders will be those who can recognize and bridge the cultural differences within their own society, as well as build bridges when interacting with other cultures of the world.

NOTES

1. Thomas L. Friedman, *The World Is Flat: A Brief History of the Twenty-First Century* (New York: Farrar, Straus & Giroux, 2004).

2. Stephen Shambach, ed., *Strategic Leadership Primer*, 2nd ed. (Carlisle, PA: U.S. Army War College, 2004): 60.

3. Mary L. Connerley and Paul B. Pedersen, *Leadership in a Diverse and Multicultural Environment: Developing Awareness, Knowledge, and Skills* (Thousand Oaks: Sage Publications, Inc., 2005): 49.

4. Franklin D. Roosevelt, "Executive Order 8802—Prohibition of Discrimination in the Defense Industry," (25 June 1941).

5. Harry S. Truman, "Executive Order 9981—Establishing the President's Committee on Equality of Treatment and Opportunity in the Armed Services," (26 July 1948).

6. Mickey R. Dansby and Dan Landis, "Intercultural Training in the United States Military," *Managing Diversity in the Military*, Mickey R. Dansby, James B. Stewart, and Schuyler C. Webb, eds. (New Brunswick: Transaction Publishers, 2001): 9.

7. Francis J. Harvey and Peter J. Schoomaker, *A Statement on the Posture of the United States Army 2006*, presented to the committees and subcommittees of the United States Senate and the House of Representatives, 109th congress, 2nd session: 15.

8. Peter G. Northouse, *Leadership Theory and Practice*, 4th ed. (Thousand Oaks: Sage Publications, Inc., 2007): 3–4.

9. Connerley and Pedersen, 49.

10. Lynn R. Offerman and Kenneth Matos, "Best Practices in Leading Diverse Organizations," *The Practice of Leadership: Developing the Next Generation of Leaders*, Jay A. Conger and Ronald E. Riggio, eds. (San Francisco: Jossey-Bass, 2007): 287.

11. Connerley and Pedersen, 92.

12. Ibid., xii, 50, 113.

13. Glen Fisher, *Mindsets: The Role of Culture and Perception in International Relations* (Yarmouth: Intercultural Press, Inc., 1988): 23.

14. Ibid., 33.

15. Marilyn Loden and Judy B. Rosener, *Workforce America! Managing Employee Diversity as a Vital Resource* (Homewood: Business One Irwin, 1991): 18–21.

16. Ibid.

17. Katharine Esty, Richard Griffin, and Marcie Schorr Hirsch, *Workplace Diversity: A Manager's Guide to Solving Problems and Turning Diversity into a Competitive Advantage* (Avon: Adams Media Corporation, 1995): 3.

18. Ibid.

19. Mark A. Williams, *The 10 Lenses: Your Guide to Living and Working in a Multicultural World* (Sterling: Capital Books, Inc., 2001): 4–9.

20. Williams, *The 10 Lenses: Your Guide to Living and Working in a Multicultural World.*

21. Ibid., 4

22. Fisher, *Mindsets: The Role of Culture and Perception in International Relations.*

23. Erik R. Peterson and William A. Schreyer, "Seven Revolutions," Center for Strategic and International Studies, available online at http://www.7revs.org/seven-revs_content.html (accessed 13 December 2006).

24. Norma M. Riccucci, *Managing Diversity in Public Sector Workforces* (Boulder: Westview Press, 2002): 29.

25. Mady Wechsler Segal and Chris Bourg, "Professional Leadership and Diversity in the Army," *Future of the Army Profession*, 2nd ed., Lloyd J. Matthews, ed. (Boston: McGraw-Hill, 2005): 705–719.

26. Remi Hajjar and Morten G. Ender, "Harnessing the Power of Culture and Diversity for Organizational Performance," *Leadership Lessons from West Point: Building Stronger Leaders*, Doug Crandall, ed. (San Francisco: Jossey-Bass, 2006): 314.

27. Riccucci, 29.

28. Dansby and Landis, xiv.

29. Richard D. Lewis, *When Cultures Collide: Leading Across Cultures,* 3rd ed. (Boston: Nicholas Brealey International, 2006).

30. Ibid., 27.

31. Ibid., 33 and 34.

32. Ibid., 101.

33. Maxie McFarland, "Military Cultural Education," *Military Review* (March-April 2005): 63–67.

34. Ibid., 66.

35. Connerley and Pedersen, 78.

36. Peter M. Senge, *The Fifth Discipline: The Art and Practice of the Learning Organization* (New York: Currency and Doubleday, 1990): 248.

37. Dansby and Landis, 24.

38. Connerley and Pedersen, 121.

39. Christopher Earley and Randall S. Peterson, "The Elusive Cultural Chameleon: Cultural Intelligence as a New Approach to Intercultural Training for the Global Manager," *Academy of Management Learning and Education* 3.1 (2004): 105.

40. Shambach, 59.

41. U.S. Department of Defense, *Quadrennial Defense Review Report*, 6 February 2006 (Washington, D.C.: U.S. Department of Defense): 35.

42. Department of the Army, "FM 6-22—Army Leadership: Competent, Confident and Agile (Washington, D.C.: Department of the Army, October 2006): 12–15.

43. McFarland, 63.

44. Ibid., 64.

45. Ibid.

10 The Strategic Leader as Negotiator

COL George Woods, U.S. Army

I have come to believe that negotiation is the single most important skill that leaders exercise during their transitions to new roles.

—MICHAEL WATKINS, *SHAPING THE GAME*

Leadership is, and always has been, a main emphasis of instruction in the Army and at the U.S. Army War College. As Watkins' statement above makes clear, negotiation is an important aspect of leadership. It may not be the *most* important skill, but it certainly is one of the most important. This chapter examines the topic of negotiation and negotiating and how the Army War College incorporates it into its core course on strategic leadership.

The U.S. Army has approached the study of leadership using a three-tiered system to describe the requisite technical, cognitive, and interpersonal skills required to successfully lead at various levels within the Army. They are the direct, organizational, and strategic levels. Each level emphasizes skill sets most essential to that level. For example, leaders at the direct level, often associated with the lower levels of the hierarchy, typically see immediate and tangible outcomes resulting from their leadership, whereas those at the strategic level may not see the outcomes for years, nor will the results be as tangible as those witnessed at the direct level.

Why is negotiating a skill typically associated with the organizational context at the strategic level? This is not to imply that negotiating skills are not important at the other levels in the organization, especially in today's complex environment. Ongoing counterinsurgency operations require use of these negotiating skills at all levels—direct, organizational, and strategic. The operational demands have caused the Army and others to reevaluate how much negotiation education and training is required in the formal schooling systems. The Army is also assessing when negotiation training and education should occur and how many resources should be dedicated to this end.

Negotiation training and education should occur earlier in an officer's career. Negotiation has been a more salient and essential skill at the strategic level. Why is this? First, leaders at the strategic level have less direct authority. They often lead and influence change and decisions across the organization but do not command most of those they rely on to achieve organizational goals. Often these organizations are themselves led by peers. Second, compared with leaders lower in the hierarchy, who interact with others *inside* the organization and whose roles and responsibilities are defined largely by rules, regulations, and operating procedures and organizational norms, strategic leaders operate in an environment where more of their time is spent interacting with and influencing others *outside* their organization. The external actors vary in values, interests, and frames of reference.

Finally, relative to leaders lower in the organizational hierarchy, strategic leaders operate in an environment that is more volatile, uncertain, complex, and ambiguous. *Volatility* refers to the rate of change in an organization's environment. *Uncertainty* and *ambiguity* affect the degree to which leaders can know, interpret, and predict the environment in which they operate. *Complexity* also affects predictability but refers to the probabilities that actions taken will cause predictable effects.

These four environmental characteristics often present problems that exceed the leader's organizational capability or authority and necessitate negotiating skills to address the problems. They also create situations in which even clearly defining what the problem is requires a negotiated agreement or, because of the inability to clearly predict a cause-and-effect relationship between actions taken and results achieved, negotiated solutions may be necessary.

For example, the Army's mission is to defend the United States and win the nation's wars. This, combined with the nation's preference to fight its wars outside national boundaries, means the Army must be an expeditionary force. It must deploy its forces where they are needed. The Army, however, is unequipped and incapable of deploying itself to places around the world to protect national interests. The Army requires support from both the Navy and the Air Force to transport its forces when and where they are needed. The Army's Chief of Staff, the senior ranking officer in the Army, has the legal responsibility to man, arm, equip, and sustain Army forces to meet these national security needs.

The Army receives funding to meet these needs. However, funding for the Army's sea and air transportation goes to the other services. Therefore, the Army Chief of Staff must negotiate with the chiefs of the other services to fulfill these needs. Simultaneously, the Navy and the Air Force also have competing missions and thus can devote only a percentage of their funding to meet these needs. Further, they have preferences regarding the size of Army forces they transport and how fast they are expected to move them. Defining these capabilities requires negotiated solutions.

Further, given the uncertainty about what potential threats the United States should prepare to meet in ten years, and given the frequency at which change occurs in today's environment, making decisions and keeping pace with the changes become a challenging problem. Defining what the threat will be, when it might become a threat, and how best to prepare for it requires a negotiated solution between interested parties. The Services have to determine which threats will likely emerge, which are most threatening, where risk will be accepted, and what forces are required to counter the likely threats. All the solutions to these issues must be negotiated. How many forces of what kind will be needed—and when? Regional combatant commanders, the war fighters around the world, also have a vested interest in this process. They have their own views of what combination of forces could and should be mustered to negate these probable threats. The Service chiefs and the combatant commanders, among many interested parties, must together negotiate solutions to balance requirements, resources, and risks.

WHAT IS A NEGOTIATION?

Negotiation "is best understood as a process of potentially opportunistic interaction aimed at advancing the full set of one's interests by *jointly* decided action."[1] Negotiation is not haggling or bargaining. Nor is it purely an exercise of power in which one side is bullied into accepting a solution.

Negotiation is not *mediation*. To mediate is "to settle or resolve differences by acting as an intermediary between two or more opposing parties."[2] Mediators "intervene between two or more disputing parties in order to affect [sic.] a settlement, agreement, or compromise."[3] Use of a third party in negotiations to mediate between two parties may be a solution to a negotiation impasse.

Imagine you are a commander serving in Afghanistan and two factions, under the leadership of two warlords, coexist in your area of operation. The two warlords are at an impasse over the use of a road that provides access to the one water source in your area of operation. You may have to facilitate reaching an agreement between the two factions because they do not seem capable of arriving at a solution by themselves. The two warlords, or their designated representatives, would be considered the negotiators in this case. They are dependent upon each other to find joint solutions to peacefully coexist within the area you command but are unable to reach an agreement. In this case, because you have established a relationship with them and have become a trusted and credible agent, you might serve as the mediator who works with them and encourages them to agree to a mutually satisfactory solution both parties will, in good faith, implement.

Negotiation is also not *arbitration*. Arbitration is a "process by which two or more disputing parties submit their differences to the judgment of an impartial person or group selected by mutual consent or statutory provision."[4] The *arbitrator* is impartial, and *empowered by both parties* to make a decision when presented sufficient data or information. The powers in this case are two or more negotiators who cannot resolve their own differences to develop a satisfactory decision both sides can live with.

One often reads about situations decided by arbitration. It would not be uncommon to read about two nations that are at an impasse on a trade arrangement or an international conflict. Unable to craft their own solution to the problem, both parties could agree to have a third party make a decision that both will honor. Often nations defer to the United Nations to serve as an arbitrator. The U.N. reviews the merits of both arguments and renders a decision. The decision made is then executed in the manner the arbitrators deem fair, just, or right.

Negotiation distinguishes itself because of the interdependence of the parties involved. Negotiating requires two parties deciding to decide. It is "the process where two or more parties decide what each will give and take in the context of their relationship."[5] Negotiation becomes a process by which "solving their problem is a means of solving your problem."[6]

To give a simple example, imagine you are a military commander in Iraq who may have to negotiate with a nongovernmental organization (NGO) representative who wants to provide humanitarian assistance to a troubled village within your area of responsibility. You are responsible for security in the area and for reducing the risk to all noncombatants. Therefore, you may be reluctant to give the NGO free reign in your area, where it might be vulnerable to attack. The NGO, on the other hand, is interested in providing immediate relief to the populace and resists military control because overt ties to the military damages the NGO's credibility with the locals. To complicate matters for the NGO representative, the area is not safe for the NGO's personnel to operate in without military support, especially in the area requiring relief.

Furthermore, you are also charged with winning the populace's hearts and minds. Admittedly, providing immediate relief to the stricken population would be an action consistent with achieving that goal. In this case, both you and the NGO leader have full decision-making authority. Negotiating the timing and support to provide the relief under safe conditions for both parties requires joint problem-solving and a negotiated settlement.

The definitions and the accompanying example highlight key aspects of negotiation. First, negotiations involve relationships. They require two or more parties engaging each other to achieve results. The parties must solve problems that neither could achieve without assistance from the other. Negotiation is an interactive process.

As the example demonstrates, both parties place value on different aspects of the problem. You, as the military commander, value control over the NGO's movement because you are responsible for the assigned area and the people in it or transiting through it. You want to maintain security and avoid providing a target of opportunity for insurgents to attack noncombatants within your sector. You know full well that if the insurgents successfully attack and kill innocent civilians and eliminate the NGO relief organization, they will use that event to discredit the U.S. security efforts in your area. On the other side, the NGO wants to provide relief to the affected citizens as quickly as possible.

Further, the NGO's association with U.S. troops affects not only its freedom of movement but also the degree of confidence citizens have in the organization. Both sides, however, value things similarly in this situation. The NGO leader values the safety of her organization and those she is responsible for aiding just as much as you do. Both you and the NGO leader value providing relief to the affected citizens as soon as possible.

WHY IS NEGOTIATING SO DIFFICULT?

Understanding why negotiations fail is a good place to start in better understanding why most people experience negotiating as an onerous, unpleasant task. Margaret Neale defines several psychological factors that can interfere with a negotiation's potential effectiveness and create unsatisfactory results. They are suspicion and a lack of trust, the myth of the fixed pie, framing, hubris, overconfidence, and the search for confirming evidence.[7]

The parties in a negotiation may not know much about the other side and lack trust in their counterpart. Therefore, fear of being taken advantage of by the other party may loom over the process. Worse yet, you may realize that you are too trusting a person and too easy a victim. You may feel as if you walk around with the word "sucker" tattooed on your forehead, and therefore you are reluctant to expose yourself to humiliation. In either case, you enter the negotiation process with trepidation and do not experience it as a positive interaction.

Most of us fear entering a negotiation because we see it as a win-lose affair. Fear of losing or of being taken advantage of stems from a misperception of the negotiation process. Many negotiators believe there is only one set of solutions in a negotiation and that someone has to win and someone has to lose—the myth of the "fixed pie." Because we think negotiating is a zero-sum game over the mythical fixed pie, it usually becomes one. Suppose we enter a negotiation with five possible outcomes. If we "win" three or more of those outcomes, we win; if we come back with two or fewer, we lose.

Often how we frame or perceive the problem affects the way we see it and further entrenches our view of the fixed pie. When we approach the negotiation process as if it is a zero-sum game, we cause our counterpart to adopt the same outlook. It then becomes the competitive process we thought it would be at the outset. The 1978 Egypt–Israeli peace treaty illustates this. Both countries dug in with incompatible positions over ownership of the Sinai Peninsula following the 1967 conflict. There seemed to be no agreeable solution. Why? Egypt framed the problem as a sovereignty issue, whereas Israel saw it as a security issue. Once these two competing frames of reference were discovered, a creative solution to the problem resulted.[8]

Hubris also influences the negotiation process. Pride and arrogance often put us, as negotiators, in competition with each other. We are motivated to take the majority of the outcomes; walking away from the negotiation with anything less damages our self-esteem. Overconfidence becomes closely entwined with hubris. We often feel more confident about what we can achieve in a negotiation and tend to underrate our counterpart's ability. In competitive contexts we believe we are more capable; our expectations are high, and we become emboldened. When both sides come to the table with these perspectives, the competitive dimension consumes the process.

Overconfidence is not a bad thing. It motivates us to act and may increase our willingness to take risks. However, it sometimes gets us to act too quickly, may prematurely truncate the search for information, and may increase our willingness to take risks.[9]

Because most negotiators enter the process seeing it as a zero-sum, competitive process, they look for confirming evidence. If I see you as a competitor, I will interpret everything you do as being competitive. Your being competitive motivates *me* to be more competitive. I must be if I want to extract the majority of the fixed pie from you. You, in turn, see me as competitive and become more competitive. You get the picture. We quickly become stuck in a downward spiral. Yet, we know negotiations can also be highly successful. How *does* that happen?

THE PRINCIPLES OF A SUCCESSFUL NEGOTIATION

Interest-based negotiation, described in the pivotal work *Getting to Yes,*[10] provides the philosophical foundation that informs negotiation education at the U.S. Army War College. Why? Interest-based negotiation has stood the test of time. Since its beginnings in 1981, the approach has spawned significant research and a tremendous following. More important, the framework works; when used correctly, it demonstrates positive results. Negotiators leave the negotiation satisfied with their results and committed to carrying out the terms of the negotiation.

Several guiding principles establish the framework for the negotiation process, including:

- ▸ Don't argue over positions.
- ▸ Separate the people from the problem.
- ▸ Discover underlying interests.
- ▸ Create options for mutual gain.
- ▸ Insist on objective criteria.
- ▸ Define what constitutes a bad deal.

Don't Argue over Positions

The first principle—***do not argue over positions***[11]—is the foundation the other principles support. Many negotiations fail when negotiators focus on positions. When this happens, negotiations become haggling or bargaining. Such negotiations often lead to unwise agreements, provide no alternatives, become an inefficient use of the negotiators' time, and usually ignore the relationship between the negotiators. Sometimes they irreparably damage the relationship. The process also becomes unmanageable when multiple parties become involved.

What is a *position*? A position is a stand on an issue.[12] Positions become the specific, tangible items that *represent* a party's interests and the opposition's interests. Positions can be thought of as a price you would seek to minimize if you were a buyer in a negotiation. Costs incurred, time invested, quantities of things produced—all can represent positions in a negotiation. Positions, the tangible representation of the parties' interests, are detrimental when they become the centerpiece around which the negotiation's outcome is measured. *Interests*, on the other hand, "are the *underlying* concerns of deeper dimensions of value that would be affected by different resolution of the issues under negotiation."[13] Often these are *assumptions that are not consciously examined.*

In the Iraq example described earlier, the NGO leader may measure her position by the timeliness and quantity of relief supplies she delivers. The commander, on the other hand, might measure his outcomes by the number of casualties experienced. The commander's desire to minimize casualties conflicts with the NGO's position of maximizing delivery. When negotiation is centered on only these positions, there is little room for agreement between the two parties in this case.

Separate the People from the Problem

Separate the people from the problem is the second principle.[14] Negotiations involve two broad categories of interests: substance and relationship. Often, substance becomes the sole focus of a negotiation. When that happens, relationships are ignored. Positional bargaining increases the probability that negotiators will ignore relationships and likely damage them. Because relationships are not acknowledged in positional bargaining, the relationships tend to become intertwined with the substance of the negotiation. Negotiations are rarely one-time affairs. Parties usually come to depend on each other in future circumstances. Therefore, relationships are important. In the Iraqi situation, both the commander and the NGO leader will likely interact throughout their tours of duty. Therefore, avoiding negotiations over positions and tending to their relationship during the process will be important.

Paying attention to perceptions, emotions, and communication, the negotiator can aid in separating the people from the problem. Acknowledging your own perceptions and estimating the other party's perceptions also helps. Self-awareness is important to understanding your own perspective and is easier to achieve. Role playing, seeing the world through the other's eyes and "putting yourself in their shoes," helps estimate their perspective. Blaming the other party for your problems damages relationships and must be avoided. Discussing perceptions on both sides also helps. Acting in a manner inconsistent with the other party's preconceptions actually helps relationships and prevents the other party from judging you based on stereotypes. Rather, the other party will see you as unique or different and will relate to you as an individual.

Negotiations involve values, and values evoke emotions. Therefore, negotiators should acknowledge their own emotions and respect the other party's emotions in a negotiation. Some recommend that negotiators be aware of their own emotions and assess the emotions the other side may be feeling. Assessing what other people feel during a negotiation, based on nonverbal cues or tone of voice, can be difficult. Instead of trying to determine what emotions your counterpart is actually feeling, researchers suggest that as a negotiator you do two things. First, manage your own emotions. Second, take the initiative by *shaping* the other party's emotions. One way to simplify managing your own emotions is to adopt a role that best fits your personality, one that provides purpose and reflects your personal beliefs.[15]

These negotiating roles may be entitled "helper," "evaluator," or "enforcer," among several others. To influence others' emotions, you can make statements that express *appreciation* toward the other party, build *affiliation* with him or her, respect the party's *autonomy*, and *acknowledge* the party's status.[16] Instead of managing your emotions and the other party's, you simply manage your own and positively influence his or hers. Other helpful tips include permitting the other side to "let off steam" and avoiding the creation of conditions in which the other party "loses face."

When you speak with a purpose and speak to help the other side understand you, you build positive relationships and create the separation of problem and relationships. Speaking about yourself and not the other person—not in a self-indulgent way, but one that helps educate that person about you—has the same effect. Avoid blaming the other party for your condition. Most important, actively listen to the other party. Doing so not only enhances the relationship but also provides an opportunity to fully appreciate the other side's perspective. By listening, you discover the other party's values, interests, and objectives. You learn things about the other party you did not know before. The effect may create opportunities for previously unimagined solutions.

Facing the problem, not the people, and building working relationships are two important principles.[17] Assuming future negotiations are inevitable means attending to relationships as an ongoing interest. Relationships built in each encounter can prevent the likelihood of impasses in later negotiations and increase the probability of reaching successful agreements.

Discover Underlying Interests

The third principle focuses on *discovering the underlying interests parties bring to the negotiation, then basing agreements on those interests.*[18] "Interests define the problem"[19] and, when used, can help you avoid arguments over positions. Interests provide the opportunity for mutually beneficial results from the negotiation. The negotiation process should seek to discover these interests in the information-gathering phase.

Let's return to the vignette in Iraq. The military commander might easily make a blanket policy (take a position) that no NGO supplies will transit the most dangerous route in his sector. The NGO representative might take an opposing position—her organization will make the humanitarian relief delivery at all costs. Although they have conflicting initial positions, looking at their *interests* unveils *mutual* interests. The NGO is interested in providing relief as soon as possible, in the safest manner, and not undermining the protection that the military provides. Similarly, the military commander wants, among other competing interests, to win favor among the local populace by eliminating or minimizing their suffering. But he must do so in a manner that minimizes the threat to the safety of the unit, the NGO, and the villagers.

Perceptions in the negotiation process are important. When negotiating with other parties, *their* perception of *their* interests is what counts. It is not what *you* think their interests should be, but their interests as *they* now see or may later come to see them. Interests also shape and are shaped by *their* perception of alternatives, *their* notion of fairness, *their* constituency pressures, and so on. To change their minds, the negotiator must create a "golden bridge"[20] to bring them *from where they are now to where you want them to be.*

As was pointed out earlier in the chapter, interests are often unexamined or unconscious. Therefore, helping the other party realize or acknowledge his or her own interests helps the party understand himself or herself better. It also helps you understand the party better. And it helps to accurately discover common interests that permit or facilitate solutions to both sides' problems. One way to help the other party discover his or her own interests, permitting you to reach a deeper understanding of those interests and create that "golden bridge" is to ask why the party thinks or feels the way he or she does. Answers to these questions will make the interests salient. Rarely do parties come to a negotiation with only one interest. Asking "why not?" to various proposals or options discussed in the negotiation process provides a mechanism to explore the other interests bearing on the problem.

Create Options for Mutual Gain

Negotiating entails both competitive and cooperative processes. The cooperative process, sometimes referred to as *integrative negotiation,* is the process by which negotiators create value and expand the "pie." The integrative process's purpose is to explore all the options that could mutually satisfy the parties' interests. Cooperating and creating value enacts the fourth principle, which urges negotiators to **invent options for mutual gain.**[21] The creative process is not foreign to most Army War College students. Military students recognize this phase as the course of action development phase in the military decision-making cycle. Most civilians recognize it as brainstorming. Many of the students have been through brainstorming sessions during their careers.

Setting rules up front to govern the creative process is essential. No one wants to give the impression he or she has committed to a decision during this phase because that freedom from commitment allows both perties to think of novel, innovative options that might not otherwise be considered. Brainstorming internal to a negotiation team (i.e., one party of the two involved) can be an effective process for estimating the other side's interests as well as clarifying your own. Although a little more difficult or riskier, brainstorming simultaneously with both parties involved in a negotiation can prove very fruitful. Sitting side by side to face the "problem," which may be posted on a board or projected on a screen, has a fascinating psychological effect on the process. The participants actually act as and feel themselves to be part of a team jointly trying to solve the problem. They often subconsciously shift from an "I" and "you" mentality and begin to use "we" as part of their speech.

Insist on Objective Criteria

Having uncovered all options, the negotiation process must transition to a competitive phase, during which negotiators *claim value,* or divide the expanded pie. This phase is also known as distributive negotiation. To divide the pie in a manner that preserves good relationships is the focus of the fifth principle, ***insisting on the use of objective criteria.***[22] "The tough distributive or value-claiming aspects of a deal can poison the negotiation and destroy business partnerships."[23]

Using fair standards both sides agree to gives both sides a common way to measure the effectiveness of proposed negotiation outcomes. Both parties can gain confidence that they will end up with a commitment they can live with. Further, using fair standards and/or fair procedures can enhance the trust experienced between the two parties with a result of enhancing the relationship.

There are many examples of standards that can be applied: market value, precedent, tradition, law, moral, etc. Standard procedures can be those already established (norms, standard business practices, protocols, etc.) or ones invented specifically for the situation the negotiators are trying to resolve. The objective is to use the negotiation process to determine which of these standards and/or procedures apply in their specific situation. Three points assist in discovering objective criteria in the course of a negotiation: (1) frame each negotiation as a joint search for objective criteria; (2) reason and be open to reason; and (3) never yield to pressure.[24]

Opposing parties in a negotiation often arrive at the table using different *frames of reference* as a way of ordering their thoughts and attitudes. These are also the heuristics that Steve Gerras elsewhere refers to in Chapter 3 of this book. *Heuristics* are the operating theories people use to simplify the complex world they live in on a daily basis. When different or mismatched frames are used within a team or between negotiating parties, the process can bog down and/or become frustrating.

Several categories of frames of reference exist: (1) substantive (what the negotiation is about); (2) loss/gain (the risks or benefits of various outcomes); (3) characterization (different expectations and evaluations of others' behaviors and outcomes); (4) process (how the negotiation will or should proceed); (5) aspiration (regarding the parties' underlying needs and interests); and (6) outcome (the parties' preferred positions or solutions).[25] *Reframing* an issue helps others see the situation from a different perspective. Defining a problem broader or narrower, bigger or smaller, riskier or less risky, or over a shorter or longer term can help in aligning frames or can minimize the differences in perspectives.

For example, you can affect people's behavior by manipulating their perspective of risk in a negotiation. People are generally more risk-averse when considering options focused on potential gains, but risk-seeking when considering potential losses.[26] Reframing the problem can change the way they see the decision. When offered a sure $100 versus a 50-50 chance of winning $200 or $0, we are more risk-averse. However, when offered a 50-50 chance of losing either $200 or $0 over a certain loss of $100, we are more risk-taking, even though the probabilities are the same in each condition.[27]

Framing each negotiation as a joint search is both an art and a state of mind. If one approaches the negotiation process as a joint search, it can become one, whereas if one assumes the opposite approach, it definitely will not become one unless the other party influences it in that direction. The art of framing negotiations in this manner comes from practice and from using good technique. Trying to understand the theories or heuristics the other party uses to inform his or her perspectives helps, as does relying on and agreeing on principles up front.

The use of objective criteria also helps interject reason into the process. By agreeing to principles and objective standards and procedures, both parties have a means to rationally measure the proposed outcomes of a negotiation. It helps to negotiate reasonably as well as to be open to reason from the other party. Further, injecting rationality into the negotiation process prevents one from yielding to the pressure or hardball tactics others may employ in the negotiation process.

Define What Constitutes a Bad Deal

The other side in a negotiation often uses pressure tactics to exact outcomes in the relationship. What can one do to protect against being pressured to yield and accept "bad" outcomes? When the other side has a more advantageous position or possesses more power and exerts it, the final principle protects the negotiator from accepting a bad deal: *To avoid a bad deal, know what constitutes a bad deal.*

Negotiators should use a concept known as the *best alternative to a negotiated agreement* (BATNA). It is the no-agreement alternative. Your BATNA "reflects the course of action you would take if the proposed deal were not possible."[28] Others refer to the BATNA as the *reservation price* (the bottom line)—the value you put on the BATNA. The BATNA is usually quantified and based on a specific number or condition that represents a trigger point. Reaching the trigger point prevents one party from agreeing to something he or she does not want to agree to.

Thinking through conditions the other party might offer that add no value to something you could do yourself or something you might find elsewhere is time well spent. Realizing that condition and knowing when it is reached prevents you from accepting a bad deal. Estimating the opponent's BATNA is also time well spent. Assessing the BATNAs on both sides of the negotiation empowers each negotiator. Forethought also gives you the opportunity to think of conditions that better your BATNA. Finding alternative sources that provide increasingly better deals increases your BATNA vis-à-vis your counterpart and defines the triggers that can cause you to walk away from an agreement. Having the option to walk away from a negotiation gives you tremendous power.[29] Realizing your counterpart no longer exercises power over you evens the playing field. Assessing both sides' BATNAs helps identify the range of possible agreements that may exist before the negotiation begins and forms an agenda for negotiators to discover in the information-gathering phase of a negotiation.

The *zone of potential agreement*, often referred to as the ZOPA, defines the range of possible solutions both parties (several in multilateral negotiation settings) can agree to with some sense of satisfaction. For example, if a seller's minimum price is well below a buyer's maximum cost, there is room for agreement. Often a ZOPA exists because multiple interests (costs, status, security, comfort, etc.) enter into each negotiation *and* the parties differ on the value they hold vis-à-vis each issue. This gives them *trading space* and creates a ZOPA where none previously existed. Sometimes ZOPAs are estimated in the preparation phase, but most often they are discovered during the negotiation itself. Approaching the negotiation process as a cooperative, creative process allows negotiators to discover or confirm the other side's BATNA and the range of options, which can lead to better outcomes.

Being armed with the operating principles Roger Fisher and William Ury recommend in *Getting to Yes* is helpful, but it is only half the battle. A negotiator should spend at least as much time preparing for a negotiation as he or she anticipates negotiating—more time spent is desirable. For the novice negotiator, preparing for a negotiation can be a perplexing task.

PREPARING FOR A NEGOTIATION

Preparing for a negotiation is analogous to a commander's preparing for a battle or an operation. The commander scouts the enemy and reconnoiters the battlefield as time and security permit. Likewise, the negotiator should scout out the other side, assess the conditions, etc. like a military officer does in the intelligence preparation of the battlefield phase in the military decision-making process. But what does the negotiation battlefield look like? Tom Colosi offers a helpful organizing framework.[30] He describes three dimensions negotiators must manage during the negotiation process: the horizontal, internal, and ratification dimensions.

The Horizontal Dimension of Negotiating

The *horizontal* dimension (Figure 10-1) is the terrain discussed to this point in the chapter. It is the process of negotiating between two designated negotiators at the table. A negotiation can range from the simplest kind, a bilateral negotiation between two negotiators, to the hardest, multilateral negotiations including three or more parties. In the horizontal dimension, negotiators can negotiate across the table or in private sessions away from the table.[31]

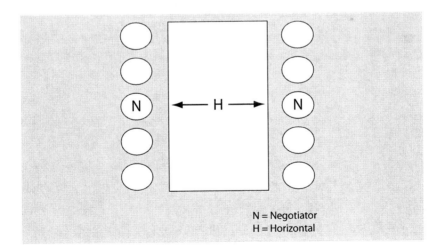

N = Negotiator
H = Horizontal

FIGURE 10-1. The horizontal dimension.

Before proceeding, some more terms must be defined. Negotiators present or discuss issues. *Issues* are items that are on the table for explicit agreement.[32] Issues may or may not be relevant to the negotiation process, but they may be perceived to be relevant. Issues can focus on both positions and interests. They may be emotionally based and, therefore, emotionally charged. *At the table* translates to the tactical (in a formal negotiating, not military, context) moves made in the formal, for-the-record negotiation sessions. This may or may not be the context in which decisions are really made. At-the-table negotiations may be as much for show as they are for substance.

Issues are also often worked *away from the table.* Away-from-the-table moves are the informal, face-to-face, intimate interactions between negotiators or negotiating parties. This venue may be where the real negotiating occurs and most of the decisions are made—if it is used. Taking a break and engaging in informal conversations over meals or at social events are forms of away-from-the-table strategies. They are, or should be, an integral part of the negotiation process.

The Internal Dimension of Negotiating

The *internal* dimension to a negotiation (Figure 10-2) concerns the membership of each party. Often more than one person accompanies the negotiator, and a team, not just an individual, negotiates. These additional team members may bring to the table financial, legal, or technical expertise. They provide specific information in the negotiating process. Often, when looking across the table during a negotiation, one thinks the other team represents a monolithic point of view. It rarely does. Neither does your side.

A way of viewing these relationships is to classify team members as stabilizers, destabilizers, and quasi-mediators. *Stabilizers* are the conciliatory members of the team. They like to avoid confrontation and conflict. They tend to trust people when trust may not be warranted. They are "soft on people, and soft on the problem."[33] When they are on your team, they may be prone to promise too much, yield to pressure, and give away the farm. *Destabilizers*, on the other hand, dislike the negotiation process and tend to distrust the other side and their fellow teammates who are "soft." They prefer confrontation through aggressive negotiation tactics.[34] Balancing these opposing dynamics and managing the team's approach to the negotiation belongs to the *quasi-mediator*, who is the team's lead negotiator in this scenario.[35]

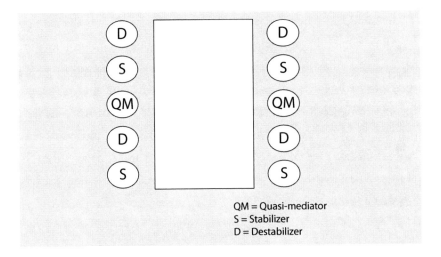

QM = Quasi-mediator
S = Stabilizer
D = Destabilizer

FIGURE 10-2. The internal dimension.

The lead negotiator/quasi-mediator has a complex task. He or she must manage both the internal and the horizontal negotiation dimensions. One of the first steps in the process, then, is to manage the internal dimension and gain a cooperative and negotiated procedure and stance prior to the negotiation—a significant part of your preparation. The procedures negotiated not only pertain to the team's internal dimensions but also affect how they behave, both verbally and nonverbally, during the negotiation both at and away from the table. You may have to establish fairly restrictive procedures if you believe either the stabilizer or destabilizer may adversely affect the process, especially in the early, critical stages when relationships are built. Procedures may affect who talks during the negotiation, what they may be allowed to say and when, what roles they play, and what they are allowed to divulge—especially when away from the table.

The Ratification Dimension of Negotiating

The final dimension the lead negotiator must manage is the *ratification* dimension (Figure 10-3). Frequently, the negotiator may not have full decision-making authority. The agent who does hold decision-making authority vis-à-vis the salient issue being negotiated is the *ratifier*. The ratifier may or may not be the lead negotiator. The lead negotiator may have constraints on the extent to which he or she can make a decision and, when those conditions are exceeded, must seek counsel and approval from the ratifier. When in possession of full authority to make a decision, the lead negotiator is also the ratifier.[36]

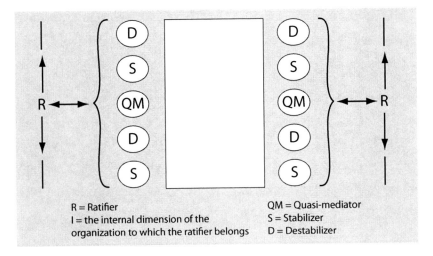

R = Ratifier
I = the internal dimension of the
organization to which the ratifier belongs

QM = Quasi-mediator
S = Stabilizer
D = Destabilizer

FIGURE 10-3. The ratification dimension.

Often, senior officers and/or their counterparts have insufficient time to attend formal negotiations with other organizations, especially when much work and time may yet have to be expended to even approach an agreement. Under these conditions, decisionmakers empower others to make decisions on their behalf.

These empowered negotiators probably won't have unlimited decision-making authority for a number of reasons. One reason might be that the issues addressed have significant political impacts the negotiator might be ill-equipped to know or anticipate, or the issues might be ones for which the ratifier simply will not or cannot delegate decision-making authority. Not all of the decisions that need to be made can be anticipated. This condition creates another consideration for ratifiers withholding full decision-making authority from the negotiator early in the process. The negotiator may have to use the negotiation process to "discover" the decisions that the negotiator and ratifier will have to consider before committing to an agreement.

Sometimes, withholding decision-making authority is a deliberate strategy in the negotiation process to "protect" the negotiator from pressures experienced in the negotiation process. By not giving the negotiator authority to make certain decisions, you can protect him or her from counterparts who have a history of using harsh tactics. It can also help control the pace of the negotiation by providing needed breaks in contact to conduct away-from-the-table moves.

When the lead negotiator and the ratifier decide to agree with a proposal on the table with the other party, the lead negotiator is empowered to close the deal. At this point, he or she can be referred to as the *closer*. Sometimes, the closer is a different person. This person may possess a particular character trait or skill needed to bring the deal to a close. Managing the complexity of all three dimensions is a tough task, especially when moving from bilateral negotiations to multilateral negotiations.

During the Korean War truce talks, two delegations met in 1951 to negotiate an armistice. The United States took the lead in representing the United Nations Command (UNC). Both sides agreed to restrict the issues to military decisions only. The U.S. delegation was initially led by Vice Admiral C. Turner Joy, commander of U.S. Naval Forces Far East, who served in this role until May 1952, when he was replaced by Lieutenant General William K. Harrison. The UNC team also included three American generals/admirals and one Republic of Korea army general. They faced a combined North Korean and Chinese team led by Lieutenant General Nam Il, the senior Korean People's Army/Chinese People's Volunteers (KPA/CPV) delegate. He was the KPA chief of staff and North Korean vice-foreign minister. He was assisted by two North Korean and two Chinese generals/admirals.[37] The U.S. government took sole responsibility for the negotiation outcomes, and the Chinese were the more influential decision-making authority on the other side. UNC instructions came from dispatches from the Joint Chiefs of Staff in Washington.

In this scenario, one can see all three dimensions at work. The horizontal dimension involved the two lead negotiators, Joy (then Harrison) and Nam Il. The internal dimensions pertained to the team compositions on both sides. Given the differences in interests between the Chinese and North Koreans, as well as between the United States and the Republic of Korea, one can imagine the challenges both Joy and Nam Il faced in managing the internal dimension for their teams. In this role they served as the quasi-mediators, managing relations between the stabilizers and destabilizers. Further, they both had to manage the ratification dimension. On the UNC side, President Truman was the "ratifier." He communicated his wishes through the cables sent through the Joint Chiefs. Likewise, Nam Il had to work through his government to the Chinese government for decisions and guidance affecting the Korean/Chinese interests.

Having identified the players and the playing field, a negotiator can begin to understand who is involved, which dimensions are critical to work and in what order, how much latitude the negotiator will be given or should be given, and where and when the negotiation should take place. Further, having analyzed the structure of the negotiation, the negotiator can begin to prepare the substance of the negotiation, knowing who the key participants are or should be and what the likely parameters will be. The three-dimensional framework helps, but it is inadequate to completely prepare for a negotiation.

A NEGOTIATION FRAMEWORK

The Harvard Law School Program on Negotiation created several frameworks to assist negotiators in preparing themselves for the negotiation process. One used by the Harvard Law School, taught in its week-long basic negotiation workshop, puts into practice the principles Fisher and Ury identified in *Getting to Yes,* using a seven-element framework that includes interests, options, objectives, relationships, communications, alternatives, and commitments.[38]

Negotiating *substance* and tending to *relationships* are very important in creating joint solutions to the problem(s) at hand. The diagram in Figure 10-4 depicts the seven elements in relation to each other. This model provides a structure to guide a negotiator's preparation. During negotiation preparation, the negotiator may reorder the elements to maximize preparation time. The major steps to focus on here are (1) determining interests, (2) developing options, (3) making choices, and (4) building relationships.

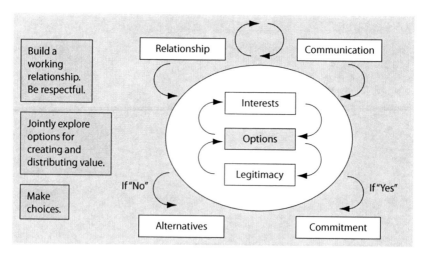

FIGURE 10-4. Harvard University Law School Program on Negotiation Seven-Element Model.

Determining Interests

Determining the *interests* involved in the negotiation on both sides of the table should be the first priority. Why? Assessing the interests you share and where you differ with an opposing party can help you determine whether there is reason to negotiate. If you have nothing in common and you cannot imagine how to reframe the problem in a way that can evoke a common set of interests, you may determine that negotiating with that specific party may not be very productive. On the other hand, determining you have little in common may be more a product of expending too little attention or time preparing for a negotiation. The negotiator should be comprehensive.

Identifying your interests and estimating the other party's may be easier said than done. It can be more complicated in practice. Acknowledging your own interests may require skills that take some practice and definitely require focused mental energy. Further, if you are the quasi-mediator on a negotiation team, gaining consensus and clarity on your side's interests may require considerable collaborative work up front. Perspective-taking aids in identifying the other side's interests. Answering three questions helps to improve your perspective-taking before and during the negotiation:

1. What are the other side's underlying interests, motivations, and needs?

2. How can the other side meet its needs elsewhere?

3. Why is the other person behaving that way?[39]

Assessing the other side's interests, motivations, and needs has some advantages. First, it increases the probability that you will avoid an impasse.

Second, you are more likely to arrive at an innovative solution. Finally, perspective-taking normally leads to creating more value in the negotiation. By assessing how the other side can meet its needs elsewhere or, in other words, determining the other side's BATNA, you better understand its alternatives and possible options, and you protect yourself against the other side's first offer.

At this point, let's discuss first offers. Gerras mentioned anchoring in Chapter 3. Anchors affect the negotiation process, too. *Anchors* are the "base figures from which negotiators add or subtract to judge offers."[40] The emergence of (or purposeful use of) anchors can have a significant effect on the outcome of a negotiation. An anchor "defines the bargaining range."[41] Often the first offer presented in a negotiation has the effect of centering the process on that position or offer. You often gain an advantage if you make the first offer, thereby establishing the range around which the outcome becomes centered. You can also counter another's first offer by making him or her back the offer up using objective criteria. The other party's offer may be outlandish, and you can reestablish a more reasonable range; or the other party's offer may be fair and may advance the process.

Back to perspective-taking: During the negotiation, asking why the person across the table is behaving the way he or she is behaving helps you to overcome *sinister attributions*[42]—attributing negative or sinister motivations to the other side. Remember the discussion on heuristics. You function by using heuristics in daily life. Heuristics are based on assumptions and biases from your life's experiences—assumptions that are often unquestioned. You are therefore prone to make these sinister attributions if you do not keep yourself in check. Perspective-taking can prevent such attributions and avoid a cycle of mistrust that could infect the negotiation process.

Developing Options

The next element concerns your focus on developing a variety of *options* you want to explore jointly in the process. In the preparation phase, you should not constrain yourself; imagining a wide range of unconstrained or innovative possibilities is time well spent. Thinking about what "things" you consider important and not so important is also valuable. The items of lesser importance to you may be valued greatly across the table. These "things" give you more options for a variety of packages in the value-claiming process. You will be better prepared to respond to these options in the value-creating phase if you have thought about them beforehand.

During the negotiation, you must remember to be patient and not jump into substance before building trust and establishing relationships. During the value-creation phase, you should emphasize the difference between inventing and deciding. It is part of managing the other side's expectations. Consider adding complexity to your negotiation. Often adding people, issues, and options creates value. Sometimes generating too many options can negatively affect the negotiation.

In seeking to optimize his or her outcomes, a negotiator may forget the essential focus of the negotiation. The negotiator must keep his or her central focus in mind. Sometimes, the negotiator may lose sight of the central focus because of overconfidence, hubris, or a misguided need to maximize the outcomes received from the negotiation. Rather than seeking to maximize the outcomes in a negotiation, the negotiator might be better served "satisficing," or accepting satisfactory outcomes, instead of searching for optimal ones.

During this phase of your preparation, keep the long view in mind. Take, for example, the case of Duluth, Minnesota's, municipal government, which since 1983 had promised and paid for lifetime health care for its retired employees. The city budgeted on a yearly basis, and when it agreed to this promise, it had no idea how much the benefit would cost the city. In 2002 the city hired an actuary, who projected the cost to the city. The total cost to support past and current city workers amounted to $178 million, more than doubling the city's operating budget. The city is revisiting solutions to avoid the crisis in which it now finds itself.[43] The obvious teaching point in this example is to consider the long-term impacts of potential options *before* you enter the negotiation process. This is an especially critical task at the strategic level, where decisions have far-reaching effects in time, scope, and resources.

Considering the possible legitimate measures that may apply during the value-claiming process is another important step in the preparation phase. First, the negotiator should determine what objective criteria could be relevant to the negotiation. Considering what the market standards are, what legal standards apply, or what fair procedures normally apply to the specific situation can guide the negotiator's preparation. Second, having considered the other side's perspective, the negotiator is also better prepared to assess what objective criteria the other side will likely accept as persuasive. Again, putting yourself in the other party's shoes helps you understand what that party will likely perceive as legitimate, or what you have to reframe to help the party see your criteria as legitimate.

The three elements in the circle in Figure 10-4 that affect the substance of the negotiation—*interests, options,* and *legitimacy*—are connected by arrows flowing up and down and between the elements. They suggest the process is iterative. As new options are generated and new criteria apply, they will have to relate back to the interests both parties bring to the negotiation. But preparing for the substance of the negotiation is just one-third of the process. Building relationships and making choices are the other two-thirds. Let's focus first on making choices, then on building relationships.

Making Choices

Earlier in the chapter, the power of the BATNA was discussed. In preparing for the negotiation, the negotiator must have a strong sense of his or her bottom line. What is the trigger that determines when you are better off *not* negotiating with a party? It is the trigger that prevents you from accepting a bad deal. The stronger your BATNA, the stronger your position at the table and the more value you are likely to extract during the value-claiming process of the negotiation. Therefore, spending time assessing and even improving your BATNA before the negotiation is vital. Finding alternative sources with which you can negotiate solutions improves your BATNA.

Always considering the other side's perspective is good preparation. Estimate its BATNA and how you may affect it in a positive way (i.e., how you may weaken its legitimately). Weakening the other party's BATNA may simply involve discovering information about its alternative sources and offering something it values that you do not value as much. This has the effect of weakening its alternative solutions to your problem. Weakening its BATNA puts you in a more powerful position when you come to the table. Whether you exercise that power and how you exercise it affects trust and the relationship, but that power does give you considerably more flexibility and confidence.

Managing the ratification dimension means you have to consider, before entering the negotiation, what authority you have to make commitments in the negotiation. If you are constrained and need more, you must negotiate with your ratifier first. If you have the authority you want, you must estimate what realistic commitments you can make and/or want to make in the negotiation. Are there commitments the other side can and will live with? Are there commitments your own side can and will live with? You should also consider who the agents that will have to execute the deal are and when they will have to execute it. Finally, trust aside, you should consider what incentives exist for compliance with the agreements. What incentives should be built into the agreement to encourage both sides to meet the obligations they commit to in the solution? These incentives, too, will have to be negotiated.

Building Relationships

Having considered the two elements associated with the negotiation's substance, the negotiator must consider how to build the bonds necessary to negotiate that substance. Assessing who the negotiator across the table will be and the possible dynamics that may result is important. One way to conceptualize the other party is to consider what role the party may assume.

Laurie Weingart categorizes these roles based on the social motives negotiators may use. *Individualists* are motivated to maximize their own outcomes and account for 50 percent of the negotiators she studied. *Co-operators*, those motivated to maximize both parties' outcomes, make up 25 percent of the negotiators studied. *Competitives*, who make up 5 to 10 percent of the field of negotiators, want to win by big margins. They are motivated to maximize the difference between their outcomes and those of their counterparts. Finally, *altruists*, motivated to maximize the other's outcomes, make up the rest of the population.[44]

Dynamics in the negotiation process differ based on the combination of negotiating styles compatible with these roles. For example, when two co-operators negotiate, they may become so fixated on maximizing the other party's outcome that they overlook their own. "Including value-claiming behaviors in their repertoire"[45] helps them to prevent this dynamic from adversely affecting the outcomes. On the other hand, when two individualists interact, they may be too ready to start claiming value before all the value between them is created and put on the table. The way negotiators counter their vulnerabilities is first to recognize their negotiating role preference and then to adopt elements of the other styles to counter their bias. Doing so usually enhances the outcomes in a negotiation.

BUILDING AND MAINTAINING TRUST

Trust is "essential to maintaining a perception of fairness. When we trust someone, we are less likely to suspect ulterior motives, traps, or deception."[46] Since most negotiations are not one-time interactions, establishing and preserving trust in the relationship is important. An agreement is best served if both parties leave the negotiation committed to honoring the agreement. Trust can be established using several techniques: actively listening, being courteous, observing customs or norms, divulging or sharing information, and acknowledging the other's interests in a negotiation. These are but a few methods that enhance trust between negotiating parties.

In discussions about trust and transparency, many frequently ask the question, "Should I tell the truth when negotiating?" Lying or deceiving another party in a negotiation leaves a negotiator vulnerable to being caught, which risks destroying any trust between the parties. Therefore, a good rule to remember is to "tell the truth, nothing but the truth, but not necessarily the whole truth."[47] The point is that you should always provide truthful information, but you should not divulge more than you need to in a negotiation. The other party has some responsibility to ask the right questions in the negotiation process. You are not obliged to give it all to them freely or without effort on their part. That said, the other major point is to always tell the truth to preserve the basis of trust between negotiating parties.

Catherine Tinsley and Kathleen O'Connor claim that "Being candid, honest and forthright about my intentions generates future opportunities for doing business, because . . . your counterparts are going to come to you with deals."[48] Establishing a cooperative reputation for collaborative negotiations creates an optimistic perspective in your partner's eyes and usually leads to better solutions than those achieved with a competitive reputation.[49] A cooperative reputation can be established by building trust, fostered by conceding small wins early in the negotiation relationship. Communicating your interests also helps build a cooperative reputation. Revealing information to others implies you trust them.

The manner in which a message is communicated can have a favorable impact when you emphasize the "how" rather than the "what." Explaining how things occur or how your interests are affected suggests a willingness to be cooperative. To cement your reputation, you must close the deal as a cooperator. One way to positively impress your reputation upon the other party is to offer a post-settlement settlement.

A *post-settlement settlement* occurs when a settlement has been reached, but one or both parties explore additional opportunities for increased gains. The initial negotiation session may have not revealed all the value possible. In a post-settlement settlement, the initial deal reached serves as the new BATNA upon which both parties negotiate to discover more value to be gained. The post-settlement settlement ensures that both parties *optimize* their benefits from the negotiation and leave nothing of value on the table. Care must be taken, however. Sometimes one party can take advantage of another during this phase. But when done properly, a post-settlement settlement can achieve a potentially better result for both parties and can enhance your reputation as a cooperative negotiator.

Trust is important, but only when it is valid. "We often enter into negotiations with an assumption of trust."[50] *Social risk* refers to the "hazards that negotiators face in dealing with an opponent's unpredictable behavior."[51] Managing social risk is yet one more task for the negotiator. Blindly accepting social risk is a dangerous proposition in a negotiation. When negotiating with a person with whom you have had little or no previous contact, you must consider managing trust as one more component of the negotiation. How do you manage trust? First, adjust your initial attitude toward trust. Do not assume the other party is trustworthy. Communicate your need to build trust in the relationship. You can also incorporate risk concerns into the negotiation. One way to manage risk is to devise contingent agreements. When certain conditions are met, the next phase of agreements goes into effect. Assess the trust/risk balance. Are you assuming more risk than the other side? Is trust warranted? Building trust incrementally helps manage this balance.

One of the most delicate conditions to overcome is restoring relationships when trust has been violated. When you have lost trust in the other side, how do you regain it? When you send signals that you do not trust the other person, he or she usually perceives it, and the relationship becomes strained. But it may also be necessary if you have completely lost faith in that person. Therefore, you must carefully weigh the advantages and disadvantages. If it is tolerable, you can chalk it up to experience and approach future negotiations more carefully with this person. On the other hand, you may have to declare your loss of good faith and rebuild trust incrementally, incorporating security controls into future negotiations with this person until trust can be reestablished.[52] You may also have to resort to including a third party to serve as a go-between negotiator or mediator[53] until trust is reestablished.

When lack of trust threatens to derail your negotiation, one solution is to stop arguing about the *structure* of the deal and instead reshape the negotiation *process*. Changing the negotiating process can help mitigate risk and make distrust less of a barrier to deal-making.[54] Negotiators can use one of three strategies: (1) make it safe to reveal reservation values; (2) agree to involve a third party; or (3) delay negotiations until data become available.[55]

Preparing your communication strategy should complement the relationship you intend to establish or preserve. In preparing for the negotiation, you estimated what the other party's interests might be. You should use this assessment to delineate what you want to learn from the other party. You should determine what questions you want to ask to discover that party's interests; how you can use or improve your listening skills to obtain the information you seek; and who will ask specific questions, if you are part of a negotiating team. Having considered what you want to learn from the other party, you should determine what you want to communicate. How do you communicate in a persuasive way? How can you avoid ambiguity in your exchanges to minimize confusion or misunderstanding?

Knowing what you want to communicate to your counterpart and what you want to learn from him or her, you should next consider with whom you will communicate and in what sequence you will communicate. Other questions help. How will you start each meeting off? Does the sequence matter? Should you start with small issues and build confidence and momentum, or should you go with the most difficult issue first, spending most of your initial energy working on it? How does your communication style or scheme complement the relationship you are trying to build with your counterpart? The answers to these questions help define your agenda and communication plan.

What happens if you say something to hurt or offend your counterpart during the negotiation? Knowing when to apologize and doing so can further the negotiation process. Apologizing can improve understanding when it helps explain your motives. Your apology may enhance trust; it can also repair damaged trust. Finally, it may prevent retaliation and improve your outcomes. Research has shown that people are less likely to strike back when the offending party apologizes. It has also shown that outcomes from such a negotiation are better than outcomes where no apology occurred.[56]

PUTTING IT ALL TOGETHER

Let's return to the example of the commander in Iraq who is presented with the issue of providing passage and delivery of humanitarian relief supplies to a stricken village. Let's assume you are the commander. You and the NGO leader have no previous relationship. You are three months into a yearlong deployment. Your best estimate is that you will remain in your assigned area of operation for the remaining time of your deployment. You have received a request to meet with the NGO leader to discuss delivering relief supplies to a village in your assigned area of operation. The village has experienced insurgent attacks recently. It has two main roads that meet in the center of town, where most of the village gathers to meet, share information, and celebrate.

You do not know much about the NGO leader, but you gather what information you can through your staff. You wonder what the best initial approach toward her will be. You could be firm and assertive, emphasizing your control and command of the village area. You could also be cordial and respectful of her role in the overall scheme of things. You decide to use the latter approach because you do not know much about her and what she wants. In your preparation, however, you estimate what you think she and her organization want to accomplish. You put yourself in their shoes and imagine what you would want to have happen if you were in her position. You also assess what you value most in the situation. You determine that although you have some differing *interests*, you also have some in common. You realize that providing assistance to a beleaguered village population will help earn the people's respect and likely gain their cooperation in identifying the insurgents living among them.

Although you want to provide relief to the suffering villagers, you also do not want to create conditions that provide a lucrative target in the village for the insurgents, putting noncombatants at greater risk of attack. The insurgents will undoubtedly use the attack to demonstrate your inability to protect the Iraqi citizens in your charge. You quickly realize that you have a few alternatives. You can prevent the NGOs from delivering the relief supplies entirely, you can cooperate with other NGOs if this one proves unreasonable (but other NGOs would not be able to arrive for another day or two), or you can negotiate with the NGO leader and potentially provide relief more quickly. The other alternatives you have thought of represent your BATNA. If the NGO leader proves unreasonable, aggressive, or unresponsive to addressing your interests, you can walk away from the deal. You are now more confident that you have alternatives that meet your need, and your communication and relationship strategy reinforces your desire to listen to the NGO leader to discover what options might be possible based on what she wants from the negotiation.

During the negotiation, you express your appreciation for the service she provides and recognize the dangers she and her organization risk in providing relief to Iraqis. You acknowledge her role as the leader of her organization and express that, within reason, you want to see if there is a mutually beneficial solution to your joint problem—how to relieve suffering without causing more—while keeping your ultimate goal of winning the villagers' popular support in mind. The NGO leader appears to be relieved and relaxes a bit. You feel that you have established rapport with the NGO leader, at least enough to engage in a productive conversation. You ask her what she wants to accomplish and how she sees you helping. In the course of the discussion, you discover that the NGO leader is under some pressure to deliver large amounts of supplies in a timely fashion to sustain the generous support of her benefactors. If this cannot be done, she risks losing funding and the ability to provide needed humanitarian relief to suffering Iraqis. She says that she would like your support in providing security and that she wants permission to use the main road. She also wants to distribute the supplies in the village's center in order to affect the greatest number of people. She also desires to announce the delivery time and place.

You express your appreciation for her interests but also express your concerns over the risk to the villagers and the NGO personnel. She was previously unaware of the dangers in this particular village and appreciates your concern for her safety and her organization's. You and the NGO leader sit down together and look at your operational map of the village. You identify the routes that have the highest risk and show her the patterns of attack over the past month. The town center has been the heaviest hit in the past three weeks. Without either of you committing to an agreement, you ask her what she would like to have happen and what she could live with. You express your optimal and minimal options. You find that there is overlap, which defines your zone of possible agreement. You discuss a supply point distribution model and a dispersed model option. You discuss various probabilities of attacks based on the distribution model to be used, the routes the supplies will transit, and whether the delivery would be announced. You balance these against the rate and amount of supplies to be disbursed. You also factor in the impact various options would have on your other security operations in the sector. In the process of brainstorming solutions, both of you discover options you had not thought possible.

Having noted all the possible contingencies you can think of, you begin to explore the criteria you would use to determine the best option for both sides. You decide to use a combination of the rate of supply, the time it would take to conduct the mission, and the probabilities of casualties associated with that option to determine the various "best" options.

The objective criteria used, based on the best estimates of two experienced leaders, prove to be a legitimate way to assess the viability of each option. Neither of you commit to the agreement until you are satisfied with the results, but you have a way of claiming value that both of you believe to be fair and reasonable. You both are pleasantly surprised with the resulting outcome. Varying the routes, times, and locations you use; giving a two-hour prior notification to the village leader about the supply distribution location; and conducting these operations over a week permits delivery of several tons of badly needed supplies. The people in the village receive enough food, water, and medicine to sustain them for a month. In addition, a joint media event that captures you and the NGO leader with happy villagers in the background really boosts your strategic communication effort in the sector and makes the NGO leader a real hero in the village and among her peers.

Negotiations can be complex, especially when you have no organizing framework to help you sort out the complexities. With the Army's enhanced peace and security efforts as well as nation-building responsibilities, strategic leaders must be skilled negotiators. Using the principles described in Fisher and Ury's work, applying the seven-element framework to aid your preparation, and using Colosi's three-dimensional framework for managing the interactions should prove helpful in preparing leaders at all levels, especially at the strategic level, to be better negotiators.

NOTES

1. James Sebenius, *Introduction to Negotiation Analysis: Creating and Claiming Value* (Boston: Harvard Business School Press, 1997): 2.

2. *Webster's II: New Riverside University Dictionary* (Boston: Houghton Mifflin, 1994): 737.

3. Ibid.

4. Ibid., 121.

5. Margaret Neale, "Winners (Don't) Take All," *Stanford Executive Briefings* (Mill Valley, CA: Kantola Productions, 2002).

6. Sebenius, 7.

7. Neale, "Winners (Don't) Take All."

8. Roger Fisher and William Ury, *Getting to Yes: Negotiating Agreement without Giving In* (New York: Penguin, 1981): 42–43.

9. Neale, "Winners (Don't) Take All."

10. Fisher and Ury, 42–43.

11. Ibid, 3–14.

12. Sebenius, 3.

13. Ibid.

14. Fisher and Ury, 17–40.

15. Roger Fisher and Daniel Shapiro, *Beyond Reason: Using Emotions as You Negotiate* (New York: Penguin Group, 2005): 115.

16. Ibid.

17. Fisher and Ury, 38–39.

18. Ibid., 41–57.

19. Ibid., 42.

20. Ibid., 48.

21. Ibid., 58–83.

22. Ibid., 84–98.

23. Robert C. Bordone, "Divide the Pie—Without Antagonizing the Other Side," *Negotiation* 9.11 (November 2006): 4–6.

24. Fisher and Ury, 91.

25. Roy J. Lewicki, David M. Saunders, and John W. Minton, *Essentials of Negotiation*, 2nd ed. (Boston: Irwin McGraw-Hill, 1997): 137.

26. Susan Hackley, "Focus Your Negotiations on What Really Matters," *Negotiation* 9.9 (September 2006): 11.

27. Ibid.

28. Sebenius, 4.

29. Adam D. Galinsky and Joe C. Magee, "Power Plays," *Negotiation* 9.7 (July 2006): 1–4.

30. Tom Colosi, *On and Off the Record: Colosi on Negotiation,* 2nd ed. (New York: American Arbitration Association, 2001).

31. Ibid., 20–22.

32. Sebenius, 3.

33. Colosi, 24.

34. Ibid.

35. Ibid., 25.

36. Ibid., 26.

37. Donald W. Boose, "The Korean War Truce Talks: A Study in Conflict Termination," *Parameters* 30.1 (Spring 2000): 102–116.

38. Fisher and Ury, *Getting to Yes.*

39. Adam D. Galinsky, William W. Maddux, and Gillian Ku, "The View from the Other Side of the Table," *Negotiation* 9.3 (March 2006): 1–4.

40. Margaret Neale, *The Stanford Video Guide to Negotiation: The Sluggers Come Home . . . Study Guide* (Mill Valley, CA: Kantola Productions, 2002): 13.

41. Hackley, 10.

42. Max Bazerman, et al., *Environment, Ethics, and Behavior: The Psychology of Environmental Valuation and Degradation* (Lanham, MD: Lexington Books, 1997): 91.

43. Kimberly A. Wade-Benzoni, "Take the Long View," *Negotiation* 9.4 (April 2006): 9–11.

44. Laurie Weingart, "Negotiating Differences: How Contrasting Styles Affect Outcomes," *Negotiation* 10.1 (January 2007): 2.

45. Bordone, 3.

46. Neale, 3.

47. Colosi, 111.

48. Catherine H. Tinsley and Kathleen O'Connor, "Want the Best Deal Possible? Cultivate a Cooperative Reputation," *Negotiation* 9.12 (December 2006): 1.

49. Ibid., 49.

50. Iris Bohnet and Stephan Meier, "How Much Should You Trust?" *Negotiation* 9.3 (March 2006): 7.

51. Ibid., 7–9.

52. Ibid.

53. Lawrence Susskind, "Find More Value at the Bargaining Table," *Negotiation* 10.2 (February 2007): 4–6.

54. Deepak Malhotra, "Dealing with Distrust? Negotiate the Process," *Negotiation* 9.3 (March 2006): 7.

55. Ibid.

56. Maurice E. Schweitzer, "Wise Negotiators Know When to Say 'I'm Sorry,'" *Negotiation* 9.12 (December 2006): 4–9.

11 Leading Change

COL Lee DeRemer, U.S. Air Force

If you don't like change, you're going to like being irrelevant even less.
—General Eric Shinseki, U.S. Army

Consider the topic of change. We live, learn, and serve in a time of unprecedented rates of change, complexity, and interdependence.[1] No life, no organization, and no environment is static. In our volatile, uncertain, and complex world, some strategic leaders impose change on the world around them; others react to change imposed on them and their organizations. Successfully leading change at the strategic level incorporates a host of essential leadership skills: visioning, scanning, and futuring; understanding organizational culture and climate; developing cultural competency; and developing strategic negotiation skills.

Entering a strategic leadership role means leaving the realm of technical competence and clearly defined responsibilities behind. The strategic leader understands that many dynamics act as change drivers in the lives of both individuals and organizations. Change drivers include (1) transnational issues, such as population migration, narcotics trafficking, human smuggling, and terrorism; (2) demographic issues, such as aging populations and changing national heritage; (3) social issues, such as declining numbers of functional high school graduates and changing cultural values; (4) an international order that is simultaneously experiencing both globalization and fragmentation; and (5) the resource implications of all of these challenges. Those who can't broaden their scope of interest to understand the impact of these issues on their organizations' ability to complete their missions effectively are probably not prepared to succeed on the strategic leadership landscape.

STRATEGIC LEADERS AS CHANGE AGENTS

The currency of strategic leaders is influence. The marketplace in which strategic leaders spend this currency is a continuously changing one. Brigadier General David Fastabend's advice in 2004, to "adapt or die," is good counsel as far as it goes. But effective strategic leaders must do so much more. Choosing to adapt is choosing to live. In the "necessary and sufficient" test, this is necessary of course, but it is not sufficient because the strategic leader as change agent wants the organization to not merely survive, but to thrive. Corporate, academic, governmental, and nongovernmental entities aspire to win in the marketplace of ideas, to win in the competition for market share or recognition for excellence. The Department of Defense engages in some of those contests; but to an even larger extent, we desire to win in demonstrating effective stewardship of the shareholders' or taxpayers' investment, and especially to win in the application of combat power and other capabilities on behalf of our nation. This was the essence of General Fastabend's message: We must adapt not merely to survive, but to win, through relevance of—and excellence in— our mission.[2] It's a timeless principle that drives businesses to success or bankruptcy and military forces to victory or defeat.

If we accept the charge that strategic leaders are in the business of change, then we should develop "dealing with change" as a personal core competency. It's worth our effort to improve our ability to **lead change** at the outset, to **manage change** from the initial idea through the many challenges all the way to completion, and to establish a climate and culture that **thrive on change** as a means of individual and group success.

Describing the change process is complicated by the fact that presenting and reading a paper are linear processes, whereas leading and managing change actually occur simultaneously and in alternating cycles of mutually reinforcing activities (Figure 11-1). Therefore, let's acknowledge at the outset that we are describing in linear fashion a change process that is complex and nonlinear.

LEADING CHANGE

Strategic leaders are responsible for creating the future for their organizations.[3] If they do not, external forces will create one. Competitors want market share; in government, other interests want budget share. Even in a perfectly benevolent world, organizational entropy will turn a finely tuned machine into disarray in time, absent sound leadership and management. History generally holds strategic leaders accountable for the effectiveness of organizations. Responsibility implies a rejection of leaving the future to chance and, instead, approaching it through a deliberate, intentional, thoughtful application of the appropriate resources.

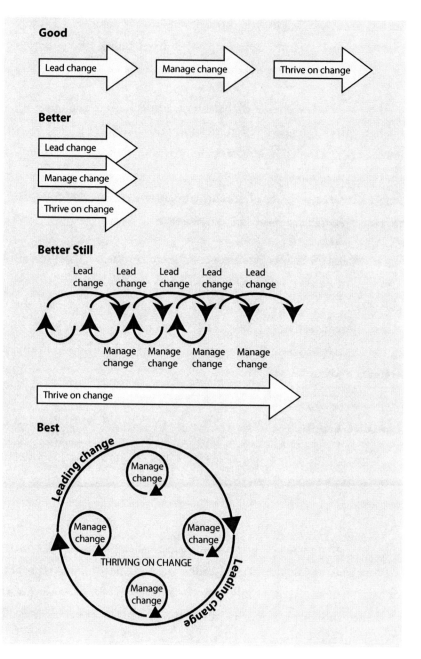

FIGURE 11-1. The change process.

As shown in Chapter 7, change agents have a vision of the future. They have spent some time scanning the environment to improve their situational awareness. They believe they understand the external and internal forces acting on their organizations, and they have some notion of the challenges and opportunities of the near- and long-term future. They're familiar with the literature on "alternative futures," and they might even have participated in "future scenario" exercises.

It is impossible to overstate the power of vision. Peter Senge argues that "few, if any, forces in human affairs are as powerful as shared vision."[4] In 1976 Steve Jobs envisioned "an Apple on every desk," and Apple Computers became a household name. In the 1960s the Boeing corporation determined to design, build, and sell a world-spanning plane, and the 747 airliner was born. In the 1930s Army Air Corps officers' vision of strategic bombing led to the building of B-17s and their planning of the air campaign that helped defeat Hitler and the Empire of Japan in the 1940s. Indeed, it appears that where there is vision, people and organizations flourish.

MANAGING CHANGE

Once a leadership team commits to a vision for the future, it is critical to sustain the momentum created by the launch, the communication effort, and the initial enthusiasm. While the leadership continues to show the way, the daily work must continue. To do so is to manage change at the level of key processes. To give in to the temptation to rely solely on unbridled enthusiasm is to invite devolution toward chaos and loss of focus. In time, enthusiasm alone will not accomplish the mission, whether it is producing and delivering a product, applying combat power, or succeeding in the social mission of a nongovernmental organization.

Managing change, then, is the daily, deliberate work of adapting the functions and processes of an organization to changing realities and the new direction. Whereas leadership defines the shape and direction of an organization, aligns people with the vision, and inspires them to attain the vision, it is management that runs the operation to enable such noble endeavors. Management is no more or less glamorous than leadership; it merely serves a different function. Planning, organizing, leading, and controlling, along with solving problems at the lowest level in the fastest manner, are essential management practices, and they all evolve during periods of change.

John Kotter suggests an eight-stage change process that is generally sequential.[5] Successful transformation efforts tend to go through these overlapping stages. The early stages are leadership-driven. They include establishing a sense of urgency, creating a guiding coalition, developing a vision and strategy, and communicating the vision for change. Although the remaining four stages still rely heavily on the top leaders to set the tone, they clearly are more associated with process management and thus on managing change. The management-heavy stages of the change process include empowering broad-based action, generating short-term wins, consolidating gains to produce more change, and anchoring new approaches in the culture.[6]

Managing change begins with a persistent sense of urgency. The effective vision statement helps generate a sense of urgency. Effective change management sustains the sense of urgency over time—not by instilling a climate of anxiety, but by reducing complacency and continuously reminding the members of the efforts and results still necessary to achieve the vision.[7]

One vital tool in sustaining a broad sense of urgency is an effectively tailored performance feedback system.[8] Many call this tool a series of *metrics*. Metrics that focus an organization on its core competencies are crucial to gauging progress toward achieving the vision and can galvanize an organization into a formidable team. In the midst of change, Secretary of the Army Dr. Francis Harvey's reminder is useful: "Ultimately, the only thing that counts is results—what gets measured gets done."[9]

Choosing appropriate metrics matters greatly. They should be relatively few; if an organization's top management is reviewing more than ten metrics on a recurring basis, the identification process has not been sufficiently selective. Metrics should be easy to gather and easy to communicate; this avoids the necessity to hire new members or divert existing members' attention unnecessarily to provide the organization's performance feedback. Metrics should be presented in a concise, simple manner that members of the organization can understand. They should be chosen based on their centrality to the success of the change effort, not so that various leadership members feel that their function is equally represented.

All members and functions are in fact important, but not all are the same; it is the mission and the change effort that must be the subject of the most frequently recurring metric appraisals. Less-frequent metric presentations should be tailored to specific functional areas, but these should not be mistaken for the metrics' effectiveness in the unit's core competencies and progress toward the vision.

As the change process reaches the empowerment stage, leaders support managers' efforts to remove obstacles, whether they are short-term problems that are wasting resources or antiquated systems or reporting structures that undermine the vision for change.[10] Another useful way to view this approach is to build a disciplined culture of freedom and responsibility. Highly functioning teams are composed of members who don't see their roles as jobs; rather, they see (and feel) responsibility. This builds the sense of ownership and commitment referred to earlier. These "trusted risk takers" show initiative, feel welcome offering innovative solutions that challenge the status quo, and are willing to cross boundaries to make improvements.[11]

Generating short-term wins and consolidating gains are two closely linked stages in the management of change. While the overall change process is somewhat linear, these two stages—once reached—are a continuous cycle that occurs within the larger picture. Planning and creating initial performance improvements demonstrate that progress is possible and desirable. Visible, meaningful recognition of those who accomplished the wins demonstrates that the leadership is serious. The increased credibility and buy-in makes this the right time to change the remaining systems, structures, and policies that don't match the new vision. There are usually many, and some will be protected by functional owners for reasons of selfishness and fear of uncertainty. Nevertheless, systems oriented to an irrelevant past need to be changed. Finally, nothing speaks louder than decisions on who is hired, promoted, and selected for leadership development programs.[12] This commitment of money, status, and responsibility to specifically identified members committed to the change vision is the most powerful and visible statement the senior leadership can make.

The final stage in the change process is anchoring the new approaches to the mission in the culture. Permanently changing culture means sustaining the production performance or mission accomplishment; sustaining the improved leadership of the early days of the change effort; and sustaining the improved management through continuous attention to discipline and the relevance of key processes.[13] Permanently changing culture means changing attitudes toward the company and philosophies of what it means to be a member of the team.

If leaders and managers can work together to change an organization's culture, they can pull the most effective lever of change. Indeed, Edgar H. Schein argues that "the unique and essential function of leadership is the manipulation of culture."[14] He adds that it is also the most difficult challenge. It requires persistence, patience, and insight into the many components and motivations that constitute the culture. Leaders and managers too under-appreciate the power of culture in their organizations. This mistake leads to unachievable visions, poorly aligned teams, and ill-drafted long-range plans that don't address required changes in the organizational culture.

A second mistake is to confuse culture with climate, values, and business philosophies. In fact, however, culture operates one level below these important concepts and largely *determines* them. Therefore, understanding culture is the key to knowing which climate, values, and philosophies are supportable.[15] Understanding an organization's culture is also the most important key to implementing a change vision.

A third mistake is to ignore culture altogether. It is the naïve leader who either takes no interest in or thinks he or she has no way to influence culture. Such a leader forfeits the change opportunity that only he or she has the chance to seize.

There is a better way: The strategic leader should be inquisitive enough to understand his or her culture, courageous enough to embrace the opportunity to influence it, and insightful enough to employ proven techniques to embed the change vision into the culture. *Embedded* change is essential to achieving the lasting change articulated in the vision statement.

EMBEDDING AND REINFORCEMENT MECHANISMS

Leaders and managers can spur lasting culture change through primary embedding mechanisms and secondary reinforcement mechanisms, as discussed in Chapter 8. The effectiveness of both categories depends on (1) their power, (2) the explicitness of their message, and (3) their intentionality.[16]

The most powerful ***primary embedding mechanisms*** are (1) what leaders watch; (2) how leaders react; (3) how leaders teach; (4) how leaders reward; and (5) who leaders recruit and promote.[17]

What Leaders Watch

This is yet another plea to align top leadership's metrics or business indicators with key processes. The items leaders watch, measure, and control serve as a focusing effort and a forcing function to bring accountability to managers and transparency to key processes at regular intervals. They provide the opportunity to make deliberate and informed course corrections to achieve the vision. Frequent minor adjustments usually avert the need for infrequent but major changes in course, which can reduce commitment to the vision and confidence in the leadership. These metrics should be part of recurring internal and external communication. Individual successes and positive organizational trends should be celebrated and rewarded, and they should drive adjustments to organizational strategy.

Leaders and managers send other powerful signals within the culture. The self-aware leader recognizes that even seemingly casual remarks and questions geared toward certain performance areas will change behavior because these comments signal the leader's priorities. In a mature culture, subordinates also interpret what the leadership does *not* respond to. In very little time, gainfully employed people with full schedules will reduce attention given to tasks that don't appear to be valued when they have other, more highly valued tasks competing for their time.

How Leaders React

When a crisis confronts an organization, its leaders' reaction often converts the experience into a strategic decision, for better or worse. Leader reactions create new norms, values, and processes. They reveal important personal traits about the strategic leader and underlying assumptions about how the organization works. Crises also have the potential to change culture because of the emotional intensity of the risk the organization and members have experienced together.[18] Crisis response—for a strategic leader, for a top management team, and for an organization—can be a crucible experience, out of which emerges a committed team with a strong bond and an unflinching commitment to the vision.

How Leaders Teach

Strategic leaders are in the business of developing people. The techniques are as varied as leadership styles, but one commonality is crucial: intentionality. Strategic leaders are constantly modeling, teaching, or coaching—even if they are unaware of it. At work, at home, and socially, what strategic leaders do and don't do communicates to lower layers of leadership what the expected norms of behavior are. If they pursue continuous learning, their subordinates will enroll in master's degree or technical associate's degree programs. If they work 80-hour weeks, the culture will reflect that expectation. If they are callous toward their associates, their subordinates will feel welcome to conduct themselves in the same way, gossiping about peers and demeaning subordinates. If they know the names of the janitor and the fellow who mows the lawn, others will consider that this might be an expectation—and develop a sense of community.

If strategic leaders don't take vacation time or military leave (because they are "just too important to the organization or the mission"), two truths will emerge. First, either they have an unrealistic understanding of their own importance to the organization, or they have cultivated an unhealthy dependence upon themselves in that organization. Second, they are raising a generation of leaders who will shortchange themselves and their families out of the valuable recharging time that vacation or leave affords.

How Leaders Reward

Effective strategic leaders and managers link rewards to results and behavior that reflect their vision, priorities, and values and the culture they seek to reinforce or create. These rewards appear in the form of pay raises, job promotions, rank promotions in military organizations, or performance appraisals that can be the source document for competitive selection processes.[19]

Schein reminds us that rewards differentiate between *espoused values* and *actual values*. Leaders and managers espouse, publish, and demand certain behaviors throughout their tenure. In some companies and organizations, these are not the real values. In these organizations, the fact that there is a difference between espoused and actual values reveals a disconnect between a rewards program offered as a formality and a pay raise or promotion system based on performance. This is dangerous territory, and leaders should avoid it by trying to constantly align reward systems with what the culture is demonstrating as the true values, and vice versa.[20]

Who Leaders Recruit and Promote

Leaders should recognize that culture also perpetuates itself through the recruitment and promotion of "like-minded" people. Consequently, leaders should understand that to promote change, they should consider finding talent and creativity within a person who has values conducive to the change. Nevertheless, leaders will also need people whose attitudes and values he or she seeks to have emulated by new hires as the leader builds a new team for the future.[21]

Promotions give an even clearer picture. Senior leadership should not promote on the basis of those who have "earned it based on past performance," but on the basis of both past performance *and* a desire to commit that performance and potential to achieving the top management team's vision for the future.

Removing subordinate leaders from positions of responsibility seems to be a more delicate matter, but it is no less important. When a strategic leader makes the difficult decision to fire a subordinate leader for failure to perform or failure to commit to the leadership team, the leader is typically 6- to 12-months late, and the organization has been waiting months for the leader to do it. Finally making this decision speaks volumes to the organization about the leader's commitment to the members and to the vision over any personal loyalties to the individual being released or to the system that erred in placing or leaving the subordinate leader in the position beyond his or her effective service.

The primary embedding mechanisms described above are supported by ***secondary reinforcing mechanisms***. These include (1) organizational design and structure; (2) organizational systems and procedures; (3) physical layout; (4) stories, legends, myths, and parables about important events and people; and (5) formal statements of organizational philosophy, creeds, charters, and visions.[22]

These secondary reinforcing mechanisms work only if they are consistent with the primary embedding mechanisms, since those embedding mechanisms affect the culture so deeply. Working together, these physical objects—structures, systems, buildings, stories, and vision statements—can reinforce the embedding mechanisms to make lasting change. However, if the embedding and reinforcing mechanisms are inconsistent, the reinforcing mechanisms will be ineffective and often counterproductive because this inconsistency will reveal differences between espoused and actual values and will cost the leadership precious credibility.[23] Another useful way to think about this phenomenon is to picture an iceberg. The 10 percent above the water line represents the surface changes of reinforcing mechanisms. These are usually the realm of management. The 90 percent below the water line represents the deeply rooted culture change that is so difficult to achieve. This is primarily the responsibility of leadership, with daily reinforcement at the management level.

Having considered the eight steps of organizational change—from communicating a sense of urgency and casting a vision for change to effecting long-term change to the organization's culture—it is time to consider how to repeat this cycle of change . . . effectively and indefinitely.

THRIVING ON CHANGE

Taking an organization through a transforming vision means permanent change—in the personnel policies and in attitudes toward the mission, the customer, and each other—so that there is no regression to the former level of performance or mindset. To discuss this changed culture, we must transition from leading change and managing change to thriving on change. Companies, military units, and nongovernmental organizations that thrive on change experience lasting change and greater success. How do they do it? By resisting complacency, avoiding impediments to change, exhibiting positive leadership, being a learning organization, hiring the right people first, focusing on strengths, developing agility and resiliency, and leading humbly.

Resisting Complacency

First, such companies, military units, and nongovernmental organizations don't accept complacency. They don't allow themselves to become comfortable. In May 2001, Secretary of Defense Donald Rumsfeld identified the danger of allowing such a climate to persist when he said, "When the people say, 'but we're doing fine,' that's exactly when institutions suffer. If they think things are going good, and they relax and don't recognize the changes taking place in the world, they tend to fail."[24] Instead of sliding backward from "good" to "irrelevant," organizations that thrive on change are prepared to make the personal sacrifices and investment in the future to jump forward from "good" to "great."[25]

Avoiding Impediments to Change

Second, organizations that thrive on change have matured enough to have a culture and teamwork that resist negative systemic response to change efforts. One such negative systemic response is pervasive bureaucratic inertia that is so powerful as to impede change or slow it to evolutionary change at best, ruling out the possibility of the revolutionary change achieved by only the top corporations or nonprofit organizations.[26]

A second systemic hurdle to change is a cultural complacency that lacks a sense of urgency, as alluded to in Secretary Rumsfeld's quote above.[27]

A third impediment to change is the simple cultural refusal to change, with the attitude that "this too shall pass." It is rarely stated explicitly, but such an organization has key individuals who expect the vision for change—and probably its sponsor/leader—to move on before the organization really has to commit to it. These informal leaders plan to "wait out the boss."[28] Military units are especially vulnerable to this attitude because of frequent rotations of officer leadership.

A fourth negative systemic response to change is to employ diversionary tactics. Such tactics include diverting the effort by creating a crisis that must be addressed first, or arguing that the timing is not right and that the leadership team should delay the change initiative until the timing is better. It is common to argue for delay with the justification that there are too many things on the agenda already. Subsets of this complaint include the plea that people are already stretched to the limit, that there are too many other problems left over from the last fiscal year or planning cycle, or that the vision for change will divert the organization from "the real work."[29]

The final negative systemic response is to deny the leader the follower-ship the leader needs.[30] At high levels of responsibility, after decades of personal growth and multiple leadership roles, some people stop growing and stop following. They are tired of growth, tired of teamwork, or insistent on following only their own agenda. These subordinate leaders have somehow risen a few levels above their last position of positive impact and are cancerous to the change vision. Younger people who don't understand the importance of followership are almost always simply the victims of inadequate training in this principle and inadequate exposure to good leadership. Unfortunately, they are easy prey for more senior opponents to change. Successive military service chiefs have emphasized the symbiotic relationship between leader and follower;[31] however, followership is still under-appreciated as a prerequisite for positive change.

Exhibiting Positive Leadership

Organizations that thrive on change reflect a positive leadership style, an affirming climate, an enthusiastic workforce, and a leadership philosophy that treats each member of the team as a volunteer.[32] With just a little analysis, we can see the importance of recognizing the voluntary nature of our organizations, from top management to the youngest hourly wage earner. The U.S. economy has been so strong for so long that both a professional force and a labor force can relocate with ease. Corporations, government agencies, nonprofit organizations, and military services therefore spend time, energy, and money to retain the talented members in whom they have invested so heavily. This trend is increasing in importance as organizations continue to downsize labor they can do without and as the percentage of functionally incompetent adults rises.

Being a Learning Organization

This is both a personal and a team imperative. Through continuous learning, individuals and organizations re-create themselves. The learning organization continually expands its capacity to create its future. Such organizations aren't satisfied to merely survive; they want to thrive. Thus, they engage in what Senge calls "adaptive learning" and "generative learning." The learning organization is populated by people with the discipline of personal mastery, who understand the systems model of interdependent organizations and processes, who share a common vision of the future, and who embrace team learning.[33]

Hiring the Right People First

Any organization can stumble through a few quarters and fail. Most organizations can survive for a few years on average mission performance and with dysfunctional processes before becoming bankrupt or irrelevant. A few make it from "good" to "great" and truly thrive in periods of change. Jim Collins reminds us that one common trait among these last organizations is that they place their highest priority on hiring the right people. This "first who, then what" mindset says that building the right leadership team is even more important than identifying what, specifically, that leadership will lead.[34]

This is an emerging truth for corporate leadership. For military organizations, in which leaders are assigned to join a team or to lead a team, the leaders often are not in position long enough to build their own team, even if they have the authority to do so. Still, understanding the primacy of getting the right leadership team in place can help leaders who don't choose their leadership team to anticipate some of the dynamics likely to occur as their existing team bonds through shared experiences.

Focusing on Strengths

For decades, the prevailing wisdom taught that leaders and managers needed to develop their weaknesses into strengths. This philosophy held that such efforts would broaden a person's skill set to better prepare the person for leadership responsibilities at higher levels. Emerging research supports a different conclusion. In top-performing organizations, leaders and managers are hired for specific gifts and exceptional interpersonal skills. Research indicates that focusing on strengthening weak areas distracts gifted individuals from developing in areas in which others already excel, and they then sacrifice the opportunity to further develop their natural strengths and pursue their passions. By breaking this older rule of leader development, companies are finding skills in individual leaders and allowing individual excellence to propel teams to new levels of performance.[35]

Developing Agility and Resiliency

Individuals and teams need agility to remain relevant and successful in a rapidly changing world. Agile leaders can lead a team through change quickly, in order to take advantage of emerging trends and increase market share. Agile followers and teams are necessary to make such a leader's vision a reality. Resiliency addresses the reality that even the best leaders and teams are surprised from time to time. Resilient leaders and teams recover more quickly than competitors do when surprised by change drivers that negatively affect their ability to complete their mission. They adjust their operating scheme and redirect resources more quickly and more effectively than others do.[36]

In a study of current trends and future possibilities, the American Management Association studied hundreds of companies. The AMA interviewed ten global companies known for their ability and resiliency in the face of change. The association identified common, achievable traits of high-performing companies that can apply not only to business but also to government agencies, nongovernmental organizations, and military organizations. They fall within five broad categories. High-performing organizations (1) anticipate change, (2) generate confidence, (3) initiate action, (4) liberate thinking, (5) and continually evaluate results.

Forty-six percent of high-performing companies not only anticipate change but also plan for in it in advance. Twenty percent of these actually induce change by forcing others to react to them. In anticipating change, agile leaders are active listeners; they encourage open dialogue and constantly reinforce the organization's core values through words, policy decisions, and personal example. Agile teams are customer-centric, always scanning the environment, and they are never complacent.

To generate confidence, agile leaders are effective communicators, actively engaged with multiple levels of the organization and consistently positive about the future. They are artful builders of organizational culture through the use of history and metaphors. Agile teams are committed to the vision, take ownership of their responsibilities, and are visibly confident in their leadership.

To initiate action, agile leaders are decisive. They create a culture and expectation of action-oriented teams and functions by emphasizing initiative, creativity, responsibility, and accountability. Their agile teams have responsive, effective key processes to get things *done*, not just "started," by making decisions at the lowest appropriate level and working across functional lines to solve problems.

To liberate thinking, agile leaders acknowledge that they don't have all the answers, ask appropriate questions, listen well, give credit liberally, and celebrate success while simultaneously presenting the team with the next challenge. With the exception of moral failure, they generally view *failure* as another term for *learning*. Agile teams innovate at all levels, continuously improve both product and processes, and involve customers regularly.

To evaluate results, agile leaders set fair goals and give honest, regular feedback. They don't dodge difficult issues or decisions. They quickly see root causes of poor performance or dysfunctional processes and effectively build teams to address them. Finally, agile leaders provide the resources necessary to implement solutions. Agile teams focus efforts on measured activity, anticipate when metrics should change, and are more interested in product and process improvement than they are in receiving personal accolades.[37]

Resilience for leaders and teams applies when the organization experiences significant failure or surprise. A resilient organization with the healthy five-part agility model described above has some key strengths that it fully expects to have to employ. Its leadership, culture, and processes are capable of "emergency response." While its decision-making cycle can be fast or deliberately slow, depending on the context, it is *capable* of being accelerated to meet the challenges posed by an emergency response. The entire organization is more committed to the organization's long-term health than its members are to their short-term personal interest. The result is a team focus that results in even stronger trust, confidence, and commitment when the organization emerges from a crisis.[38]

Leading Humbly

This is a radically countercultural mindset. However, Collins argues persuasively that the most effective transformational leaders—those he calls "level 5 leaders" in *Good to Great*—have an extraordinarily high degree of personal humility. It's not that they lack ambition; to the contrary, these men and women are driven to the point of sometimes being "consumed" by their vision. They are also very strong-willed people, but this is not the same as being stubborn. Note this study in duality: Their ambition, willpower, and unwavering resolve are directed toward the institution—the mission and the vision—and are *not* for self-aggrandizement. They genuinely place the interests of their people above their own interests.[39]

A strategic leader's role is not to "make the trains run on time." It is to "lay new track," to drive the organization to higher levels of performance always and to chart a new direction when appropriate. The strategic leader who can excel in this central role as change agent has the opportunity to greatly improve organizations and lives.

Choosing to reach for this level of performance has implications for leaders, managers, and organizations. The leader must seek to manage (read: change) culture. The leader must have the emotional strength, depth of vision, self-awareness, and objectivity necessary to change culture. Finally, management processes and leadership decisions must protect those who are so creative and innovative that they occasionally make leadership uncomfortable, to promote the culture of agility and resiliency described earlier.[40]

Such leaders, managers, and teams embrace their vision, understand their organization's strategic situation, and know themselves. They can create organizations that effectively lead change and manage change in a simultaneous and mutually reinforcing effort, with synergistic results. Indeed, one might even conclude that they *thrive* on change.

NOTES

1. Peter M. Senge, *The Fifth Discipline* (New York: Currency and Doubleday, 1990): 68–74.

2. David A. Fastabend and Robert H. Simpson, *Adapt or Die* (Washington, D.C.: Department of the Army, 2004): 2.

3. Gordon R. Sullivan and Michael V. Harper, *Hope Is Not a Method* (New York: Broadway Books, 1996): 44.

4. Senge, 206.

5. John P. Kotter, "Why Transformation Efforts Fail," *Harvard Business Review* (March–April 1995): 61.

6. Ibid.

7. John P. Kotter, *Leading Change* (Boston: Harvard Business School Press, 1996): 162.

8. Ibid.

9. Francis J. Harvey, *Soldier Magazine* interview (March 2005): 13.

10. Kotter, "Why Transformation Efforts Fail," 61.

11. Jim Collins, *Good to Great* (New York: Harper Collins, 2001): 124–126.

12. Kotter, "Why Transformation Efforts Fail," 61.

13. Ibid.

14. Edgar H. Schein, *Organizational Culture and Leadership* (San Francisco: Jossey-Bass, 1996): 317.

15. Ibid., 314.

16. Ibid., 224.

17. Ibid., 224–225.

18. Ibid., 230.

19. Carl Builder, "Can We Talk?" RAND Corporation briefing on culture to USAF Long Range Planning Board of Directors, Washington, D.C., 18 April 1996.

20. Schein, 233–235.

21. Ibid., 235.

22. Ibid., 237.

23. Ibid.

24. Donald Rumsfeld, *The New York Times* interview, 16 May 2001.

25. Collins, 1–16.

26. Warner W. Burke, *Organization Change* (Thousand Oaks, CA: Sage Publications, Inc., 2002): 111.

27. Ibid., 111–112.

28. Ibid., 112.

29. Ibid.

30. Ibid., 113.

31. John J. Jumper, *Leadership and Force Development* (Washington, D.C.: Department of the Air Force, 18 February 2006): 7.

32. Jerry White, Address to Altus Air Force Base (Altus Air Force Base, Oklahoma, 9 February 2001).

33. Senge, 3–16.

34. Collins, 41–49.

35. Marcus Buckingham and Curt Coffman, *First, Break All the Rules* (New York: Simon & Schuster, 1999): 141–176.

36. American Management Association, *Agility and Resilience in the Face of Continuous Change*, a webinar produced by amanet.org, 15 November 2006.

37. Ibid.

38. Ibid.

39. Collins, 17–40.

40. Schein, 326.

PART IV

Gettysburg:
A Case Study in
Strategic Leadership

12 Gettysburg: A Case Study in Strategic Leadership

COL Mark Eshelman, U.S. Army, and
COL James Oman, U.S. Army

Located 30 miles south of the U.S. Army War College is the Gettysburg battlefield. As a pivotal battle in the American Civil War—the war that affirmed our identity as a united nation—the battle of Gettysburg has particular significance for our institution, which is charged with educating and developing strategic leaders. As military professionals, many of our staff and faculty have combat experience and can identify with those who fought at Gettysburg in 1863. What happened at Gettysburg is part of our heritage, and when we remember and use it to develop strategic leaders, we honor those who fought and died there.

This chapter addresses many of the teaching points we offer to our students and the visitors to whom we give the Gettysburg staff ride. Since its founding in the early 20th century, the Army War College has conducted staff rides at the Gettysburg battlefield. The Gettysburg campaign provides insights into the theory and practice of war, strategy, and leadership.

What is a staff ride? Typically, an Army War College historian leads a small group of 20 to 30 participants on a walk through the battlefield. On terrain where the battle took place, our historian discusses what happened, why it happened, and how. We use the history of Gettysburg as a means to explore the role of leadership and to synthesize and evaluate our teaching, much as business schools use the case study.

As Army War College senior battlefield historian Len Fullenkamp has said, what we choose to think about on the battlefield determines the value of the time spent there. While much of the historic detail is interesting and many of the vignettes make the trip enjoyable, many are of little substantive importance to educating senior leaders because they focus on nineteenth-century tactical-level historical lessons. From a leader development perspective, much of what we choose to consider relates to time-tested and enduring theoretical principles that derive from the unchanging aspects of human nature.

Up to now, this book has described various aspects of contemporary strategic leadership theory and practice. We now consider the relationship between that theory and practical application through the historic lens of what took place at Gettysburg in July 1863. We focus on how those leaders dealt with the infinitely complex and dynamic environment of battle in order to draw lessons that future strategic leaders might find useful.

BATTLE OVERVIEW

The staff ride begins with an overview of the campaign's strategic context. Not only does it familiarize participants with the events leading up to the battle of Gettysburg but, more important, it also provides a contextual lens that can be used to frame discussion on the battlefield. One cannot think of the leadership decisions made at Gettysburg in isolation from the strategic context of the war. The overview also gets participants thinking leadership and strategy, thus preparing them to engage in dialogue both on the battlefield and later in the classroom.

The battle of Gettysburg took place two years into the American Civil War—a war that, at the time, was essentially at a strategic stalemate. For the most part, the Confederacy had retained the initiative in the eastern theater while the Union was more offensively minded in the west. The overall southern strategy was to remain on a strategic defensive, defending forward in an effort to wear down the Union, drain northern resolve, and hopefully bring a foreign ally into the war. On the other hand, the Union was conducting a strategic offensive focused on the military defeat of the Confederate armies, the maintenance of an effective naval blockade, and on supporting efforts to divide the Confederacy along the Mississippi River.

President Abraham Lincoln consistently sought defeat of the Confederate army despite enduring a succession of unsuccessful commanders. He intuitively understood the need to attack and destroy the southern army. As a center of gravity, the loss of the Confederate army would ultimately lead to its defeat. By the summer of 1863, Lincoln had chosen Major General George Meade to become the fifth and final commander of the Army of the Potomac. When considering Meade's success at Gettysburg, and criticism of him in its aftermath, we should remember that he had been in command only three days when he fought one of the most important battles in American history. Meade was still forming his staff, yet he would perform well. Later, in the spring of 1864, Lieutenant General Ulysses S. Grant would ably fill the position of commander in chief of the Union army and finally provide Lincoln a commander who would relentlessly take the attack to the Confederate army.[1] But it was Meade who commanded the Union army during those three fateful days in early July of 1863.

It is important to consider why General Robert E. Lee, Commanding General of the Army of Northern Virginia, brought his army north to eventually fight at Gettysburg. The campaign was not Lee's first attack north; he had conducted limited offensives earlier in the conflict as a means to retain initiative and keep the damages of war off southern soil. Prior to July 1863, Federal victories had been few and far between, public support of the war was waning, and it seemed likely that Lincoln's upcoming reelection bid would fail. Lee thought a decisive win in Union territory would further erode northern morale and perhaps force a negotiated settlement. By 1863 it was also becoming more difficult for Lee to feed and equip his army on southern land that had been fought over for more than two years. In the rich farmland of Pennsylvania, his army could forage on northern supplies. Finally, even though it was unlikely that France or England would enter the war as Confederate allies following Lincoln's Emancipation Proclamation, there may have been some hope of that outcome should Lee carry the day in Pennsylvania.[2]

Although these factors influenced Lee's desire to take the war into Pennsylvania, there was disagreement among Confederate leaders about whether a northern offensive was the best course of action. Lee argued for an offensive in the East, avoiding suggestions from President Jefferson Davis to shift forces from the Army of Northern Virginia to reinforce Confederate armies in Tennessee or Mississippi.[3] The disagreement highlights the importance of strategic leader negotiation. Operationally, Lee argued for the invasion of Maryland and Pennsylvania, maneuvering in south-central Pennsylvania to capture the state capital, Harrisburg. That would cut the Union line of communication and supply down the Susquehanna

River and threaten Washington, Baltimore, and Philadelphia to force an engagement with the Army of the Potomac. He would fight a tactical battle against the Federals if he could fight it on favorable terms.[4]

There were problems within Lee's army, however. The Confederate army's organizational structure proved to be a significant factor in the battle. Lee's aggressive, capable, and reliable corps commander, General Thomas "Stonewall" Jackson, had been killed at the battle of Chancellorsville just two months before Gettysburg. The loss of Jackson and Lee's struggle to identify capable commanders led Lee to reorganize his army from two very large corps into three smaller corps. Richard Ewell was promoted and given command of Jackson's Second Corps, and A.P. Hill was also promoted and given command of the newly formed Third Corps. Working with two generals new to the responsibilities of corps command affected Lee's decisions at Gettysburg. It is a leadership issue we carefully consider.

Figure 12-1 shows a map of the primary points of interest on the Gettysburg battlefield trip.

DAY 1—MCPHERSON'S RIDGE AND THE REYNOLDS STATUE

The first stop on a typical Gettysburg staff ride is at the equestrian statue of Major General John Reynolds on the Chambersburg Pike just outside the village of Gettysburg. It is here that Brigadier General John Buford, commanding a division of Union cavalry, deployed his force midday on June 30, 1863. Shortly thereafter he made contact with elements of the Confederate army under the command of Major General Henry Heth, which quickly withdrew. The significance of this stop centers on the subsequent actions of Buford and Reynolds, the First Corps commander. Buford was able to fuse intelligence reports from his scouts, local citizens, and his own observa-

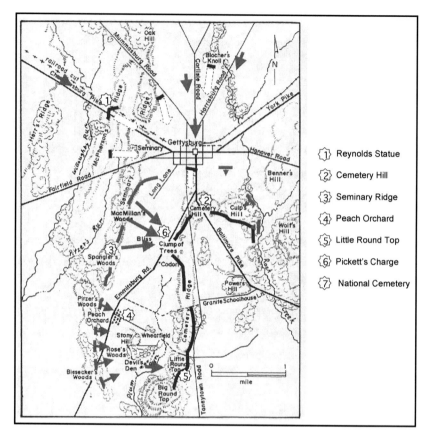

FIGURE 12-1. Gettysburg battlefield.

tions to determine a fairly accurate picture of the Confederate force to his front, predicting they would attack in strength the next morning. Buford is also credited with appreciating the value of the terrain and recommending that reinforcements be brought forward rapidly so a battle could be fought on ground favorable to the Union. Reynolds agreed and passed this assessment on to Meade, who immediately directed the Army of the Potomac to concentrate at Gettysburg.

From a leadership point of view, what we discuss here sets the stage for the rest of the staff ride. We emphasize from the beginning of the ride that senior commanders must be comfortable making or at least willing to make decisions with incomplete information in a volatile, uncertain, complex, and ambiguous (VUCA) environment. Buford was able to function in a state of uncertainty and ambiguity. He synthesized the incomplete information available to him, analyzed it, and was willing to make a timely decision to recommend that the Union army fight at Gettysburg.

Another important aspect of this engagement concerns the tactics employed by Buford's cavalry. Early in the war, Burford gained an appreciation for how technology, particularly increasing weapons lethality, would change cavalry tactics. Buford was realistic and adaptable, and he realized that fighting dismounted offered many tactical advantages. At Brandy Station, he had dismounted most of his division to cooperate with an infantry brigade.[5] To improve force survivability, Buford sought to have "dragoon tactics" adopted by cavalry throughout the army. He was unsuccessful but nonetheless trained and fought his own division using those tactics. Several of our historians think that had any other cavalry unit been on McPherson's Ridge July 1, it would have been unable to delay the Confederates.

Another leadership challenge is never to lose perspective on the big picture. An example is Heth's and Hill's actions following the June 30 excursion into Gettysburg. They received reports of contact with elements of the Army of the Potomac. Both men were skeptical, and Heth refused to believe that any portion of the Union army was nearby. This resulted in his request to Hill (who approved it on the spot and forwarded the information to Lee) to march on Gettysburg the next morning, not understanding that pushing ahead would decisively engage Lee's army. Heth's attack the next morning failed to overcome Buford's cavalry quickly, and it decisively committed the Confederate army.

Heth is widely believed to have lost perspective, at least in part because of a strong desire to obtain supplies reportedly available in Gettysburg. It is impossible to know what Heth was thinking and important to acknowledge that his immediate superior, Hill, certainly influenced the outcome. It is, however, plausible to conclude that Heth ignored information that did not support a preconceived course of action he was determined to act upon. Edwin Coddington writes that an observer at the time thought a "spirit of unbelief" clouded the thinking of most, if not all, of the officers in Hill's corps, leaving them unprepared for the battle that followed.[6] The lesson for leaders is not to get caught up in the interesting or urgent events of the moment, but to remain focused on important matters and the overall purpose of an operation.

DAY 1—CEMETERY HILL

One of the most significant leadership considerations of the staff ride involves the actions that took place on Cemetery Hill late on the first day of the battle. Confederate forces attacking from the north of town began to roll up the Union line that had formed during the late morning and early afternoon as a result of Buford's delaying action. Confederate General Ewell arrived on the battlefield with his Second Corps as Union forces were withdrawing through the village. As Federal forces were organizing a defensive line from Culp's Hill to Cemetery Hill and down Cemetery Ridge to the south, General Lee was observing from Seminary Ridge west of town. Lee concluded that there was an opportunity to seize Cemetery Hill before Union forces could organize themselves. He gave Ewell a discretionary order to take Cemetery Hill "if he found it practicable" but not to become decisively engaged until the rest of the army could be concentrated.[7] Ewell chose not to attack, a decision that historians have debated and soldiers have studied ever since. At the Army War College, we consider several points of view and in conclusion suggest that these actions demonstrate the impact of the loss of Stonewall Jackson vis-à-vis the team-building role of a strategic leader.

Comparing Ewell and Jackson, we consider how the personalities of leaders matter. Lee was accustomed to Jackson's aggressive interpretation of his orders. We make the point that if Jackson had received an order to do something "if practicable," he would have gone to extraordinary lengths to find a way to accomplish the mission, essentially interpreting "if practicable" to mean "if possible." Those words meant something very different to Ewell; as a division commander under Jackson, Ewell was accustomed to detailed and specific orders and was held strictly accountable for closely following them. In his first campaign as a corps commander, Lee gave Ewell less detailed guidance—what we might call "mission orders" today, where a subordinate is told what needs to be done but is not told how to do it. Ewell may not have understood the nature of his new relationship with Lee or grasped the need for more flexibility in the discharge of his duties and a consequent need to demonstrate increased initiative and aggressiveness.

We also consider, in the wake of Lee's reorganization of the army, that Ewell was new to corps command and that the transition from division to corps command during the Civil War was particularly difficult. A division commander had fairly decent situation awareness. He could see most, if not all, of his forces and the battlefield affecting his fight. Not so with a corps commander, who required new skills: an ability to envision the battlefield and the confidence to intuitively make decisions amid much greater uncertainty. In more ambiguous, uncertain, and complex battle spaces, many successful Civil War division commanders failed to make the transition to corps level.

In any event, a realistic situation analysis would have caused any commander in Ewell's place to carefully consider mounting an attack. The day's fighting had reduced the combat effectiveness of Ewell's corps; most units had suffered casualties and were disorganized. They were tired from long marches and suffering from heat, effort, and lack of water. It would have taken time to organize the attack; it was evening, and night was approaching. The strength and disposition of Federal forces on Cemetery Hill was unknown, and the difficulty of gaining situation awareness was compounded by the town, which obscured the view. The town's layout, with a narrow maze of streets, was another unknown and would have to be negotiated to quickly get to the Union lines. In addition to the many reasons for Ewell to question the feasibility of seizing Cemetery Hill, we already noted that he may not have understood Lee's intent.

In terms of team-building and decision-making, staff ride participants should consider how Lee dealt with Ewell. Did he fail to realize Richard Ewell was not a Stonewall Jackson? Did he still operate as he had with Jackson? These questions address the tension between empowering subordinates to exercise initiative versus specifying exactly what is to be done and controlling their actions. The questions suggest that a senior leader must consider the personality of the subordinate to whom he is giving a discretionary order, particularly early in their command relationship. Subordinates are certainly expected to adjust to a superior's leadership style, but Ewell was new in the position, and the relationship was still developing. We suggest that perhaps Lee failed to alter his own leadership style even though new circumstances required doing so.

DAY 2—SEMINARY RIDGE

At some point, usually on Seminary Road, the War College staff ride stops to consider General James Longstreet's Day 2 failure to aggressively pursue Lee's intent to attack the Union left. After the engagements of July 1, Lee concluded that he had little choice but to give battle and continue the attack. He gave Longstreet, his friend and the ablest and most experienced corps commander, the mission to move along a covered route and attack to seize the lightly defended high ground that secured the Union left flank. Longstreet did not agree with Lee's decision, and his subsequent behavior has been a matter of controversy ever since.

A master at defensive operations, Longstreet was a superb tactical commander who we suggest thought tactically and not strategically. Longstreet wanted to maneuver around the Union left flank to the south, threaten Washington, establish a strong defensive position on favorable ground, and force the Union to attack in order to secure the capital. Failing to win that argument, he proposed a tactical envelopment of the Union flank and an attack from the rear. Failing to win his second argument with Lee, it seems Longstreet developed an attitude that resulted in a lost opportunity for the synchronized attack that Lee envisioned on July 2.

It requires strategic leader competency to manage the strong personalities of subordinates who are experienced senior leaders themselves, and we suggest that a strategic leader must appreciate the various points of view of the people with whom he or she interacts. One aspect of that skill (which also happens to be a critical thinking skill) is identification of underlying assumptions. An operative assumption for both Lee and Longstreet may have been that they were considering courses of action from the same perspective. Had one commander or the other considered that their perspectives were different—that Lee had a more strategic perspective than Longstreet—there might have been an opportunity for one or both of them to deal more effectively with the situation. As things turned out, while historians may debate what was in each commander's mind, there can be no doubt that what Lee envisioned—an early and aggressive attack on the Union left—did not take place.

Dealing with disgruntled subordinates has been the bane of leaders throughout history, and Meade had such a problem with one of his subordinate commanders, General Dan Sickles. The most significant exchange between the men at Gettysburg occurred in the vicinity of the Peach Orchard over Sickles' arguably poor decision to relocate his Third Corps from its assigned position along Cemetery Ridge to the higher ground of the Peach Orchard, well forward of where he was told to be and leaving a gap in the Union line. Learning of Sickles' displacement as Longstreet attacked, Meade's subsequent actions to reinforce the line were effective and successful. Most War College historians think Meade's performance has been undervalued, and indeed, maligned by history.

The reader must first understand that Meade and Sickles were very different. They also despised each other. Sickles was a corrupt Tammany Hall politician who drank excessively and "enjoyed the company of loose women." Before the war he had shot and killed his wife's lover and had subsequently become the first person ever acquitted of murder using a temporary insanity plea. After the war he was appointed minister to Spain and was widely reported to have had an affair with the queen. After losing a leg at Gettysburg, he had it preserved. As a member of Congress in the 1890s, he would allegedly end a night of drinking by taking his women friends to look at the leg. To this day, the Third Corps monument at the Peach Orchard has an empty space for Sickles' bust, which was not erected because of his efforts to embezzle monies from the New York State Monuments Commission.[8]

Meade was the antithesis of Sickles: very disciplined, strait-laced, and formal. He had the added challenge of not getting along easily with others. Not long after Gettysburg, Meade had a run-in with a journalist, who then organized his colleagues to quit writing stories favorable to Meade; the result was that Meade did not receive the acclaim his leadership probably warranted.[9] His leadership challenges were further compounded by the fact that Sickles and General Dan Butterfield, the Army of the Potomac's chief of staff whom Meade had inherited (and whom he was unable to replace for lack of a willing replacement) were close friends and very loyal to Meade's predecessor, General Joe Hooker. Coddington describes them as "an intimate trio in Army circles," with connections to nationally powerful politicians and newspapers.[10]

Even before the war ended, Meade's enemies tarnished his reputation. In 1864, before the distinctly partisan Congressional Joint Committee on the Conduct of the War, Butterfield mischaracterized the orders Meade had given at Gettysburg to develop a contingency plan for withdrawal from the field in case the battle went poorly. Insinuations were made before the committee and elsewhere that Meade had wanted to retreat and had to be persuaded to stay and fight. The day after Meade testified before the Commission, a story appeared in the *New York Herald* accusing Meade of nearly losing the battle and praising Sickles for saving the day. The articles appeared under the pen name Historicus, but were sponsored by Sickles himself.[11] We are again reminded of two cautions about history. First, any account is merely one interpretation of events, and in some cases it may be intentionally false or misleading. Another point worth considering, particularly with regard to our collective memories of historical events, is that the first stories to gain acceptance, even if later proven wrong, are hard to displace. Meade spent the latter years of his life struggling to refute his enemies' stories, and it seems his reputation still suffers today.

Other aspects of events at Gettysburg also reinforce a need to apply critical thinking and keep an open mind when using history to inform judgment. We often suggest that staff ride participants read Michael Shaara's book *Killer Angels*. It is a historical novel largely based on speculation about what might have happened. The book is plausible and provides a good perspective on several leadership topics, though much of what is described almost certainly did not happen as described.

Colonel Joshua Chamberlain, whom we will study next, provides another example of how history can be slanted toward a particular viewpoint. Chamberlain was a genuinely heroic combat leader, as well as an outstanding communicator who told his story well after the war. These factors and his prominence in books like *Killer Angels* have probably led to an inordinate amount of credit being attributed to him for the defense of Little Round Top. Other leaders, such as Major General Gouverneur K. Warren, Colonel Strong Vincent, and Colonel Patrick O'Rorke also played crucial roles. As Keats said, "beauty is truth, truth beauty," and it is enough for us to understand that we must be careful about how we use history.

DAY 2—LITTLE ROUND TOP

A favorite stop on the staff ride is Little Round Top, and the July 2 actions that occurred there provide a rich opportunity to discuss a variety of leadership topics. The Little Round Top hilltop was key terrain that anchored the left end of the Union line. Yet at midday on the second day of the battle, with only a signal station on the hill, it was not well secured. Fortunately for the Union, Major General Warren, Meade's chief of engineers, arrived just in time to see Confederate forces forming to attack. Warren recognized the vulnerability and quickly took action to set in motion a series of events that resulted in Union reinforcements, eventually eight regiments, occupying the hill. The best-known engagement involved the 20th Maine, commanded by Colonel Chamberlain. After repelling several assaults and running out of ammunition, his creative thinking resulted in an out-of-the-ordinary but successful bayonet assault.

The July 2 fighting at Little Round Top provides one of the best opportunities at Gettysburg to explore the importance of shared vision to a senior leader. With our instruction grounded in a military context, we often link shared vision with commander's intent. *Commander's intent*, as the term is used in the U.S. Army today, is essentially the commander's distilled vision for a particular operation. We define it as "a clear, concise statement of purpose," what must be done with respect to the enemy and terrain to achieve the desired end state.[12] Commander's intent provides a framework for subordinates, particularly those who are isolated from the commander, to act independently in the spirit of the mission. It is all about subordinate initiative and enabling subordinates to act consistently with the commander's vision. Actions at Little Round Top provide a set of nested examples.

The vision that shaped events at Little Round Top was Meade's clear intent to defend and hold. It empowered Warren to issue orders, consistent with Meade's vision, that would normally have been generated by the chain of command. The study of battle command teaches us that commander's intent becomes particularly important in uncertain and ambiguous environments, where subordinate initiative is especially critical to operational success. When Warren found Little Round Top relatively undefended but threatened, he acted based on his understanding of Meade's intent and decided to divert the forces moving toward the Wheat Field. The common understanding between Warren and Meade cascaded down another two levels with Warren's guidance to Colonel Vincent, whose order to Chamberlain to "hold that ground at all hazards"[13] reflected Meade's intent as a shared vision among the Union leadership. Meade's intent ultimately empowered Chamberlain to defend the hilltop and was thus instrumental in holding the Union defensive line.

Compare the clarity and focus of Meade's intent and vision with Lee's intent to take Cemetery Hill "if practicable" but "to avoid a general engagement until the arrival of the other divisions of the army."[14] Meade's vision unleashed the initiative of several subordinate commanders. It allowed the Union to secure key terrain before the Confederates could do so and then to repel several attacks. Ewell, on the other hand, seems to have been uncertain about his authority and may have misunderstood Lee's intent. Gettysburg was a close-fought battle, and it may be that Meade's shared vision (as it influenced events at Little Round Top on July 2) or the lack of such a shared vision between Lee and Ewell (on July 1) was responsible for the outcome.

As demonstrated in earlier chapters, there is an important connection between shared vision and organizational culture. The strategic leaders who built today's Army leveraged organizational culture to institutionalize commander's intent and make it a routine aspect of how business is done. New soldiers—enlisted and officers—are taught to exercise initiative from their earliest days in the Army and to use the commander's intent as a guide. It is embedded in the orders process, where it is a mandatory part of the five-paragraph operations order. It is read verbatim and often elaborated upon by the commander during the operations order briefing.

It is the focus of rehearsals and back-briefs. Over time, use of commander's intent in the planning and execution of American military operations has become institutionalized and is part of "what right looks like," a defining characteristic of organizational culture.

Little Round Top is also a good place to highlight the value of diversity and creative thinking, as discussed in earlier chapters. Joshua Chamberlain was a rare and inspiring individual, and his background demonstrates the value of encouraging diverse opinions and ideas. Not a career soldier, he had been a college professor of rhetoric before the war. Amazingly talented, he was a strong leader, as evidenced by the fact that after the war he became a four-term governor of Maine and later distinguished himself as president of Bowdoin College. Unbounded by the conventional military thinking of the time, this creative and effective leader came up with a nonstandard solution to the problem of running out of ammunition in the midst of multiple assaults by superior forces: He fixed bayonets and charged the enemy. Different backgrounds result in different and often fresh perspectives and ways of doing things. Perhaps even more important, by definition diverse perspectives ensure the avoidance of groupthink.

Chamberlain's actions also demonstrate the team-building benefits of valuing diversity. The circumstances of his Little Round Top defense were all the more unusual because about one-third of his soldiers were enemy prisoners assigned to his command the day before. Chamberlain treated the men with dignity and respect, motivating the prisoners to fight with him. Not only can diversity enhance creativity, but respect for subordinates who are a bit different, or whom others disregard, often pays dividends when times get difficult. Chamberlain's ability and willingness to induce prisoners to fight with his regiment distinguishes him from commanders who would have seen them solely as a burden.

Another often-cited example of Chamberlain's respect for others and its strategic benefit occurred at the end of the war. After negotiating Lee's surrender in April 1865, General Grant picked Chamberlain to be the officer in charge of the official surrender ceremony and to receive the Confederate weapons and colors at Appomattox Courthouse. Chamberlain showed his respect for the defeated Confederates by ordering his men to carry arms as the Southern army passed. Historians frequently cite that act of respect as a major contributing factor to the achievement of Lincoln's vision of a magnanimous victory that allowed for true conflict resolution and the healing of our nation.

DAY 3—PICKETT'S CHARGE

The climax of the battle and of the staff ride takes place on the open field between Seminary and Cemetery ridges just south of town. After attacking the Union right on the first day and the Union left on the second day, Lee decided to attack the Union center on the third day of the battle. He directed a frontal assault preceded by a two-hour artillery bombardment using cannon from all three of his corps. At about 3:00 p.m. on July 3, the assault began with nine Confederate infantry brigades advancing across 1,500 yards of open ground. Although some Confederates penetrated the Union line, the attack faltered and was beaten back. The fighting that occurred at the center of the Union position has subsequently become known as the high-water mark of the Confederacy because it is considered to be the closest the South came to winning the war.

This portion of the staff ride typically begins at the Virginia Monument on West Confederate Avenue and includes walking the ground across which the Confederate brigades attacked. About 20 minutes after starting out, the Confederate assault reached the copse of trees that was the focal point of the attack. At this stop we typically discuss some of the most strategic aspects of senior leadership: leading change and the creation of adaptable, learning organizations.

Throughout history, successful armies have been forced to adapt to changing circumstances or risk defeat. In that regard, it is a strategic leader's responsibility to establish an environment conducive to adaptive change. In the summer of 1863, the Union army demonstrated many characteristics of a learning organization. One example is the forced withdrawal of the Union army through the village of Gettysburg on July 1. Contrary to some accounts, the army did not break and run; it conducted a rather orderly withdrawal that included disciplined volley fire to cover the retreat. Only two months before, at Chancellorsville, the same Union forces in a similar situation had broken and run from the enemy.

Another example of the maturation of the Union army was the growing confidence of the soldiers in their leaders, especially at the brigade and regimental levels. Chamberlain and the other Federal commanders at Little Round Top are examples.[15] Army of the Potomac leadership from regimental to corps level continued to exercise effective command in spite of the many commanders lost in action. Assumptions of command during the heat of battle were frequent and well executed without significant loss of combat effectiveness. Conversely, some question whether repeated success may have put Lee and his army into a state of complacency that inhibited adaptation.

Many of the commanders War College historians identify as most adaptive at Gettysburg learned from past experience. Most belonged to the Union army. Meade had observed General Hooker at Chancellorsville and had concluded that Hooker had failed to employ all available forces to avoid defeat. Meade resolved to exert tighter control at Gettysburg, and he did. Sickles' occupation of the Peach Orchard, for better or for worse, came about largely as a result of his experience at Chancellorsville. Although individual leaders learned from experience, there was no institutionalized process to standardize learning across the army. It is a senior leader's responsibility to embed processes that will improve performance across the entire organization. One of the most effective ways to achieve this today is through the After Action Review (AAR).

The Army's use of the AAR is a contemporary practice of leveraging culture to create a learning organization. Introduced in the mid-1970s, the AAR is conducted at all levels of command. Immediately after an event, the participants collectively review what should have happened, what did happen, and why, to identify strengths to sustain and weaknesses to improve. The purpose is to improve soldier, leader, and unit performance. It took over a decade for the AAR to gain full acceptance in the Army; it became commonplace about the time of the First Gulf War in 1991. Many soldiers who experienced the rejuvenation of our Army from the "hollow Army" of the 1970s credit the AAR with being one of the key components of the turnaround. Today the AAR is firmly embedded in the Army's culture, as demonstrated by soldiers taking time to conduct them in combat. They are organizational habits in that soldiers often do not feel a sense of closure or consider an operation complete until after the AAR. Army leaders have thus changed their culture to institutionalize a process that helps ensure the Army remains a learning organization that can adapt rapidly. Although the Union army at Gettysburg did not have this sort of embedded process, it did demonstrate several attributes of a learning organization.

Perhaps the clearest signal of the Union army as a learning organization occurred at the culmination of Pickett's Charge. Federal soldiers remembered the lessons of Fredericksburg, where wave after wave of massed Union infantry were repulsed by dug-in Confederates armed with contemporary weapons. As the Union soldiers repelled the attack, they realized it was their turn to administer the same lesson, and they took up the chant: "Fredericksburg, Fredericksburg, Fredericksburg. . . ." These indicators of a maturing Federal army were visible on the battlefield, but some Army War College historians question whether Lee and his commanders recognized the change in technology; if so, there is little evidence they adapted to keep pace. Given the outcome at Gettysburg, it is worth considering.[16] While lessons from the past are critical, we converse with staff ride participants about the senior leader responsibility to take an organization into the future and lead change. As General Eric Shinseki, former Army Chief of Staff, taught the Army, a viable organization must be postured in the present so that it will ready and relevant in the future.

The two great forces requiring strategic-level adaptation are changes in technology and changes in the geopolitical environment. The Civil War occurred at a time of great technological change. Nineteenth-century innovations included the steam engine, leading to revolutionary changes in sea and land transportation. Interchangeable parts were revolutionizing industry. The telegraph was revolutionizing communications. Advances in weapons technology included increased accuracy and repeating and breech-loading weapons that resulted in increased volume of fire. Today's leaders face the challenge of integrating a plethora of new technologies into the force. The importance of environmental scanning to strategic leaders of the Civil War is intuitively obvious and remains relevant. According to former Army Chief of Staff General Gordon Sullivan, it is the strategic leader's responsibility to turn technological advantages from potential into strategic achievement.

Strategic leaders have the responsibility to integrate new technology into an existing organizational baseline. Established, complex organizations do not possess the resources to enter a new technological era and build an ideal force from scratch. Leaders, instead, inherit organizations that already exist, along with the sunk costs and investments of the past. One construct used to bring about organizational change categorizes potential solutions to new requirements as falling into one of these domains: doctrine, organizational structure, training, materiel, leadership development, personnel, or facilities. At Gettysburg, change in the Union army can be seen in several of these domains.

In terms of materiel change, both North and South used emerging technologies like the railroad and telegraph. However, by this point in the war, the North's industrial might was finally being leveraged to practical advantage. At Gettysburg, Buford's cavalry had integrated Sharps repeating rifles into the organizational baseline. Rifled, breech-loading cannons, with extended range and accuracy, though not a weapon of choice, were present on the battlefield. Particularly significant to educating today's strategic leader is the linkage of these materiel developments, enabled by industrial might, to the fluidity and dynamism of systems thinking.

A strategic leader's function is to manage complex organizations, systems of systems where the systems are legion; the aforementioned materiel and industrial might of the North is an example. The North had a much greater capability not only to produce materiel such as weapons and ammunition but also to transport them and, more significantly, to develop a complex logistical system to support the army. Without the industrial capacity of the North, the South had to rely on whatever weapons and equipment it could obtain, resulting in cascading effects and adverse consequences that can be illustrated by comparing the artillery with which the armies were equipped. The South had fewer cannons but a greater variety of calibers, presenting more complicated supply problems than those faced by the North, which relied on fewer standard pieces requiring less variety of ammunition. Over the strategic long haul, the effectiveness of northern systems and industrial might outweighed other advantages the Confederacy had. It is the responsibility of senior leadership to manage systems, and we suggest that the Union was more competent in doing so.

Another aspect of adapting to the future involves the doctrinal bridge between the theory and practice of war. It is the strategic leader's responsibility not only to integrate emerging technology but also to adapt procedures accordingly. Already mentioned is Buford's adoption of dragoon tactics as a doctrinal adjustment to account for emerging changes in the conduct of war. On the other hand, Pickett's Charge tragically illustrates the failure of leadership to adapt doctrine to changing times. The astute military leader, such as Buford, who is scanning the environment, strives to anticipate strategic change driven by technology and to proactively evolve doctrinal practice before he has to react to change after it has occurred and he has consequently suffered tremendous battlefield losses. The goal should be for doctrinal change to lead technological change and not vice versa, as was commonly seen at Gettysburg, throughout the Civil War, and indeed throughout history.

In addition to materiel and doctrinal changes, Union army organizational changes are apparent at Gettysburg. General Hooker, Meade's predecessor, had strong organizational skills, and much credit belongs to him. One of his more significant contributions was creating the Bureau of Military Information, essentially an intelligence fusion cell that gave Meade what we now call information dominance throughout the Gettysburg campaign.[17] Hooker also created a system of distinctive unit patches and markings that soldiers wore to identify units in the chaos of battle. Another organizational change involved increasing the size of Union staffs to deal with expanded and faster-paced operations.[18] It should be noted that Lee, as well as the Federal commanders, recognized the need for larger staffs, but only the Union army had the resources to implement the change. The benefits of these organizational changes could be seen at Gettysburg.

The Pickett's Charge venue also provides an opportunity to point out the importance of strategic leader consensus-building. Meade convened a council of his commanders on the night of July 2, 1863, to review events of the following day, solicit input, and develop a plan of action. Contrary to usual procedures of the day and likely because he had been in command for less than a week, Meade felt the need to involve his subordinates in the decision-making process. In doing so, he contributed to their ownership of the plan and achieved some level of buy-in, thereby enhancing a sense of shared vision. War College students have usually spent most of their careers at the direct and organizational levels of leadership, and we suggest to them that inclusive leadership that involves consensus-building is more typical of strategic-level leadership. The more senior a leader, the more important consensus-building and subordinate buy-in is to the organization's success.

NOVEMBER 19, 1863—PRESIDENT LINCOLN'S GETTYSBURG ADDRESS

The strategic significance of the Battle of Gettysburg was solidified November 19, 1863, when President Lincoln delivered the Gettysburg Address. The site of Lincoln's remarks at the National Cemetery is typically the last stop on our staff ride. In a famously short set of remarks (271 words in less than two minutes), Lincoln transcended the battle to associate the war and its purpose with one of the nation's most fundamental values: justice.[19] Lincoln associated the war's purpose with the nation's founding in 1776 and the values articulated in the Declaration of Independence. Our historians always emphasize that Lincoln linked the war to the Declaration of Independence rather than to the Constitution, which made allowance for slavery. Lincoln addressed the nation's most fundamental values. He called for a reconciliation of the nation's strategic deeds with its lofty words and for the nation to finish the war and live up to its ideals. We consider the degree to which justice and fairness are required components of conflict termination in order to win the peace that follows war, raising linkages to our ethics instruction.

There is also a linkage to the strategic leader's vision and decision-making in that Lincoln's focus throughout the war had been on maintaining the integrity of the nation. By this point in the war, he was convinced that to achieve reunification, slavery had to be ended and the South's social institutions fundamentally changed. Thus, on January 1, 1863, six months before Gettysburg, the Emancipation Proclamation was implemented, freeing slaves in all rebelling states and effectively abolishing slavery. Having decided that the Northern strategy must change and having taken steps to effect that change, at Gettysburg Lincoln established a new political context for the war. He gave the battle political meaning and charted a new course for the war and the nation.

The Army War College is fortunate to have the Gettysburg battlefield in such close proximity to Carlisle. Through our frequent use of the staff ride, the legacy of the American soldiers who went before us and fought at Gettysburg, such as Meade, Chamberlain, Buford, Lee, Longstreet, and many more, continues. With the proper use of the staff ride, the experience of these leaders from our past helps to develop our leaders of today. The richness of the battlefield experience allows us to examine almost every aspect of strategic leadership that we teach.

NOTES

1. The Army of the Potomac (and its predecessor) was commanded in turn by Irvin McDowell (1861), George B. McClellan (1861–1962), Amos P. Burnside (1862–1863), Joseph Hooker (1863), and George G. Meade (1863–1865). The commanding generals or generals-in-chief of the Union army during the Civil War were Winfield Scott (1861), George B. McClellan (1861–1862), Henry Halleck (1862–1864), and Ulysses S. Grant (1864–1865).

2. Slavery was already illegal in both England and France, so regardless of whether the strategic leadership of either country would have deemed it to be in their interest, entering the war to fight alongside the Confederacy would have been difficult for domestic political reasons.

3. Edwin B. Coddington, *The Gettysburg Campaign: A Study in Command* (Dayton: Morningside Bookshop, 1979): 5.

4. The credit for this synopsis, as well as the factual basis for most of this chapter, belongs to the War College's corps of historians. The leadership lessons of Gettysburg have been honed by our historians for decades. Therefore, it is important to acknowledge all War College historians, past and present, who have contributed to the body of knowledge presented in this chapter.

5. Coddington, 65.

6. Coddington, 263–264.

7. Jay Luvaas and Harold W. Nelson, eds., *Guide to the Battle of Gettysburg* (Lawrence, KS: University of Kansas Press, 1994): 50.

8. For more information about General Sickles, see Thomas Keneally, *American Scoundrel: The Life of the Notorious Civil War General Dan Sickles* (New York: Anchor Books, 2002).

9. Coddington provides a balanced characterization of Meade, 210–213.

10. Coddington, 219.

11. Coddington, 338–348.

12. Department of Defense, *DOD Dictionary of Military Terms*, 8 August 2006, available online at http://www.dtic.mil/doctrine/fel/doddict (accessed 16 October 2006).

13. Luvaas and Nelson, 85.

14. Ibid., 50.

15. See also Coddington, *The Gettysburg Campaign: A Study in Command*.

16. While we want staff-ride participants to think about learning organizations and consider the Union army as an organization, we do not want to overstate the case. For example, the Union army took tremendous casualties later in the war from frontal attacks, such as those at Cold Harbor and Petersburg.

17. Edwin C. Fishel, "Command Decision: Colonel Sharpe's Critical Role at Gettysburg," *North & South* 3 (1998): 14–29.

18. John B. Wilson, "Maneuver and Firepower: The Evolution of Divisions and Separate Brigades," *Army Lineage Series* (Washington, D.C.: Center of Military History United States Army, 1998): 14.

19. There is more than one version of the Gettysburg Address because the speech was recorded by different observers. The 271-word count comes from the Bliss version, the only one to which President Lincoln affixed his signature.

Afterword

During World War II I was suddenly pulled out of my training division in Arkansas and flown to Honolulu to join a brand-new military history project. Under the leadership of General Marshall, a military history program was being developed that put emphasis on combat history at the very lowest level—platoon engagements from day to day and even hour to hour. To collect information, officers and enlisted men would be interviewed in groups or singly before a planned operation, during lulls in the actual operation, and in lengthy and numerous sessions after the operation.

The essence of this whole effort was to discover leadership strategies—leadership from the top, from the bottom, and from every level in between. I was especially interested in this program because in college and graduate school I concentrated on the theory and practice of leadership.

Sooner than we expected, our little military history group found ourselves embarked on the invasion of Saipan, where we were to test our theories and approaches. There were only two of us gathering information this early in the game, a lieutenant and myself, a sergeant. I was happy to be a "noncom" because I thought it might be easier to talk with GIs in combat.

Halfway through the Saipan operation, I was detached from my division and dispatched by plane to Guam, where an operation was already under way. I was taken to the command ship, but the Navy did not know what to do with me. I didn't blame them—I was still in my stinking fatigues, unwashed and unshaved. They dumped me on shore. Soon I was watching operations from command posts wherever possible. Later I met with officers and GIs in groups or individually.

What did I learn from these experiences, including later operations in the Philippines and Okinawa? I learned about leadership at all levels. It was interesting to discover how leadership differed among lieutenants and GIs, sergeants and privates, and captains and colonels, who all had unique roles and memories. It was fascinating to watch all this play out in group meetings following the operations. Since these island battles were conducted by relatively small units and were brief operations, we could review critical episodes from hour to hour. It was amusing to hear a lieutenant tell the story from his perspective, only to be followed by a platoon sergeant who would tell a different story, and then a private would say, "No, Sarge, we didn't attack on the right flank. I led the guys over that little hummock on the left, and did we ever get our asses shot off!"

This experience in the Army fortified my basic theory of leadership: leaders should mobilize followers so the followers themselves become leaders. This depends on the standards and values under which the followers are mobilized. In the military the ends and means are relatively simple: victory by the lowest cost possible. At home it is much more complicated, but I believe that we have strong and meaningful democratic values stemming from our Declaration of Independence and Bill of Rights. Instead of a simple leadership hierarchy governed by sergeants and lieutenants, we have numerous and complex levels of leadership by parents, teachers, and bosses, intermingled and vitalized by children, students, and employees—all tested by democratic values entrusted to us by the brilliance of the founders so long ago. In short, democratic practices ensure and enable the potential transformation of followers to leaders—crucial to the future of our democracy and made possible by enlightened civilian and military leadership.

James MacGregor Burns
Williamstown, MA
September 2008

Index

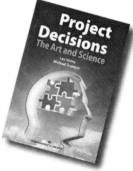

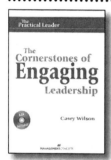
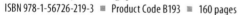
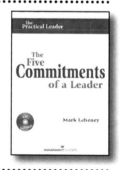